Interpersonal
Approach
To
Psychoanalysis

Interpersonal Approach to PSYCHOANALYSIS

Contemporary View of HARRY STACK SULLIVAN

BY GERARD CHRZANOWSKI

GARDNER PRESS, INC., New York
Distributed by Halsted Press
Division of John Wiley & Sons, Inc.
New York • Toronto • London • Sydney

GARDNER PRESS, INC.
19 Union Square West
New York 10003

Distributed solely by the Halsted Press Division
of John Wiley & Sons, Inc., New York

Library of Congress Cataloging in Publication Data
Chrzanowski, Gerard, 1913-
    Interpersonal approach to psychoanalysis.
    Bibliography: p.
    Includes index.
    1. Psychoanalysis.   2. Sullivan, Harry Stack,
1892-1949. I. Title
RC504.C5   1976   150',19'570924   77-1951
ISBN 0-470-99071-6

Printed in the United States of America

Acknowledgments

I wish to express my appreciation to Dr. Otto Will for reading the original manuscript of this book and offering helpful suggestions for its final version. I am also indebted to Mr. Donald Stewart for his thoughtful and effective way of keeping my prose in line. Additional assistance was offered by my wife Ruth who worked with dedication and skill in organizing a number of chapters, and by my daughter Romola who provided substantial help in preparing the material for publication.

Dr. Ralph Crowley generously offered the use of Sullivan's complete bibliography as published in *Contemporary Psychoanalysis* with the permission of Academic Press, the journal's publisher.

I also feel indebted to many of my colleagues here and abroad for making me clarify my concepts and my numerous students for asking challenging questions.

Finally, I want to express my gratitude to my teachers Clara Thompson and Frieda Fromm Reichman who first encouraged me to formulate many of the ideas presented here.

Contents

Preface

This book serves a dual purpose: first, to present a critical exposition of the study of interpersonal relations which is Sullivan's definition of the field of psychiatry; second, to expand Sullivanian psychiatry beyond its present theoretical and clinical boundaries to include a change in the concept of Self.

A central theme of the book is to view the Self as being rooted in a network of relatedness to one's fellow human beings rather than in an a priori structure. Harry Stack Sullivan's pioneering work has provided us with the original frame of reference underlying this point of view. Part I addresses itself to an elaboration of Sullivan's basic tenets. Included is a critical evaluation of the fundamental assumptions pertaining to an interpersonal theory of therapy. Reference is made to significant changes in both Sullivan's theoretical structure and in his clinical approach.

Part II deals predominantly with modifications in interpersonal theory and practice as they have emerged since Sullivan's death. Special consideration is given to the impact of ecological considerations, to a clinically applicable formulation of an interpersonal Self as a means of transcending energetic principles, as well as an experience-close area of therapeutic observation.

There has been increasing psychological concern with the formulation of a Self in classical and neoclassical psychoanalysis. The emergence of Ego psychology has given new impetus to bringing the Self into a focal theoretical and therapeutic position. This trend is evident in the titles of numerous psychoanalytic publications that assign this word a prominent role. Among others, we are familiar with:

> *The Self and the Object World* (Jacobsen)
> *The Analysis of the Self* (Kohut)
> *The Privacy of the Self* (M. R. Khan)

The Divided Self (Laing)
Self and Others (Laing)
The Self (Moustakis)
The Undiscovered Self (Jung)
The Intrapsychic Self (Arieti)

It should be emphasized, however, that all extant conceptualizations of the Self are based on the principle of a unique, individual personality. The formulation of an interpersonal Self thus constitutes a bold step into novel theoretical and clinical territory. Baldwin's notion of the Self as a "looking glass" and G. H. Mead's pioneering formulation of Self in *Mind, Society and Self* presaged the interpersonal theory of therapy, whereas Kurt Lewin's psychological field theory enlarged the scope of a therapeutic two-way relationship. Finally, it became necessary to bring the ahistorical concept of a field in line with a developmental scheme.

What has emerged is an ecological model of the Self as a comprehensive unit consisting of an integral biologic and social network. It means that the core of a person can never be extricated from its organic and social moorings without producing artefacts. There is a ceaseless interpenetration between a person's individual endowment and that person's prevailing mode of physical and social existence. This point of view calls for a basic reevaluation of many current theoretical and clinical aspects of psychotherapy, and it requires that the emergence of "the interpersonal Self" be traced from Sullivan's initial formulations (see "Illusion of Individual Personality") to its theoretical and clinical conceptualization at the present time.

The implications resulting from these changing concepts of the interpersonal Self are discussed in detail, particularly their clinical applicability; for they pertain mainly to a newer conceptualization of the therapeutic alliance. Significant modifications have taken place regarding the vicissitudes of transference and countertransference as well as the range of psychopathology. Brief references are continually made to comparative points of view in the mainstream of psychoanalysis and psychotherapy.

Sullivan died in 1949 at the age of 57. Since that time

psychiatry, psychotherapy, and psychoanalysis have undergone drastic changes. Admittedly, some of his conceptions have not stood the test of time; yet many of his original formulations found their way into present-day psychological and psychoanalytic conceptualizations—a fact made more remarkable by his inability to publish a single book in his lifetime except the five William Alanson White Lectures under the title *Conceptions of Modern Psychiatry* (Crowley #59 and #97). Sullivan's seminal principles can easily be recognized in modern conceptions of group and family therapy, in milieu therapy, in social psychiatry, and in transcultural studies. His developmental scheme with emphasis on a cradle-to-grave life cycle has been popularized without giving credit to its originator, and the same holds true for his pioneering revision of the "mirror analyst" model, which has increasingly been applied in classical psychoanalytic practice. There are other areas in which Sullivan led the way without receiving adequate recognition, but equally vexing is the attitude of those disciples of Sullivan who feel he no longer needs to be taught since most of his ideas have become the common heritage of contemporary dynamic psychiatry.

I disagree with this point of view, and I consider a systematic tracing of interpersonal formulations to be of distinct theoretical and clinical value. A major aim in this respect is to highlight the evolution of a theory of therapy and its clinical applicability in psychotherapeutic practice. In the end, every psychological theory must transcend the initial formulations of its creator. My purpose is not to indulge in a personality cult, but to give due credit to the creative revisions made by Harry Stack Sullivan. At the same time we need an on-going appraisal of workable as well as non-workable principles stemming from his original conceptualizations.

Much confusion has resulted from the interpretation and misinterpretation of interpersonal terms. There is a tendency to view the concept interpersonal as a superficial, surface mode of contact in contrast to internalized experiences that are frequently referred to as "depth psychology". The concept of an interpersonal Self is intended to bring the actual clinical issues into better focus.

There is growing evidence that the language of psychoanalysis and psychotherapy has more hindered than helped in clinical practice. Terms stemming from outmoded theoretical constructs have been dogmatized and have complicated open-ended intraprofessional communication; they have also interfered with therapeutic communication. The situation is not improved by coining new terms unless we bring them in tune with workable clinical procedures that can be checked and verified by others.

Much confusion has been created by thinking in traditional psychological metaphors without clarifying their present-day therapeutic implications. Plain, descriptive language has receded into the background, with excessive reliance on a pseudoscientific terminology. Furthermore, technological language in the field of psychotherapy has been politicized by monopolizing psychological terms for party-ideologies of the so-called schools of thought.

In contemporary psychoanalysis and psychology the Self has regained a new wave of popularity. At the same time the metaphor Ego has been widely incorporated into everyday language.

The dictionary tells us that Self refers to a person or object with respect to individuality. The term in daily language is used with regard to one's own person, one's own self, one's nature, one's character, and one's personal interests.

As for "Ego" in common usage, the dictionary defines it as the I or self of any person who is thinking, feeling, and willing, and distinguishing itself from the selves of others and from objects of its thought. In contrast, the psychoanalytic term Ego is postulated as that part of the psychic apparatus which mediates between primitive drives of the Id and the environmental realities.

Freud's innovative, psychological genius had a penchant for the metaphor. His language relied heavily on analogies in his constant search for a scientific foundation of his psychoanalytic conceptualizations. The assumption of psychic energy, the designation of a psychic apparatus with structures akin to anatomical entities, the definition of neurotic conflict as a clash between Id impulses and Ego defenses must all be understood as brilliant metaphors rather than clinical facts.

It should be appreciated in this connection that Sullivan's keen interest in language and communication compelled him to transcend nonworkable terms by coining a psychiatric language of his own. He was not very successful in this endeavor and was accused of creating neologisms rather than communicable, clinically useful verbal tools. His very precision in choice of words got in his way as well as a reluctance to illustrate with sufficient clarity his need to introduce innovative terminology.

For instance, Sullivan objected to the term neurosis and suggested that it be relegated to medical history along with ancient mythological concepts such as humors. (At one time the cardinal humors of the human organism were considered to be blood, yellow bile or choler, phlegm, and melancholy or black bile.) After all, the term neurosis has direct reference to neurons or the organic nervous apparatus. This is all very well and deserves to be dealt with, but the substitution of the cumbersome term parataxis (introduced by Dom Thomas V. Moore) for the outmoded term neurosis is of dubious value. The concept of parataxic distortions is discussed in detail in this book. We are dealing here with a generic term related to interpersonal fields of maladjustment and maladaptations.

Sullivan referred to parataxic distortions as follows: Besides the psychiatrist-patient dyadic integration there is in "the parataxic situations also an illusory two group integrated of psychiatrist - distorted - to - accommodate - a - special 'you' pattern and subject reliving - an - earlier - unresolved - integration - and - manifesting - the - corresponding - special 'me' pattern. The shift of communicative processes from one to another of these concomitant integrations may be frequent or only occasional."[1]

The foregoing makes it clear why throughout my text efforts are made to shed additional light on Sullivan's interpersonal language as well as on attempts to bring his terms in line with prevailing points of view. Though some may be discouraged by Sullivan's style, readers are, of course, urged to read him in the original and at length.

Again, my purpose is not merely to repeat Sullivan's conceptions of psychiatry. Instead, a broad outline of interpersonal formulations is offered, and their present-day clinical applicability are discussed. Thus the dual nature of the book is both logical and necessary.

Throughout this work, my conviction that psychiatry, psychoanalysis, and psychoanalytic psychotherapy are firmly anchored in their respective sociocultural mediums will, I hope, become apparent. The psychological Weltanschauung above and beyond clinical, empirical observations must always be dealt with.

Much of the material presented here is taken from notes used in teaching the contributions of Harry Stack Sullivan over a period of more than 25 years at the William Alanson White Institute, as well as in lectures given at other institutions in the United States and abroad.

Finally, a biographical sketch of Sullivan's life has been included.

Gerard Chrzanowski

Part I
SULLIVANIAN
PSYCHIATRY

CHAPTER 1

Sullivanian Psychiatry – Basic Assumptions

Epistemological Considerations

Sullivan defined psychiatry as the study of interpersonal relations. His aim was to create a sounder epistemological foundation for clinical observations than Freudian metapsychology permitted. In particular, he focused attention on a larger transactional field by including cultural, societal and other environmental components in his developmental, operationally oriented scheme. His initial model came from the field of sociology and was rooted in George Herbert Mead's formulation of the genesis of the Self. What emerged was a novel view of a sociopsychological Self emancipated from its intrapsychic moorings. Some limitations on the transactional model were imposed, however, by relying on a mechanical tension-relief principle as motivating human behavior. Nevertheless, Sullivan enlarged the scope of clinically valid observation by transcending a strictly intrapsychic point of view and developing a newer type of Self psychology. His innovative approach preceded and somewhat parallelled the emergence of Ego psychology. The latter, although containing a similar goal, did not detach itself from the unfortunate confinement of its earlier metapsychological speculations about the nature of man. Sullivan's psychological, transactional Self can be said to be an independent formulation of Ego psychology, without some of its more severe restrictions.

In grossly oversimplified form, it can be said that the focus of the Freudian therapeutic model is inherently an intrapsychic conflict. It means a clash between the intractable Id and the reality-oriented Ego. In a larger sense the conflict may be transposed to the inherent nature-nurture antithesis or to the opposing motivations of Individual and Society. Be that as it may, the classical theory singles out the individual as being torn between his impulses and his internalized adaptation to external value systems. Classical analysts are instrumental in a reactivation of early wishes, fantasies, and strivings against the background of formative forces within the transferential experience.

A major shift in therapeutic considerations took place when the unique individual receded as the object of study and the interpersonal field took its place. Now it was no longer internal conflict, neurosis or psychopathology, that stood in the foreground, but rather cognitive distortion which reflected warped Self appraisals, relating to communication, and to constructive integrations with others. The detailed exploration of the manifestations of anxiety and of the complex functioning of the Antianxiety system became areas of paramount clinical significance. Human similarities were accorded greater importance than deviations from universally human behavior. An ecological model of existence and growth was eventually introduced as a construct to enlarge the therapeutic field. This permitted a more detailed study of interpenetrating or transactional human behavior within the context of prevailing conditions. Transference and Countertransference were placed in a more reciprocal system than in previous conceptions. The role of the analyst was redefined as the participant observer, and individual personality was declared to be an illusion.

Sullivan's interpersonal theory centers on three pivotal epistemological considerations. It includes a developmental approach, a transactional field-oriented model as the domain of psychiatric study, and an operational point of view. Sullivan conceives of an overall cradle-to-grave life and time space with distinct evolutional epochs, or stages, representing optimal periods in which innate capacities can be anchored. The sequential unfolding of native endowment requires biological maturation as well as environmental support and stimulation. Sullivan's transactional model includes a field theoretical approach beginning with the Faraday-Maxwell model of the electromagnetic field and leading to a far reaching ecologic construct. The operational approach assumes clinical significance as illustrated in the principle of participant observation, that is, the emphasis on observation as a means of being part of what is observed. The analyst's role is defined in terms of the participant observer, that is, a transactional model which places the analyst in a basically non-authoritarian position and makes him an essential part of the therapeutic partnership. It includes the analyst as an integral part of all therapeutic operations, while offering him a degree of detachment as a safeguard against an alliance with the patient's neurosis or psychosis.

The leitmotif of Sullivanian psychiatry is the One Genus Postulate. It emphasizes the conviction that everyone is much more simply human than otherwise and that human personality is, above all, specifically human rather than anything else. The aim of the One Genus Postulate is to build up data for a science not of individual differences but of human similarities. Sullivanian psychiatry concerns itself with the study of ubiquitously human phenomena. To Sullivan, "the differences between two instances of human personality — from the lowest grade imbecile to the highest grade genius — are much less striking than the differences between the least gifted human being and a member of the nearest other biological genus." The most succinct expression of this approach is found in *Conceptions of Modern Psychiatry* (p. 16): "In most general terms we are all much more simply human than otherwise, be we happy and successful, contented and detached, miserable and mentally disordered or whatever." This conception stresses the fact that there is nothing to be found in even the most severe mental disorders that is not a partial ingredient of every human being's experience.

Current behavior patterns are considered to be influenced by emotional patterns in the formative years, as personal experiences with significant people in the past invariably form a major foundation for on-going relations with other people. In Sullivan's view, to be cut off from human relations is tantamount to the emergence of mental disorders. The cultural medium constitutes a network of interpersonal relationships that are required for the maintenance of specifically human qualities. This concept has been widely misunderstood. It does not run counter to the principal of individuation, or with the existence of individual biologic and psychological endowment. Neither is it a social formulation of psychological phenomena that stands in contrast to depth psychology by de-emphasizing the inner life of a person. Rather, interpersonal theory considers the transactional nature of both endo- and intrapsychic processes and views the separation of internal ideation and external interpersonal events as a genuine artefact. The individual, his nuclear family, and the prevailing culture form a dynamic transactional field that does not permit the isolation of inner life from its outside habitat.

Key Postulates of Interpersonal Theory

As previously stated, the theory of interpersonal relations can be most broadly described as adhering to three fundamental tenets: (1) developmental; (2) field oriented-Transactional: (3) operational.

THE DEVELOPMENTAL PRINCIPLE

Development represents a gradual unfolding, a series of changes, or phases that an organism undergoes in evolving to a mature state. In the field of psychiatry, development consists of a series of biologic, sociocultural, and relational stages that although separate are closely interdependent in covering an individual's entire life span. The psychiatric spotlight rests on detailed data reflecting how a person comes to be who he is at a given time in his life, that is, the step-by-step transformation of the newly born child into a human being equipped to live with and among other people.

One major developmental problem reflects the fact that many people are not able to live adequately in the social organization in which they have been trained to live. Much of human life is concerned with matters of cultural definition, that is, values, prejudices, beliefs, and expectations. Every human being experiences distressing sensations called anxieties, which are utilized by all cultures in training the young and which are subject to certain cultural variations. Sullivanian psychiatry considers anxiety to be the most significant element in the coding and incorporation of experience during all development phases.

The interpersonal point of view conceives of past, here and now as well as the near future, as all-encompassing aspects of a person's total life space. Successive phases of development allow innate capacities to emerge and flourish at particular intervals, while past experiences can be modified by positive human encounters. This stands in contrast to the classical psychoanalytical approach, in which the past is viewed as stored inside a person behind a wall that shields the initial experiences from the vicissitudes of life. The influence of the past on current attitudes, behavior, and thoughts is recognized in interpersonal theory as only one dimension of the developing person. Childhood, adolescence, and adult life form a continuum of experience leading to modifications and adaptations depending on the human, sociocultural, and physical environment. These developmental epochs are way stations, in which the prevailing milieu can bring about a range of optimal to marginal growth or lead to missed opportunities, which may become cumulative and increasingly resistive to ameliorative efforts. Human personalities are in a state of ongoing interpenetration with their overall milieu. In this respect, interpersonal theory is a much more open-ended system, lacking the deterministic aspects of Freudian theory. Traditional psychoanalysis has little concern with the present life situation of the individual — his prevailing human integrations, his socieconomic, his sociocultural setting, or his physical environment. Although not entirely ignored, they are not sufficiently stressed as independent, formative factors in development. Neither is there much consideration of the immediate future playing an active part in the way the past is viewed. Furthermore, the concept of "becoming" as part of the epigenetic process is largely missing, for the notion that the individual acquires qualities on the basis of new experience is in contrast to the model of determinism. Indeed, the possibility of forming new capabilities and the capacity for transformation are given scant attention in the classical scheme.

Developmental epochs are an integral part of interpersonal theory; the process of a developmental scheme is conceived of as a "biologically ordained serial maturation of capabilities." Inherent in the concept is a firm belief that education and training cannot be successfully applied in advance of biological maturation. Timing is considered to be of the utmost significance. Premature training tends to misfire, while belated training usually leads to inadequate educational experiences. Experience of a valuable kind can occur only at a time when the organism is maturationally ready for it. As Sullivan formulates it (*Interpersonal Theory of Psychiatry,* p. 371 Crowley #123), "If experience is definitely unsuited to providing competence for living with others, at [a] particular level of development the probabilities of future adequate and appropriate interpersonal relations are definitely and specifically reduced." Appropriate experiences, on the other hand, lead to the development of specific competences at particular stages. Sullivan continues, "Seen from this viewpoint, not the early stages only, but each and every stage, is equally important in its own right, in the unfolding of possibilities for interpersonal relations, in the progression from birth toward mature competence for life in a fully human world."

This developmental scheme is a sequential stage concept with maturational plateaus indicating a readiness for new experience. Infancy, childhood, juvenility, and adolescence are all periods when the organism shifts gears to new levels of competence. At such times there is an optimal opportunity to combine maturational readiness with environmental encouragement. Severe warps in early development may seriously interfere with constructive experiences later on, and traumatic events of a previous period may be corrected by favorable experience, particularly in the preadolescent era.

Sullivan's developmental scheme represents an ongoing process in which past, present, and future events are closely interwoven. Early interpersonal circumstances affect here and now happenings, that in turn cast a shadow on things to come.

The nature of experience throughout the lifespan is a key element in shaping the boundaries of a person's Self-esteem, that is, organization of processes within the Self indicative of self-respect. Self-esteem is a state of relative freedom from anxiety that serves as a major guideline in integrating human relations. A good measure of Self-esteem tends to promote interpersonal intimacy, while a distinct lack of Self-esteem encourages hateful integrations, that is, situations characterized by a reciprocal undermining of one another's assets.

All experiences are organized along cognitive modes of perception. Sullivan postulates three basic modes of experience (proto-, para- and syntaxic) which pertain primarily to the individual elaboration and personal coding of thought, ideation, and imagery.

It can be said that the organization of experience accounts for as well as reflects the major events in a person's lifespan. Sullivan distinguished between experience in the private and public mode as outlined by P.W. Bridgeman. He did not consider experience in the private mode to be of psychiatric interest, because it is not directly observable and accordingly is outside the field of psychotherapeutic concern. On the other hand, experience in the public mode is connected with the principle of communal existence and lends itself to checking and verification.

The interpersonal term experience is defined in the broadest sense possible and refers to each and all instances of encountering or undergoing a wide range of events. Experience like a giant tent, covers everything that impinges on the human organism — conscious as well as unconscious phenomena; verbal, preverbal, and nonverbal communications, continous and disconnected thoughts; actions; and biologic and social events.

In the interpersonal scheme experience always mediates a person's relatedness to the world he lives in. Experience is defined as the inner component of an event without necessarily representing the event as such. The actual event and its symbolic representation may differ in major aspects. The a priori event and its inner elaboration takes place in different modes of experience. The integration of experience takes place in three distinct cognitive modes. Initially, we have the prototaxic mode of experience, which consists of a series of undifferentiated, fleeting sensations. There is no stable frame of reference and no capacity to conceptualize time or space. Prototaxic experiences are generally preverbal, usually beyond recall, and are related to autistic phenomena. A breakthrough of prototaxic modes of experience occurs later on in life mainly in psychotic states.

Parataxic experiences contain the bulk of symbolic and metaphoric integrations with an inadequate awareness of sequential processes and logical consistency. They cover daydreams, nightdreams, and a wide field of unverified perceptions.

The third cognitive category is in the syntaxic mode, that is, experience that can be verbally communicated and be subjected to consensual validation. There is an experiential and a referential component to language. The former is symbolic in nature, akin to the language used in poetry or involves the use of a metaphor. By contrast, referential language relates to the common tongue, which permits checking and verification. It means that when one refers to a particular timepiece as a clock, one's neighbor knows precisely what is meant.

DEVELOPMENTAL EPOCHS

In Sullivan's scheme, Infancy is a developmental epoch extending from birth to the maturation of the capacity for language behavior, that is, the use of words that can be generally understood. Infancy is the period of the closest empathic linkage between mother and child which brings about either reciprocal cooperation characterized by tenderness and satisfaction, or anxiety-fraught integrations. Experiences during Infancy are coded along tender or anxiety-permeated transactions respectively in terms of "good mother" or "bad mother" perceptions, which in turn are linked to "good me," "bad me" or "not me" self-images. During Infancy, cognitive phenomena are mainly of a prototaxic nature in view of the state of primitive symbol activity of a preconceptual level.

The new faculty that ushers in childhood and leads to the waning of infancy is the capacity for communicable language. It is the first encounter with experience in which verbal meanings can be consensually validated, i.e. the syntaxic mode of experience. At that time in the course of normal development, baby talk and autistic utterances begin to recede while referential langauage gradually takes their place. Other phenomena connected with the epoch of childhood are the manifestations of adaptational, protective devices, referred to as security operations by Sullivan. We are dealing here with "fail safe" operations in the face of prolonged, severe anxiety. The source of the anxiety is at this stage of development directly related to the mothering person, on whose cooperation the infant must rely for survival. Sullivan conceived of an empathic induction of anxiety by the mother whose anxiety may have been unrelated to the infant (anxiety producing situations between the mother and her own interpersonal circumstances). One mode of security operation in a state of maximum tension is the emergency dynamism of Apathy which leads to a major attenuation of all the tensions of needs. Another emergency measure in the face of prolonged intense anxiety, is the phenomenon of somnolent detachment which is a close relative of apathy. Different terms are used, however, to account for different types of security operations later in life.

New adaptational devices of efforts to cope with anxiety come into play as the maturational process progresses. Sullivan creates a construct called the Self-system which is a lifelong ingredient of human existence functioning as an antianxiety device. During childhood, more complex Self-system activities come into play, in conjunction with required behavior, which are part of the necessary process of acculturation and socialization.

The transition from childhood to the juvenile era occurs in Western civilization somewhere at the time of kindergarten and early school experience. One of the new abilities characteristic of this epoch is the capacity to cooperate with other children as well as with authority figures. The element of competition and compromise assumes a central position. A desire to belong to a group makes its appearance together with the fear of ostracism and the evolution of social judgments. Concepts of reward and punishment, justice and fair play as well as needs for prestige all begin to make themselves felt.

Interpersonal theory assumes that in our society the development from infancy through the juvenile period constitutes a phase of major dependency on the home and parents. The capacity to see oneself in a three dimensional way is not given so far. Personality development, for the better part, has not transcended a vital need for approval and acceptance, and experience is still predominantly in parataxic and prototaxic cognitive modes of experience, which to a large degree precludes genuine mutuality. Accordingly, the potential adult capacity to care for another person in a basically nondependent fashion does not exist yet.

The period of preadolescence represents a particular milestone in maturation. It ushers in the need for human closeness and intimacy. Juvenile cooperation and playing the rules of the game becomes an intricate process of "We-ness" or collaboration. Hopefully, somewhere between the ages of 8 and 10, a chum has been found as a partner to explore the world. If all goes well a genuine sensitivity to the needs of a peer develops with a strong desire to expand one's personal horizon. The world as rumored and the world as is are subjected to the searching view of two young people. Parents and authority figures are recast in a more objective light, and feelings of personal worth become a significant topic of mutual concern. Up to the developmental phase of preadolescence the capacity to be closely attuned to the well being, Self-esteem, and needs of another person in a spirit of reciprocity, of sharing, of nondependent, nonpossessive concern does not exist. This need for interpersonal intimacy and the freedom to integrate appears as a new faculty at that phase of life. Intimacy is defined as an interpersonal situation that aims at validating all major components of personal worth. The preadolescent capacity for intimacy is seen as a further evolution of the syntaxic mode of experience that made its initial appearance at the threshold of childhood.

A word should be said here about the experience of a

universal human phenomenon — loneliness. In its full impact it is encountered only in preadolescence and afterward. There are rudimentary components of this particular feeling tone that permeate all developmental epochs. In infancy it probably has some manifestation in the need for tenderness, and in the desire to be held or to be talked to in a soothing way. This kind of need extends into childhood, when the need for adult participation in activities becomes more pronounced. In the juvenile era the need for compeers and the need for acceptance or avoidance of ostracism come to the fore. The culmination of all these components evolves in preadolescence in the need for intimate exchange with a fellow human being, a chum, a friend, a loved one.

Early and late adolescence bring sexuality into conscious awareness. The shift in the intimate need is now directed toward a partner of the opposite sex if all goes well. In the scheme under discussion lust as an outright sexual need does not occur until puberty. Under favorable developmental circumstances lust and intimacy do not lead to a compartmentalization or separation.

Every step in the evolutional ladder is considered a distinct stepping stone to the next level of development. Difficulties at an early level will tend to cause difficulties at subsequent levels. But again, constructive experiences may ameliorate earlier damage. Ordinarily, preadolescence is the last way station at which a spontaneous favorable personality transformation may take place. A troubled preadolescence tends to leave a person with lifelong disadvantages in dealing with other people, particularly with regard to experiencing interpersonal intimacy.

Durable personality traits emerge during the developmental process which, of course, takes place within a particular interpersonal setting. Thus culture, society and family all play a part in furthering or in inhibiting innate capacities.

DEVELOPMENT OF THE SELF AND SELF-SYSTEM

The cognitive modes of experience play a major part in the organization of the Self and Self-system. There is a reciprocal relationship between the content of consciousness, that is, the scope of personal awareness — and the level of anxiety. In Sullivan's formulation the Self is made up of constructive interpersonal integrations evoking feelings of Self-esteem and approval by significant people. In other words, the part of the personality that is experienced as "I," "myself," "my body," is a "good-me" Self. It pertains to a positive transaction with a significant person indicative of "euphoria" or relative freedom from anxiety. In the presence of moderate or slowly rising anxiety the personality is experienced as a "bad-me" Self. It falls within the realm of parataxic distortions or neurotic manifestations. When anxiety is severe or comes on without warning, we are dealing with a "not-me" symbolization of the Self. The latter experience includes the manifestations of profound mental disturbances like horror, loathing, panic, eerie sensations, and a host of perceptual distortions. In "good-me" personifications the Self is in full communal contact, observing, responding and using its creative potential. "Bad-me" evokes a truncated Self, a state of partial observation and a measure of parataxic distortions. "Not-me" experience for all practical purposes precludes meaningful observations; there is only a minimal or nonfunctioning Self with a preponderance of prototaxic manifestations.

It should be appreciated that cognitive patterns play a formative as well as a maintenance role in the development of the Self. "Good-me" is the result of tender cooperation in the initial mother-child relationship. It entails a "good-mother" experience that does not per se reflect the qualities of the mother as mothering person, but rather indicates a positive interplay between mother and child. "Bad-me" originates opposite "angry" or "nasty-mother," whereas "not-me" is related to "evil-mother." Again, the reference to "angry" or "evil-mother" is the experiential coding of transactional phenomena and not a statement about the mother as such.

In contrast to the Self, the Self-system is an anti-anxiety device designed to protect the Self and to permit a degree of functioning even in the presence of medium to medium severe anxiety. Culture, society, family, and personal surroundings are all incorporated in the dynamics of the Self-system or Self-esteem maintenance system. The following diagram indicates the types of integration which are related to Self-system activity and resulting levels of Self-esteem.

The Evolution of the Interpersonal Self According to the Organization of Experience

Modes of Cognition	**Proto-** Preverbal Beyond recall Autistic	**Para-** Experiential Symbolic Metaphoric	**Syntaxic** Referential Consensually validated
Anxiety Gradient	**Severe** (NOT ME) "Evil-mother" No observing ego Absolute tension Dissociation Horror, loathing, panic Absent Self	**Moderate** (BAD ME) "Nasty-mother" Tension Partial observing ego Parataxic distortions Discomfort Truncated Self	**Mild** (GOOD ME) "Good-mother" "Euphoria" Fully observing ego Total Self
Self-System (Anti-Anxiety System)	**Failure of Self-System** No Self-esteem Breakdown of security operations Total insecurity Instantaneous transference Psychosis	**Active Self-System** Low Self-esteem Security operations Selective inattention Somnolent detachment Apathy, lethargy Sterile bickering Belittling	**Relatively In-Active Self-System** High Self-esteem Intimacy Supportive open channel of communication
Outcome	Psychosis	Severe to moderate neurosis	Mental health

A TRANSACTIONAL FIELD-THEORETICAL MODEL

The social sciences have widely used the principles of field theory, whereby all the parts which constitute a field are interdependent. The incorporation of these broad epistemological considerations within the framework of interpersonal psychiatry has aptly been referred to as an attempted fusion between psychiatry and the social sciences. As stated in *The Interpersonal Theory of Psychiatry,* page 13 "the actions from which psychiatric information is derived are events in interpersonal fields which include the psychiatrist." Patients who are observed, manipulated, or treated as mere objects without the direct involvement of a dedicated psychiatrist will not contribute information of psychiatric value. Valid psychiatric data cannot be obtained except by a person specifically trained as a participant observer in therapeutically geared interpersonal situations — the psychiatrist. Also, a setting is required that safeguards the patient's dignity and self-esteem, and aims specifically at enhancing his feelings of personal worth.

OPERATIONALISM

Operationism or operationalism was first introduced by P. W. Bridgman in *The Logic of Modern Physics.* In essence, operationism holds that the operations or steps required to obtain information about a particular event constitute an integral part of the event to be observed. For instance, the thermometer used in measuring a temperature has a temperature of its own which becomes part of the overall operation of measuring temperature. Historically, the operational approach had a certain fascination for the behavioral psychologists who incorporated this principle into their theory. Operations are steps that can be described and that, within reason, can be repeated by others in following the operational outline.

Operationism has introduced a mechanical, pseudoscientific way of thinking in psychology that leads it right back to the old days of Wilhelm Wundt who preceded analytic psychology. However, the operational influence in psychiatry has been different in that it focussed attention on listening and observing as interventions which do modify what is being observed: an observer can never be a neutral object in an observational field.

At this level of conceptualization we move away from the original behavioristic, mechanical formulations of operationism. We are no longer dealing with measurements, instruments, objects, and related parameters. Rather, our emphasis shifts to specifically human attitudes and emotional components as they interpenetrate within the therapeutically geared alliance. Instead of patient and therapist as separate units, we are more attuned to the evolving relational patterns between the parties, rather than to an exclusive focus on the patient's inner life. Instead of emphasizing psychopathology or neurosis, we address ourselves more to the human commonality of the participants in an open, communicative endeavor designed to encourage the patients to cope with himself and others under the prevailing conditions.

In highly abbreviated form, then, interpersonal theory has been outlined as developmental, field-oriented, and adhering to an operational point of view. Interpersonal theory justifies its inclusion in the framework of an Ego psychology in view of its genuine appreciation of the human organism's adaptational capacity. It stresses the active reaching out, or intentionality, of the growing child in his particular interpersonal setting. There is an adherence to structural[2] concepts without reliance on a topographic[3] point of view.

The Artefact of an Immutable Self

Interpersonal theory distinguishes between two different conceptions of Self. One pertains to a process related to an elementary goal of human striving, the other to a Self as a self-contained unit. Individuation is often confused with the concept of an atomistic Self, one of mankind's most cherished illusions. The immutable Self may be viewed as an artificial verbal construct similar to that of the Ether, which was falsely thought to have been an element of the heavenly bodies. This is not to deny anyone his private inner world, his native endowment, his one of a kind fingerprints, or other more or less durable aspects of identity. It merely emphasizes the observable, relational phenomena pertaining to the Self as an experiential matrix rather than as the core of human existence. The Self is perceived as the content of consciousness during a person's socialization, acculturation, and the formation of his relational patternings. Sullivan defined the Self as the part of personality central in the experience of anxiety. The Self is postulated to be more or less coterminous with the information directly available to the individual; this formulation resembles that of modern information theory.

Interpersonal theory postulates that each individual has a variety of personal responses to others that are directly related to his developmental encounters with significant people. A major part of therapy consists in expanding the observational and communicative field when multiple facets in the patient's personality become engaged with the psychiatrist as a real and distorted person. Treatment *per se* is an ongoing interpersonal process in which the therapist participates. His method of observation and his expectation of a legitimate therapeutic goal tend to modify attitudinal and emotional roots of current behavior and have an impact on the immediate future.

Ecology and Interpersonal Relations

Sullivan was greatly concerned in achieving a rapprochement between Operationalism as a basically mechanistic and behavioristic model and Transactionalism as a dynamic, relational human phenomenon. In a paper "The Illusion of Individual Personality", initially presented in 1944 and posthumously published in *Psychiatry* in 1950 (Crowley, pg. 118). Sullivan changes a key aspect of his epistemological considerations. He places psychiatry as the study of interpersonal relations on an ecological foundation. His new model of psychiatry opens the door to far reaching modifications in terms of theory and practice. Some of the implications connected with the ecologic concept of psychiatry will be discussed in Part II of this book.

Ecology has a dual meaning, and it embraces biologic as well as sociologic aspects. In the biologic sense it deals with the relations between the organism and its life-sustaining environment, particularly, the interpenetration and interdependency of the human organism and its physiochemical milieu.

The sociologic aspects of ecology focus attention on man's relatedness to his social institutions, with emphasis on the interrelatedness between the individual and his fellow men. Strictly speaking, sociologic ecology concerns itself with the spacing of people, with institutions and their resulting interdependency. Ecologic studies in social psychiatry have concerned themselves with the interconnection of population movements within urban communities and the incidence of mental illness, but many of these studies reached an impasse, since they could not distinguish clearly between cause and effect. Do slums produce a higher percentage of emotional disturbances in people or do disturbed people have a tendency to drift toward slums as part of their downward social movement? For our purposes, however, it is only important that we note the inclusion of both biologic and sociologic phenomena into the ecologic concept.

In the ecologic frame of reference, interpersonal theory is a statement about man's interdependence with his human and sociocultural environment. It follows that man in isolation eludes meaningful observation and is subject to distorted inference by the observer. Meaningful data about a given individual can be obtained only if he is observed in a natural habitat, one designed for living with and among other people, since specifically human characteristics unfold exclusively in such a setting. To illustrate the ecologic concept, Sullivan uses the example of the oxygen-carbon dioxide interchange in the process of inhaling and exhaling. He points out that the human organism has an extremely limited storage capacity for oxygen. Accordingly, human life is dependent on an almost uninterrupted flow between oxygen and carbon dioxide in the body and atmosphere. Sullivan transposed the ecology principle to the field of psychiatry by postulating the necessity of a more or less continuous contact between people in a humanly compatible environment. He contended that specifically human qualities were highly labile and required an open-ended channel for their potential growth and enduring survival. Insulation and isolation from the mainstream of life was tantamount to mental illness. This concept is related to the phenomenon of sensory deprivation, where the organism deprived of sensory input cannot survive intact. Meaningful contact with others is thereby considered to be an elementary biological need; the felt component of this need is loneliness.

One may want to add here that the ecologic concept pertains predominantly to here and now transactions. The mutual relations between organisms and their environment relate to an ongoing process. They do not concern themselves with the history of an individual organism or the developmental data of a particular person. In contrast, interpersonal psychiatry insists on a longitudinal, sequential scheme of transactions between organism and environment as an essential element in the ecologic process. It transcends the ahistoric approach of ecology and adds an additional dimension to what goes on at the present time.

CULTURAL ECOLOGY

In his psychiatric theory of therapy, Sullivan referred to three principles which he transposed from the field of biology. (The frame of reference is a book by Seba Eldridge, *The Organization of Life,* Thomas Y. Cromwell, New York, 1925.) They were expanded, clarified, and formed the background to his controversial paper on "The Illusion of Individual Personality." They pertain to:
1. Communal existence,
2. Functional activity, and
3. Organization.

In essence, these principles point in the direction of an absolute human necessity for a basically uninterrupted interchange with an environment, which includes culture. To Sullivan, culture is an abstraction pertaining to the world of people and their ongoing, viable integrations with others. In whatever form it takes, the cultural medium constitutes a network of interpersonal relationships that are required for the maintenance of specifically human qualities.

This concept has been widely misunderstood. Again, it does not quarrel with the existence of individual biologic and psychological endowment, nor a measure of self-determination or intentionality (an existential term referring to the organism's capacity to engage the environment actively). The illusion of individual personality represents a postulate of cultural ecology that focuses on the desired goal of acquiring existential competence in a fully mature, human world. We are not dealing here with a figure of speech, an analogy, or an allegorical reference, but rather with a basic epistemological principle.

The formulation of man's inherently communal nature makes the conceptualization of a person as a self-contained unit invalid. An individual stripped of his life-sustaining matrix is an illusory notion. The matrix is at all times a permanent component of the person it encloses in the form of fellow human beings, of culture, society, and physio-chemical elements. Man is interdependent with the above mentioned media and cannot survive without them any more than he can go on living without water, food, or oxygen. Accordingly, man's organization is rooted in the never-ending interplay between the person and the totality of the environment that characterizes a human life. The process of acculturation and socialization plays a significant role in development, since the prevailing ecologic phenomena in the personal environment of the growing individual lead to an unfolding, blocking, or stunting of his innate capacities.

Many aspects of theory and practice of psychotherapy must be reevaluated once psychiatry is viewed from an ecological perspective. First, the concept of the Self as an unalterable core of individual personality becomes rather meaningless when we apply the concept of a fluid, interpenetrating system with reciprocal channels of interchange. The question of what is inside or outside, intrapsychic or extrapsychic no longer can be formulated since there is a constant interchange going on between the internal and external locations depending on the moment in time and place when the observation is made —

that is, complementary processes in which internal and external phenomena are closely intertwined with somewhat indefinite and adaptable boundaries. In many instances the distinction between core phenomena and field phenomena depends largely on the viewer's platform and the element of time. We may observe the same process at different times when the activities at the core level appear to be more prominent than the transactional aspects. Accordingly, the distinction between intrapsychic and interpersonal is, in great part, a phantom problem. (Max Planck illustrates a phantom problem by facing an audience and indicating the obvious arrangement of left and right side from his particular position; he then points out that the opposite is true from the audience's point of view since the order of left and right is reversed in their seating arrangement. The phantom problem consists of the attempt to determine the "real" left and the "real" right side.)

The concept of transference is changed by viewing it as a two-way phenomenon in a field rather than as an intrapsychic, self-generated form of behavior. Transference is not merely a carryover from the past; it incorporates the other person's response to the distortion.

The here and now dyadic encounter is appreciated as a dimension in its own right against the background of early interpersonal situations. The past, present, and immediate future are interrelated, and transferential distortions pertain as much to the adult person as to the predominantly regressive, infantile aspects of the personality as theorized in classical psychoanalysis. It is most doubtful that we can ever make contact with the pristine child once a person has reached the adult phase of life (see Schachtel's concept of childhood memories). Finally, the ecological point of view focuses attention on the personality of the analyst as a therapeutic instrument that is constantly monitored by detailed self-observation.

Generally, the ecological model calls for an altered conceptualization of the therapeutic process. It mandates a focus on the interpersonal process above and beyond the patient's individual difficulties. What becomes most significant is the evolution of a communicative network in which complex messages receive uncomplicated feedback within a field of expanding personal rapport. Thus, the way is paved for an open-ended system of interchange.

Tensions and Energy Transformations: The Tension of Anxiety

Sullivan is of the opinion that "what anyone can observe and analyze becomes ultimately a matter of tensions and energy transformations" ("Towards a Psychiatry of Peoples" p. 368, Crowley #109). He rejects the notion of psychic energy and considers physical energy as the only kind of energy involved in human transactions. He adheres to the postulate that energy is the ultimate reality in the universe, that all material objects are manifestations of energy, and that all activity represents the dynamic aspect of energy. Sullivan adhered to Alfred North Whitehead's doctrine of organism, with its particular emphasis on process as an actual entity.

Thus energy, as described in Sullivan's theory, refers to strictly physical manifestations in its two forms, potential and kinetic.

Tension is a potential for action, whereas energy-transformation is the prequisite for action. Euphoria and tension are polar constructs designed for the organismic concept of energy-transformations. They represent extreme states of utter well-being or freedom from tension at one end of the pole to the utmost degree of tension at the opposite pole. The level of euphoria and tension are in reciprocal relation.

Sullivan postulates an intimate connection between experience, tension, and energy-transformation: "Whatever else may be said about experience, it is in the final analysis experience of tensions and experience of energy transformations." (*The Interpersonal Theory of Psychiatry*, p. 35). Accordingly, experience, in all cognitive modes, is of tensions and of energy-transformations. Tensions arise from needs seeking satisfaction as well as from the experience of anxiety.

The satisfaction of needs leads to relaxation, whereas the tension of anxiety aggravates all other tensions and precludes the possibility of satisfying needs. From infancy on human beings lack the capacity for action toward the relief of anxiety, which is an unmanageable tension that cannot be disposed of in any form or fashion.

Sullivan was much impressed with the notion of dynamism, which is defined as the smallest useful abstraction which can be employed in the study of the functional activity of the living organism, or "the smallest enduring pattern of energy-transformations which recurrently characterize the organism in its duration as a living organism." (Page 103 *The Interpersonal Theory of Psychiatry*) The dynamisms of particular interest to the psychiatrist are the relatively enduring patterns of energy-transformations that recurrently characterize the interpersonal relations.

The energetic principles imbedded in Sullivanian psychiatry are not inherently different from Freud's psychic energy. It should be understood that libido to Freud is an energetic reality, just as energy to Sullivan is a physical reality. In both theories a mechanistic energy transformation system prevails that is not directly applicable to human existence, that is, both theories rely on the first law of thermodynamics with its tenet of the preservation of energy. It does not matter whether the energy is libidinal or physical in nature, since physical laws taken from the natural sciences are not directly applicable to the vicissitudes of human behavior. We know today that energy plays a minor part in communication and that we cannot reduce all of human behavior to tension, tension relief, and energy transformation. Sullivan's later ecologic model transcends his concept of energy transformation, and deals with a living-system equilibrium, in as much as ecology concerns itself with the interpenetration and interchange between the living organism and its total life-sustaining environment. Unfortunately, this change in his thinking was never explicitly expressed.

Anxiety

The interpersonal concept of anxiety is the only significant formulation dealing with anxiety on a purely psychological basis, by rejecting the assumption of a neuroanatomic under-pinning. The experience of anxiety stems exclusively from in-terpersonal situations, and the tension induced by anxiety does not lead to energy transformations. We are dealing with a dis-junctive interpersonal experience that is not compatible with Self-esteem and communal security. In other words, Sullivan's construct of anxiety is that of a phenomenon that isolates the individual from all integrating tendencies. Anxiety is exclu-sively man-made and is an emotionally induced relational barrier.

Disruptive and destructive in every respect, anxiety inter-feres with meaningful communication, precludes intimacy, hinders creative thought processes, and leads to profound human malintegrations. Sullivan's postulation leaves no room for existential, humanistic, or potentially constructive aspects of anxiety. To him, anxiety in all its manifestations is harmful and antithetical to human progress. It usurps every available physiological pathway and is highly indiscriminate in its choice. Sullivan considered the experience of anxiety to be empathi-cally acquired from anxious people who have direct contact with the growing child.

From a clinical point of view, there is merit in viewing all aspects of anxiety as pathological. Interpersonal theory makes a genuine contribution by reserving the concept of anxiety for those interpersonal experiences that have irrationally lowered the person's Self-esteem. Thus there is a distinction between constructive and destructive anxiety. Legitimate guilt, ques-tions of conscience, morality, loyalty, and related reality prob-lems belong to the former category, in as much as they induce distresses of varying degrees, and are better grouped with fear reactions than anxiety. We stand to lose a great deal clinically by placing universal human conflicts in the realm of psychopathology. It may be argued that all human conflicts are real, and indeed they are. However, a major question is raised: Does a here and now problem stem from an unavoidable ex-ternal situation, or does it trigger off distress related to past experiences, with the concomitant distortions and exaggera-tions?

The aim of therapy is not necessarily to diminish a person's anxiety. Actually, there is some legitimate doubt that this can ever be done. Rather, the goal is to educate the patient about the great variety of disguises and irrational attitudes that indicate the unnoticed presence of anxiety, and to loosen the rigidity of the Self-system, which has the function of avoiding anxiety. People can learn to function in the presence of moderate anxiety without immediatly taking refuge in self-defeating security operations. A detailed discussion of anxiety in Chapter 2 provides the needed amplification.

The Similarity Principle

The similarity principle in interpersonal theory implies that the basic characteristics of the human species are dominant over the multitude of deviations in people's behavior, whether the people are mentally ill or well. What matters most is what people have in common, not the extent of their foibles, peculiarities, and malfunctioning. It also means that repetitive patterning takes precedence over individual isolated acts, thoughts, or events, regardless of how dramatic or unique an individual performance may be. The behavior of every person occurs within the spectrum of basically human attitudes. Mental illness, then, is viewed as an integral part of the human situation, and an unfortunate aspect of human existence. It is considered to be a miscarriage in human relations or, more specifically, an end state of anxiety-fraught experiences with significant people in the process of acculturation. The major problem in malfunctioning is to be sought in failures pertaining to quantity and timing of responses in interpersonal situations.

The similarity principle has considerable significance in the therapeutic situation. It treats mental disorders as inadequate and inappropriate modes of living with and among other people. The deviation is not considered to be an illness but rather a valid though deviant mode of existence. It is the result of prolonged exposure to warped relational experiences with people who have had a major impact on one's life.

The primary encounter between patient and doctor takes

place on the level of their common humanity, stressing the similarities of their respective experiences and dealing with the relatively intact part of the patient's personality. It is essential that the psychiatrist not participate directly in the patient's pathology, lest he enter the disturbed system, thus depriving himself of a functional, therapeutic platform. Similarity, as outlined here, implies the constant search for a mutually meaningful pathway of communication.

The Tenderness Principle

The tenderness principle is a noninstinctual postulate conceiving of collaborative human integration as a foundation for relatively anxiety-free experiences. Although a predisposition for tenderness undoubtedly is present in human beings, tender behavior on the infant's part requires an atmosphere between mother and child that is relatively free of anxiety. A transactional model underlies the tenderness principle in which the respective needs of mother and child reinforce each other while setting up a workable system of communication. A favorable cycle develops if all goes reasonably well. The infant's expressed needs evoke an appropriate response in the mothering person who in turn experiences tenderness in her ability to satisfy the infant's requirements. A corresponding feeling of relaxation and well-being on the part of the infant furthers collaboration in the task at hand. It stands to reason that the nature of this earliest person to person encounter has a powerful impact on future interpersonal patternings.

The principle of tenderness has a wide area of clinical applicability. For once, it focuses our attention on the mother-child relationship as taking place in a field, rather than thinking of it in terms of two potentially separate units. Furthermore, it does not unduly concern itself with value judgements about motherly love, the infant's appreciation of the love, and so forth. The concept of tenderness and collaboration places a different emphasis on conventional concepts of early child-rearing.

In the therapeutic situation, the postulate of tenderness suggests a transactional model that concerns itself with the needs of both patient and doctor. It is customary in the analytic process to speak in terms of "the analysis taking." Our thinking has undergone many changes in this direction since Freud laid the foundation for his initial concept of an analytic situation. The notion of finding a key to unlock the patient's unconscious and to transform unbridled, instinctual forces into meaningful interpersonal alliances still has some clinical meaning in a sophisticated way. But the concept of bringing light into darkness and of liberating the inner core of a person has distinct limitations, particularly its adherence to a biological therapeutic model. It implies that, in one form or another, attempts are made to deal with the patient's internal "sickness," whether it is considered to be moral, social, or biological. The picture changes significantly, however, once we conceive of mental disorders as difficulties of living that result predominantly from faulty human integrations. The principle of tenderness, then, aims for a collaborative endeavor as a therapeutic goal in its own right. Hopefully, it implies an evolution of intimacy in a relationship of growing equality. Tenderness is conceptualized as an intricate interplay of attitudes and behavior. It at once evokes the freedom to communicate basic and often unrecognized needs, and facilitates the capacity to respond adequately and appropriately to those needs that are compatible with the nature of the therapeutic relationship. In other words, "an analysis taking" may now be illustrated in the old saying, *manus manum lavat* (one hand washes the other). When applied to therapy, this concept transcends the conventional role relationship between patient and doctor by fusing it into a cohesive unit. It liberates us from the stereotyped tyranny of such concepts as love, warmth, kindness, gratitude, and related global terms.

Interpersonal Theory: A Historical Perspective

Interpersonal theory is the only American theory of psychoanalysis. The emphasis on its American origin is significant because it reflects certain aspects of the particular culture that have been tributary to the theory. The notion of activity, process, and — most of all — the results it can bring are deeply rooted in the American culture and attuned to the national temperament. At one time this approach was stamped with the label of pragmatism which originated with William James, John Dewey, W.C. Pierce, and others. It rests on the assumption that practical, workable considerations are more significant than theoretical constructs. The concept fell into disrepute with the overemphasis on workability, and it reached a nadir in its political application. This should not blind us, though, into condemning pragmatism in toto by seeing it mainly as a process of dehumanization and mechanization. There is a technical aspect to all human endeavors including psychotherapy. Pragmatism seen from this vantage point may be viewed as a clinical process. Translated into psychological thinking, it implies that whatever benefits the patient is good clinical procedure. Plainly, such a concept leaves the door open to serious abuses in unilateral decisions as to what is best for a person in distress. It also runs the risk of fostering manipulative procedures, and it skirts the periphery of behavioristic models.

Some of these doubts can be dispelled when we look at interpersonal conceptions within the Zeitgeist of the 1920s and 1930s when the framework of the theory evolved. The United States was in the midst of the great Depression. It was the time prior to the rise of the Third Reich in Germany, which dramatically shifted the center of psychoanalysis from the Old to the New World. The large-scale flight of European psychoanalysts to the United States had not occurred yet. Psychoanalysis consisted of a small, cultish group practitioners who tipped their hat to Freud on a short visit to Vienna. The public was generally unfamiliar with psychoanalysis, and attention to the field was drawn mainly by the so-called neo-Freudians. Revisionist movements sprang up in all directions. Sullivan, as one may guess, was as unhappy with the prevailing concepts in traditional psychiatry as with those in classical and neoclassical psychoanalysis. It was clear to him that psychiatry did not deal with diseases in the nature of medical entities like pneumonia, scarlet fever or kidney disorders. Early in his

professional career he realized that psychiatry is always concerned with processes of living that are inefficient, and with
tensions producing patterns that lead to loss of Self-esteem.
He also appreciated that attitudes of conservatism tend to
reinforce the tyranny of outmoded dogma, whereas avant
garde attitudes lack tolerance for anything that is not novel.
The resulting intolerance toward the old as well as for the new
causes prejudices and complications in living. A major task in
life is to acquire a broad tolerance of oneself and others, which
aids in accepting people as they are. Mental disorders constitute in many respects a required conformity with artificial
social stabilizers and social values and are characterized by
their basic predictability in contrast to mental health, which
always involves a distinct element of unpredictability.

Generally, the American culture has overstressed material
advantages, consumption, obsoletism, and the inherent
promise of happiness for all. There has been a tendency
toward hero worship, Horatio Algerism and basic trust in the
rightness of the cultural values. Under the prevailing circumstances, there is but slow progress in accepting the necessity for recognizing the significance of knowledge pertaining
to the observable realities of the human situation and the
intricacies of group life.

There have been a number of modifications in the adaptation of European-bred psychoanalysis to the American culture. However, this process has taken a different direction
from the conceptualizations of interpersonal psychiatry with
its specific roots in the prevailing cultural setting.

Culture and society have placed central emphasis on individuality as an inviolable aspect of humanity. The dogma of
individual personality (similar to the ancient notion of the
earth as the center of the universe) resists strongly different
points of view. Actually, there never has been a denial on
Sullivan's part of personal identity, inner mental life, and
related considerations. Sullivan's approach aims to dispel the
illusion that any aspect of human existence can be studied in
isolation apart from its communal components and insulated
from the observing person. It means that the psychiatric
method of observing makes the psychiatrist an interacting
participant in the therapeutic process There is a clearer de-

finition of the respective roles of therapist and patient in their relational, emotional, communicative encounter. The potentially curative bond is the mutual reliance on their common humanity above and beyond the realm of respective maladjustments. A lessening of complex communications and the emergence of a relatively uncluttered field of contact can point to successful integration.

Admittedly, the above-outlined difference are not in the nature of right or wrong, but are intended to highlight the progressive aspects of the evolving interpersonal concepts in the therapeutic endeavor. Basically, we need to transcend older epistemological considerations by updating our psychotherapeutic attitudes and by bringing them in tune with a larger part of the world in which they manifest themselves.

A Distinction between Intrapsychic, Transactional, and Interpersonal Views

Psychotherapeutic approaches cover a wide range of prescriptions for classes of maladaptations which are not clearly defined. There are a number of mental disorders with relatively clear-cut symptoms; others represent a mixture of classical manifestations, and a large group of people defy conventional nosological boundaries. In recent years the necessity for diagnostic clarification has become increasingly apparent. Proper diagnosis serves a host of purposes. It is a prerequisite for interprofessional communication, for allowing legitimate comparative considerations as well as for learning and teaching various aspects of psychotherapy. At the same time, diagnosis includes, within reason, an inherent statement about what attitudes may be expected of a particular person in respective life situations.

A problem of our time is the way in which events of daily life have been indiscriminately psychologized. There is major evidence that psychoanalytic concepts have permeated our prevailing culture and that the culture has found a channel into the essence of psychoanalytic theory and practice. This reciprocal pollution has reduced many clinical terms to the state of generalized slogans. Immaturity and insecurity, repression and rejection, low self-esteem, narcissim, frustration tolerance and so forth are merely a few examples of sloganizing psychoanalysis. Accordingly, we encounter increasing difficulties in focusing attention on those attitudes and behavior patterns that reflect distinctly psychological difficulties and are potentially accessible to various forms of psychotherapy.

Today we have a number of conceptual approaches pertaining to a variety of psychotherapeutic procedures. But here we address ourselves mainly to the terms transactional, interpersonal and intrapsychic. These three formulations are a shorthand for models encompassing a set of precepts, and they represent hypothetical constructs designed to guide practitioners in the field of psychotherapy. Each has its own assumptions as well as its built-in prejudices, dogmas, and contradictions. Indeed, it has become common practice to use the terms interpersonal and transactional interchangeably. This indiscriminate way of lumping diverse concepts together is unfortunate. The differences between these concepts far outweigh superficial similarities.

On a dictionary level "inter" is a prefix meaning between, among, mutually, reciprocally, or together such as in intermarriage. It does not refer to a blending or interpenetration. On the other hand, the prefix "trans" means across or beyond as in transcultural. The term transactions is widely used in the conceptualization of a field. It originated in Maxwell's work in physics and found its way into philosophy and sociology. Kurt Lewin introduced the field concept into social psychology, and Sullivan applied it to his interpersonal theory of psychiatry. It could be argued that Sullivan conceived more a transpersonal than interpersonal point of view. Furthermore, he overstressed the behavioristic principles of operationism in his earlier formulations. Nevertheless, there are certain basic assumptions associated with interpersonal theory that need to be stated in their own right, for they involve a radically different frame of reference. To capsulize our previous discussion, the principle of interpersonal relations may best be understood by reference to the concept of ecology as applied to the field of human relations, where it has been given inadequate attention so far, There is no justification in assuming that ecology refers solely to environmental factors: what goes on *between* people within the framework of their natural habitat must also be considered.

Interpersonal formulations always include biologic and social data, in a developmental perspective related to here-and-now events. The individual history of both participants is a significant dimension of their present encounter.Their respective life histories and personality formations constitute major ingredients of the current transactional field. Each personality contains a repertory of responses that come into play when an interpersonal situation becomes integrated. Cognitive distortions tend to prevail when the disruptive experience of anxiety distorts concepts about oneself and others.

Further clarification may be had from Sullivan's suggestion (*Interpersonal Theory*, p. 18) that we "study neither the individual human organism nor the social heritage but the interpersonal situations through which people manifest mental health or mental disorder."

This formulation reemphasizes his conviction that people are not static units with fixed personalities, but acitivity-bound organisms. The past and the present intertwine on a person-to-person basis as well as on a sociocultural level. It is the direct impact of other people, however, that determines the quality of the interpersonal integration regarding anxiety-free or anxiety-fraught situations. In the first instance there is a state of well-being; in the latter situation painful malintegrations prevail.

The term — intrapsychic — properly belongs in the domain of classical psychoanalysis. The prefix "intra" means within, and intrapsychic refers to everything that is located, originates, or takes place within the mind — the totality of conscious and unconscious mental operations.

Interpersonal psychiatry concerns itself more with the process that characterizes a particular encounter between people within the boundaries of their respective personalities. As stated by Zetzel and Meissner (in *Basic Concepts of*

Psychoanalytic Psychiatry, New York, Basic Books, 1973): "Interpersonal relations and their vicissitudes thus take precedence over intrapsychic conflicts and their vicissitudes. The traditional psychoanalytic approach, however, tries to keep the focus on intrapsychic conflicts and the mental processes and forces that give rise to them. The psychoanalytic and the interpersonal approaches, therefore, in a sense look in different directions. This by no means implies that they are therefore contradictory or essentially divergent in their theoretical formulations."

An overemphasis on intrapsychic versus interpersonal phenomena may be seen by some as a Cartesian leftover, since there is an obvious link between the inner and outer world of people. Furthermore, what is intrapsychic and what is interpersonal depends frequently on time factors rather than on inherent processes. On a practical basis, however, the intrapsychic point of view deserves special consideration, because it reflects a widely held psychoanalytic orientation.

Clinically speaking, it refers predominantly to a person's inner life regarding thoughts, impulses, and feelings that take place largely outside a person's awareness. Freud's focal attention on unconscious processes makes a person's inner life the sphere in which the most significant psychological action takes place. In this frame of reference overt manifestations are to be examined with scepticism since they tend to conceal inner conflicts. What meets the naked eye — the surface appearance — is deceptive and frequently covers a complex underground system that operates on an unconscious basis.

Initially, Freud conceived of a system of layers whereby the unconscious by way of the preconscious would emerge into conscious awareness. This scheme (the topographic theory) defined the therapeutic task as bringing the unconscious to the force and exposing it to rational consideration. It was later transcended by introducing the structural theory with the Id, Superego, and Ego as points of reference. In this newer organizational scheme the Id represents the psychological motor for the entire mental apparatus. The Id is conceptualized as the reservoir for libidinal energy. By contrast, the Ego is powerless. Its major function is the adaption to reality, whereas the Superego deals with familial and cultural prescriptions.

Furthermore, Freud formulated two elementary psychical processes in conjunction with his study of dreams, referred to as primary and secondary process. The former centers around wishful, primitive thoughts and is guided by the pleasure principle; in contrast, the latter follows the reality principle.

In Freud's intrapsychic scheme there is an eternal battle raging between Id impulses pressing for discharge and Ego defenses warding off their conscious awareness. This struggle between darkness and light bears some allegorical resemblance to the image of Christ and the Devil locked into never-ending battle. It also reflects the central theme in Goethe's famous poem, which depicts the internal conflict of Dr. Faust (see G. Chrzanowski, "The Changing Language of Self," *Contemporary Psychoanalysis,* Vol. 7, No. 2, Spring 1971). Freud's "intrapsychic man" has difficulty resisting the devil's temptation, which promises gratification by ignoring the consequences of uncontrolled behavior. An element of redemption is offered, however, when man is capable of recognizing his instinctual strivings and manages to gain conscious control over them. Freud's basic metaphors are religious and moral in character and are couched in an atmosphere of heroism and personal drama. The hero is always in the center of events, but he is burdened with a mortal body that is ill equipped to deal with temptation.

In contrast to Freudian metapsychology, interpersonal theory has dispensed with many metaphors. Sullivan's "interpersonal man" is predominantly a public figure. He has no hiding place in the unconscious, and he is always an integral part of each and every interpersonal situation in which he participates. The nature of "the interpersonal Self" is relatively amorphous until the person is engaged in activities with others. The individual relies on a never-ending process of defining himself rather than on stable, inherent qualities. Accordingly he is much less rooted in past metapsychological symbolism. A durable frame of reference centers around specifically human phenomena that are shared by all mankind. They take precedence over intrinsic or extrinsic events of a sporadic nature.

In fairness, we should appreciate that Freud's intrapsychic

point of view did not foreclose his consideration of a larger perspective, as his introduction to *Group Psychology and the Analysis of the Ego* makes evident: "Only rarely and under certain circumstances is individual psychology in a position to disregard the relations of this individual to others. In the individual's mental life someone else is invariably involved as an object, as a helper, as an opponent and so from the very first, individual psychology is at the same time social psychology — in this extended but entirely justifiable sense of the word."

We also should remember that Freud's work has been transcended by the contributions of Ego psychology. Freud himself had attempted to accord the Ego a larger measure of independence in his later writings without changing his basic model of the Ego as a derivative of the Id. Hartman's conceptualization of a "sphere within the ego that is free from conflict" accords the Ego greater autonomy. The resulting point of view is that the Ego is potentially active (endowed with intentionality) rather than constituting a largely reactive system. In the new scheme of Ego psychology the boundaries between intrapsychic and interpersonal are somewhat less rigid, with the dichotomy between a primary and secondary process less pronounced. Nevertheless, the classical Ego psychologists are unduly burdened by their adherence to the notion of psychical energy and by clinging to certain metapsychological formulations that have not stood the test of time.

To reiterate; interpersonal, transactional and intrapsychic phenomena coexist to a large degree. Each approach highlights a particular dimension of the overall process. It is unfortunate, however, that in present usage each term represents a particular ideology or psychoanalytic school of thought. The terms are no longer applied in a descriptive way. Instead they encompass specific doctrines with reference to certain principles that are taught and advocated in a partisan spirit. Accordingly, communication breaks down when we shift from one concept to the other. The lines of demarcation between interpersonal, transactional and intrapsychic data have become unduly rigidified and dogmatized. Much benefit could be gained in interchanging ideas from different vantage points by using terms outside of their ideological stereotype. At present, every practicing analyst requires some theory of therapy as a guideline for assisting people.

Causes of Mental Disorders

One of the great preoccupations of psychological thinking in the past has been the search for singular causes of mental disorders. In some instances there was a determination to find an organic, biologic basis for disturbances of the human mind. In other instances focal attention rested on an exclusively physiochemical foundation for psychiatric illness. On a strictly psychological basis it was popular to isolate one-dimensional causes. At one time sexual repression was considered to be the cause of every neurosis, but the role of sexuality in our society has significantly changed without necessarily reducing the frequency or intensity of mental disorders. Parents were singled out as favorite targets, and excessively hissed at as villains in many forms of psychotherapy. Next, it was the family that carried the major causative burden of neurosis and psychosis. Finally, the primary blame fell on society and culture.

It is clear today that each and all these factors play a part in the formation and maintenance of mental disorders. We have become more sophisticated in thinking of multiple variables, both biologic and sociocultural, as contributory agents to human maladaptations. What has emerged with increasing clarity is the significance of personal integrations between people, the quality of human relatedness, the network of communicative channels, and the evolving capacity for intimacy. The evolution of optimal development depends largely on the timing and opportunity for unfolding one's innate individual and human capacities in a supportive interpersonal and socioeconomic setting in which personal dignity and self-esteem are rooted. The preoccupation with single causes recedes into the background once we think in terms of transactional processes whereby the very essence of a person is in a constant state of interpenetration with other people, social institutions, and physiochemical components. We are always dealing with a large interconnected unit that cannot be objectively dissected into separate parts.

The Nature of the Therapeutic Process: Classical Psychoanalysis Compared to Interpersonal Theory

Interpersonal theory and classical psychoanalytic theory differ in many aspects of the therapeutic process, including the conception of the analyst's role, the nature of the analytic process, the goal of therapy, and the technical procedure.

Initially, in classical psychoanalysis the analytic process is centered around the vicissitudes of the transference as a means of overcoming the patient's resistances. Based on the principle of the repetition compulsion, the patient would reexperience his past by undergoing a transference neurosis, which eventually would be resolved by interpretation. Transference is interpreted as a genuine reliving of the past and a distortion of the figure of the analyst. Positive transference diminishes transferential distortions and assists in overcoming resistances. The recollection of early memories and forgotten or repressed material must be of a spontaneous nature. A questioning, structuring, or organizing of the material by the analyst is discouraged. Patient and analyst listen to the emerging material, which is implemented by cautious interpretations. There is a neutral, passive analytic ambience that encourages the regression in the form of an infantile transference neurosis. The goal of classical therapy is to deal with neurotic conflict — an unconscious clash between an Id impulse seeking discharge and an Ego defense warding off the impulse's direct discharge or access to consciousness. The technical procedures of classical analysis are interpretation and free association. According to Greenson (*The Technique and Practice of Psychoanalysis,* Vol. I, University Press, Chicago, 1972), "interpretation is still the decisive and ultimate instrument of the psychoanalyst, while free association has remained the basic and unique method of communication for patients in psychoanalytic treatment. These two technical procedures give psychoanalytic therapy its distinctive stamp. Other means of communication occur during psychoanalytic therapy, but they are affiliated, preparatory or secondary, and not typical of psychoanalysis." This focus on free association, interpretation, and insight stemmed from Freud's abiding faith in the liberating force of truth. These methods were considered the essential pathways to psychological truth, and a skilled analyst could decode perceptions and symbolic operations in a way that brought the true events to the fore.

Interpersonal theory views these tenets of classical psychoanalysis as being hampered by a number of epistemological inaccuracies. First, as previously mentioned, it is questionable whether anyone can reconstruct the past in true historical perspective since the perception of the past is influenced by here and now encounters as well as by the anticipation of future events. Second, there has not been any adequate documentation for the assumption that the intrapsychic pathway is a beacon to psychological truth. One need never argue about a search for the truth. What matters is where one expects to find it, and how one can potentially verify one's findings. Interpretations and insights are subjective and not factual statements; free association is not an internal phenomenon independent of its own workings and its interpersonal setting. Internal as well as external components connected with the associative process have a decisive effect on the associations produced. It is difficult, therefore, to consider free association and interpretation the decisive and ultimate tools for psychoanalytic therapy.

In interpersonal theory the therapeutic transaction is conceived as the process of highlighting distortions and miscommunication rooted in the past that are activated and modified in the here and now. It rejects the notion that a neurosis or sickness inside a person can be cured by the "medicine" of insight. Anxiety and the attempts to deal with it are explored with the aim of widening the scope of observation for both therapist and patient. Verbal and nonverbal communication are expanded through the process of checking and verifying messages, leading in time to the capacity for intimacy. Regression is not considered part of the therapeutic precess, in that a focusing on the past does not necessarily require a reliving of the actual events. Historical data are not merely used for the purpose of reconstruction. Rather, they serve as a guideline for the patterning of past, present and future interpersonal integrations.

The Therapeutic Transaction

Central to this conception of the therapeutic transaction is the reformulation of the role of the analyst. Freud viewed the analyst's role as analagous to that of a surgeon, who performs his task without involving his personality in the procedure, or to a mirror, reflecting the patient's behavior. The analyst functioned as a catalyst rather than a participant in the therapeutic alliance. In recent years Freudians have emancipated themselves in many respects from the notion of a mirror analyst who remains totally aloof and anonymous. Today the classical analyst is cast in the role of a benevolent, concerned parental figure who wishes his "analytic child" well. according to Greenson, "he is a physician and a therapist, a treater of the sick and suffering, and his aim is to help the patient get well." However, "the medicine" he prescribes is insight, carefully regulating the dosage. The relationship between analyst and patient is viewed as a "working alliance," a concept that refers to a relatively undistorted, rational relationship between patient and analyst designed to promote therapeutic operations. This notion, however, is still rooted in the principle of expecting the patient to play the rules of the game, to be cooperative for his own good, and to bow to interpretations and the resulting insight as an ultimate truth. Viewing the analyst as a treater of the sick who doles out insight in carefully prescribed dosages reinforces a basically authoritarian "medical model."

The necessity for a basically parental, authoritarian formulation of the classic therapeutic alliance lies in a number of interconnected assumptions. The rationale for this attitude is the quest for objectivity and for a basic truth. It rests on the hypothesis that pristine fantasies, wishes, and irrational impulses can be tapped in pure form by the method of free association. A major purpose of therapeutic neutrality is, presumably, to facilitate the reconstruction of the past without bias. The classical psychoanalyst is expected to keep his personal characteristics under cover as a means of fully drawing out the patient's personality. The interpersonal therapist is largely deprived of this insular status and can no longer be placed in a neutral corner as a catalyst mirror or an objective ambassador of reality. Neither can the therapist be viewed as a coathanger for the patient's transference neurosis. He is defined as a skilled observer who participates in the therapeutic situation by monitoring his own responses and judiciously sharing them with the patient. The psychiatrist as observer can never be a neutral figure. He is always an interacting participant in the therapeutic process, a "participant observer." Sullivan was keenly aware that the process of observing invariably modified the object of observation (a principle of physics) and that all observational data including strictly physical acts required an appreciation of the observing instrument. He was aware, too, of P. W. Bridgeman's remarks that we deal with a twofold aspect of the problem of understanding: the process of understanding the world around us and the problem of understanding the nature of the intellectual tools with which we attempt to understand that world. In other words, the observer's mode of thinking about his observations is always part of what he observes.

Sullivan redefined the respective roles of analyst and patient by placing them in a distinctly more reciprocal frame of reference. The potentially curative bond is considered to be the mutual reliance on the common humanity of the patient and therapist, leading to a lessening of complex communications, the emergence of a relatively uncluttered field of contact, and, eventually to more successful interpersonal integrations. Sullivan's interpersonal therapeutic model thus supports an egalitarian relational pattern significantly modifying the authoritarian doctor-patient pattern of classical analysis. A major part of therapy consists in expanding the observational and communicative field when multiple facets of the patient's personality become engaged with the psychiatrist both as a real and a distorted person. Treatment per se is an on-going interpersonal process in which the therapist participates. His method of observation and his expectation of a legitimate therapeutic goal tend to modify attitudinal and emotional roots of current behavior and have an impact on the immediate future. The conceptualization of the "working alliance" in classical psychoanalysis calls for some elaboration because the necessity for a basically parental, authoritarian formulation of the classic therapeutic alliance lies in a number of interconnected and dubious assumptions.

It has been appreciated by a number of Freudian analysts that the request for helplessness and submission from the patient may foster indiscriminate, even masochistic acceptance of whatever is offered. Accordingly, increasing emphasis has been placed on indicating concern, courtesy, thoughtfulness, and a measure of controlled compassion. The principle is similar to requesting parents, teachers, and other authorities to treat minors, minorities, or employees with dignity and respect. Nobody would want to argue the validity of a basically human approach in all nonegalitarian situations. It does not change the fact, however, that the "tilted" or "unequal" model entails a lopsided notion of the working alliance.

This consideration brings us back to the underlying hypothesis for the classic analytic model and its present-day modifications. Freud's unshakable conviction that the truth sets people free is admirable and inspiring. Freud was also driven by a need to stay within the boundaries of science as he understood them in his constant search for reality, objectivity and logic in the psychological domain. Here we must appreciate the fact that scientific truth is never static lest it turn into dogma. Pre-Copernican astronomers demonstrated that the sun rotated obligingly around their own homes, and that a substance called Ether held the constellations in place. Apparently, present day traditional psychoanalytic practice is still centered on a scientific truth of the past which calls for some basic modifications. Free association, interpretation, and insight were pronounced to be the essential pathways to psychological truth, which required a complex methodology to support the hypothesis. It enshrined the intrapsychic conceptualization as the proven seat of coded perceptions and symbol operations that a skilled analyst could decode in a way which brought the true events to the fore.

In a similar vein Freud's worship of rationality and his crusade against unmasking irrationality complicated his task of constructing psychoanalytic postulates. It was difficult for Freud to conceive of any constructive components of irrationality [see Chrzanowski "The Changing Language of the Self," *Contemporary Psychoanalysis,* Vol. 2, No. 2, 1971 and "The Rational Id and the Irrational Ego," *Journal of the American Academy of Psychoanalysis,* 1(3), 1973]. To Freud, the irrational remained a metaphor for rampant sexual and destructive aggressivity, but there is no legitimate reason to assume that opposition to rationality per se stamps thoughts and actions as destructive.

In summary, it can be said that the classical tenets of psychoanalysis are hampered by a number of epistemological inaccuracies. There has not been an adequate documentation for an intrapsychic pathway as a reliable beacon to psychological truth. Accordingly, we are not justified in considering free association and interpretation to be the decisive and ultimate tools for psychoanalytic therapy; and interpretations and insights are subjective formulations of events rather than factual considerations. Some specific modifications in analytic practice come to mind when we include these views.

For instance, traditional psychoanalysis considers free association to be an internal phenomenon independent from its own workings and from its interpersonal setting. It minimizes or denies the impact of internal and external components connected with the associative process. But what of people with neurotic difficulties who are frequently more attuned to nonverbal than to overt verbal communications? They often learn to "read between the lines" in the process of giving information about themselves. The analyst's reluctance to reveal his personal expectations and feelings does not prevent patients from picking up a host of nonverbal signals and promptings.

Adapting therapeutic technique to a newer epistemological model does not imply a discarding of many procedures that have proven to be useful. The couch—traditional symbol of psychoanalysis — has not become obsolete. It tends to relax many patients, helps them to concentrate on the task at hand, and constitutes a worthwhile experience.

In the mainstream of Freudian psychoanalysis there is a need to insulate the patient from the vibrations of daily life so that he can pay the fullest attention to his past. Implicit in the method is a mandate for analytic passivity. This atmosphere of the "faceless" observer and the neutral, passive, analytic ambience encourages the manifestation of regression in the form of an infantile transference neurosis. Central in the procedure is the interpretation of transference as a genuine reliving of the past and a distortion of the figure of the analyst. Positive transference diminishes transferential distortions and assists in overcoming resistances. The recollection of early memories and forgotten as well as repressed material must be of a spontaneous nature. Questioning, structuring, or organizing the material by the analyst is discouraged. Patient and analyst listen to the emerging material, which is implemented by cautious interpretations.

In short, classical psychoanalysis considers itself to be the method suited to dealing with problems due to repression and related defensive mechanisms. The idea is to reactivate basic, developmental conflicts by reproducing the infantile neurosis in a setting of objectivity and nonneurotic support. The interpretation of transference manifestations, triangular or oedipal problems, and the need to work through the conflicts rather than act them out are among the keystones of the classical therapeutic procedure. Regression is considered to be a sine qua non in the resolution of neurotic conflicts. In essence, the conflict is seen as residing inside of the patient while the analyst encourages the problems to come to the fore. The therapeutic task then is to expose the patient to his irrational wishes, resist their gratification, and assist him in achieving a better and more mature integration.

As time went on Sullivan transcended the Freudian conceptual framework not by rephrasing Freud's discoveries, as claimed by some, but by finding a newer epistemological foundation for the understanding and ameliorating of human maladjustments. Little is gained by pointing out in detail what Sullivan accepted or rejected in classical psychoanalysis. He himself warned against translating his conceptions into psychoanalytic language. Sullivan was an ardent student of the physical and social sciences. His search was for a new platform for the study of man in exploring the field of human relations. He found, in the sociologist George Herbert Mead's formulation of "The Generalized Other," a model for his dynamic notion of an on-going two-way process in human relations. *Mind, Society and the Self,* together with the concept of introjected, eidetic, or internalized people became the forerunner of the interpersonal or ecologic Self. The notion of an eidetic[1] image differs significantly from the intrapsychic construct of an introject as an actual replica of a past person rather than a parataxic distortion. The latter refers to a cognitive process that affects an ongoing interpersonal situation by permeating the transactional field and leading to warped integrations as well as to faulty perceptions of them.

A major shift in Sullivan's formulations consisted of his increasing emphasis on process as a continuous-action phenomenon or series of changes taking place in a definite manner. It led away from closed-system concepts to open-ended ones, and it transcended the deterministic Freudian model. Furthermore, Sullivan no longer considered the individual human being to be a reliable object for psychiatric exploration. He recommended the ecologic human process between man and his total environment as a more appropriate unit of study. His thinking along these lines was strongly reinforced by the construct of Field theory. Sullivan's essential innovation was the recognition that psychiatric manifestations are not the result of internal, intrapsychic events isolated from their overall surroundings. His focus of exploring psychiatric phenomena was always on the multitude of transactional events within the prevailing field. By no means does his interpersonal scheme emphasize social phenomena to the exclusion of all other considerations. The concept of social factors and cultural components must be appreciated as the ever present, always integral part of human existence.

CHAPTER 2

Basic Theorems of Interpersonal Psychiatry: Anxiety, Parataxis and Related Phenomena

Cognition and Anxiety

Cognition and anxiety assume a complementary role in interpersonal theory. Both reflect experiential events and are subject to the quality of rapport between the individual and his human environment. There is a lack of agreement in defining the process of cognition in a universally acceptable fashion. The major controversy, similar to the definition of anxiety, centers on its operational vicissitudes. Sullivanian psychiatry tends to view both phenomena as not present at birth and places particular emphasis on anxiety as an acquired interpersonal tension without any organismic underpinning. Anxiety controls the content of awareness and determines what is represented in the Self. Cognition pertains to the boundaries of external and internal perception as well as to the personalized coding of the informational data.

The mediation of experience and the way experience shapes information about oneself and others is a central consideration of interpersonal formulations. In that respect we are dealing with the input of information, the processing of information, and the storing of information. Developmentally it is the ability to conceptualize, generalize, and personalize information that makes up the structure of cognitive phenomena.

Cognition, that is, the way we have personal knowledge

about ourselves and the world around us, is intimately connected with the experience of anxiety. It serves as a restrictive and distorting agent of a person's development as well as the person's ongoing observational acumen. What can be observed about oneself and one's reflected appraisal of oneself in the eyes of others depends largely on the intervention of anxiety or its relative absence. The experience of anxiety has a longitudinal root as well as a here and now manifestation.

A distinction should be made between attributes or characteristics of the human organism that are relatively fixed compared to the more pliable manifestations. It stands to reason that the clinical field of psychiatry deals predominantly with what is capable of change rather than with fixed entities. The organism itself is in a constant state of transformation and modification in a process of transaction with its human and physiochemical environment. In accordance with hereditary, developmental, and existential factors, a cognitive map evolves that reflects the sum total of experiential data as they have been individualized and personalized. Accordingly, cognition develops along two interrelated but independent lines: the sequential unfolding of inherent human capacities and the interpersonal impact of the developmental process as dictated by personal experiences. The result is a mixture of relatively undistorted and distorted cognitive structures.

Cognitive distortions are conceived predominantly as telltales of early anxiety-fraught experiences, whereas relational integrations or interpersonal encounters take place within the evolving field of contact with another person and the concomitant level of anxiety aroused by it. In intensely anxious contacts primitive, preverbal cognitive processes come to the fore (prototaxic). Moderate anxiety evokes warped and distorted cognitive representations (parataxic), whereas mild anxiety leads to relatively uncomplicated, consensually validated cognitive manifestations (syntaxic).

Prototaxic or autistic experiences belong largely to the group of undifferentiated, nonverbalized phenomena (referred to as primary process in classical theory) and are found in profound mental disturbances. Parataxic experiences make up the bulk of neurotic syndromes. Included in this cognitive parameter are both transference and countertransference manifestations as well as events occurring in the state of dreaming. We are dealing here with a high degree of human malintegrations in the form of misperceptions, projections, and related security operations. Syntaxic experience represents an ideal goal of human contact.

General Meanings of Anxiety

Anxiety is a prominent consideration in the great majority of psychotherapeutic theories and in their clinical application. Nevertheless, much controversy surrounds the formulation of anxiety and its position in the hierarchy of psychological phenomena. Interpersonal theory has placed the implications of anxiety in everyday life and in psychiatry first on its list as a key factor in human relations. Sullivan's initial formulation of the meaning of anxiety has led to strong criticism of its basic premises. It has been distorted to the analogy of a "Typhoid Mary" syndrome whereby the mother as the carrier of an evil germ called anxiety transmits it to her innocent offspring. Actually, Sullivan conceived of an inherent human inadequacy to cope with the man-made tension of anxiety, but views it as an interpersonal umbrella that covers every aspect of life.

It has often been said that Freud erred in injecting a notion of pansexuality into classical psychoanalysis, whereas Sullivan made the mistake of introducing pananxiety into his brand of psychiatry. Libido theory does, indeed, permeate all psychoanalytic considerations. Similarly, the theorem of anxiety is forever present in the interpersonal frame of reference.

Psychiatric Definitions of Anxiety

The psychiatric dictionary definition of anxiety also fails to tell us whether we are dealing with a chronic psychic tension in mental disorders or with particular anxious reactions to objectively harmless situations.In other words, "anxiety" in psychiatric terminology as well as in everyday language refers to a feeling tone of discomfort without explicit reference to its nature, origin, or basic implications.

Psychiatric dictionaries such as English and English or Hinsie are aware of the diverse meanings of anxiety in psychiatric, psychological, and psychoanalytic usage. Each school of psychoanalysis clings to its own private definition. One theorist's anxiety is another theorist's fear. Freud interchanges both *Angst* and *Furcht* in some of his writings.

One of the major difficulties in discussing anxiety is the fact that the term has come to mean very different things to people. Indeed, our daily language does not make a particular distinction between anxiety and fear. Webster's Dictionary defines anxiety as "distress or uneasiness of mind caused by apprehension of danger or misfortune," but the definition does not concern itself with the question of whether the apprehension of danger or misfortune is real or illusory. The Webster's definition concludes that anxiety is "a state of apprehension and psychic tension found in most forms of mental disorders." Anxiety is, or has been viewed as an inherent existential phenomenon, as a potential source for creativity and humanity, as a displacement, an unwanted calamity, a sickness or a royal road to mental health. There is a conceptualization of physiological anxiety as well as a behavioristic model of anxiety, and any number of combinations between the concepts mentioned. In addition, we refer to circumscribed areas of anxiety as phobias and to anxieties involving a person's physical health as hypochondriasis.

It is not sufficiently appreciated that although anxiety reflects a universal human experience, each person experiences anxiety in his own individual fashion. Accordingly, we encounter major difficulties in communicating the experience of anxiety because its conceptualization is extremely vague and everyday language has an inadequate vocabulary for the shadings and individual nuances of an ubiquitous human phenomenon.

The twentieth century has been described in its earlier phases as the Age of Anxiety, then as the Era of Alienation. Now, toward its waning years, it may well have turned into the

Age of Lethargy, Mediocrity, and Inauthenticity. It does not mean that the future of mankind is bleak and that new generations are a bunch of hapless human beings with minimal realistic expectations for a better life in a viable environment.

Let us assume that the so-called Age of Anxiety has receded at the present time. We may not have any reliable yardstick to determine whether anxiety has actually become less of a focal aspect in human existence — it may have merely gone underground, taken on a differenct guise, or people may have become more immune or outright insensitive to it. Much of this speculation depends on how we view anxiety, but most practitioners in the field of psychoanalysis and psychotherapy report today that they are consulted by a distinctly smaller number of people with acute anxiety symptoms than in years past. In part we can attribute this state of affairs to a tremendous increase in the consumption of tranquilizing chemicals. We also find that Freud's crusade against repressed sexuality has been successful beyond expectations. Actual sexual frustration as a source of anxiety (the rule in the past Victorian era) no longer is a significant factor in modern life. Also, the metaphor of penis envy as a manifestation of unequal rights for women is in a militantly remedial phase and unlikely to be a major cause of widespread anxiety. A lessening of authoritarian practices in the home with a changing role of the nuclear family has reduced certain problems or conflicts that were considered to be potential causes of anxiety. In sum, our society has undergone a distinct metamorphosis in many respects. It is conceivable that some traditionally anxietogenic factors have been reduced or eliminated, but it is also possibe that the change has affected primarily the phenotype or the mode of manifesting anxiety rather than the basic anxiety.

We realize, too, that changes in the nature, manifestation, and origin of anxiety characterize the history of mankind as well as the developmental phases of individuals — the anxiety of primitive man differs from the anxiety of modern man. Many ancient mysteries have been stripped of their threatening qualities by the advance of scientific knowledge. Numerous menacing phenomena of nature and illness have been tamed or conquered. When it comes to the individual, it is

evident that the anxieties of childhood, adolescence, adult life
and old age show significant modifications. The focal areas of
concern shift with different developmental phases in spite of
the fact that life without a measure of anxiety is inconceivable.
However, we are in one respect dealing with variations in the
nature, quality, manifestations and causes of anxiety; in
another, with a universal human anxiety throughout the entire cycle of life imposed by its vagaries, independent of the
evolution of mankind, the development of individuals and
their particular life experiences.

Neo-Freudian Formulations of Anxiety

It is obvious that psychology cannot unduly concern itself
with the human condition per se or with universal existential
anxiety. What concerns us in the field of psychotherapy are
mainly the conditions under which people manifest anxiety by
functional paralysis and by unaccountable acts of incompetence, malintegration, and self-defeating manifestations.
Some representatives of neo-Freudian schools of thought believe that the anxiety is the result of becoming an inauthentic
person, giving up one's personal freedom or failing to seek
self fulfillment. In this frame of reference the anxiety is an
outcry against having sold out, having betrayed one's basic
humanity, ignored one's personal endowment, talent or potential, and having abdicated one's autonomy to familial,
societal, political exploitation. Seen from this point of view,
anxiety is conceptualized as an essentially healthy manifestation like pain and fever designed to alert and hopefully protect the individual against loss of his human and biologic
intactness.

Other classical and neoclassical schools of thought consider anxiety to be a basically harmful condition that must be
removed, diminished, constructively channelled, or coun-
teracted. Conflicting ambitions, unrealistic expectations, or
primitive drives are often used as explanatory causes of anxiety. A major goal, then, is to achieve mastery over the irra-

tional by gaining insight in the crippling effects of defenses or symptoms that are synonymous with the presence of anxiety.

In most classical and neoclassical thoeries anxiety is the dragon's tooth or the neurotic illness that needs to be fought in order to restore mental health. To Horney, for instance, anxiety is the core of every neurosis and indicates that the person is living against his natural grain. Behind the mask of anxiety Horney sees repressed hostility, resentment, and aggression — the telltales of lack of warmth, security, and love from parental sources. The result is alienation, interpersonal insulation, and the culturally reinforced quest for glory, with resulting thralldom to an idealized image. Anxiety subsides and neurosis wanes when the real Self prevails over the inauthentic Self.

To Fromm, anxiety occurs when man turns his back to freedom and becomes a mechanized tool of the dehumanizing methods of production. He becomes but an object on the general market, while his inherently human strivings for loving, creativity, and tolerance for man's innate separateness and isolation are stunted. Anxiety turns self-assertion and natural aggression into destructiveness. The result is a dehumanization from a love for life to a love for death.

The reader is referred to the vast literature available on the subject of anxiety. There are numerous excellent presentations pertaining to psychological theories of anxiety (among others is the well-known book by Rollo May, *The Meaning of Anxiety*). Rather than discuss various points of view, a brief sketch of some of the highlights of classical compared to interpersonal formulations of anxiety is offered.

Current Discrepancies Between Classical and Interpersonal Views of Anxiety

The basic discrepancies in the respective concepts are best illustrated by pointing to current classical versus interpersonal views on anxiety before comparing Freud's and Sullivan's initial formulations on the topic.

Some modern analysts of the classical school of thought believe "that the interpersonal dimension of human interaction is not, strictly speaking, opposed to psychoanalytic thinking."[1] For instance, to better understand clinical aspects of anxiety Zetzel and Meissner recommend an approach that combines both interpersonal and intrapsychic assumptions. The classical authors are of the opinion that a one-sided inter-personal as much as an exclusively intrapsychic approach to an anxiety-ridden patient restricts the clinical understanding of the problem at hand. Their recommendation is for taking both components into account as a means of rounding out the picture.

The suggested rapprochement between interpersonal and intrapsychic tenets rests on their opinion that the two approaches look in different directions. They consider inter-personal theory as an extension and a development of object relations theory within psychoanalysis, and they conclude that "it can thus be viewed as a special subdivision of psychoanalytic theory which can be readily be integrated with the basic assumptions of psychoanalysis."

Certainly, the mushrooming of different schools of psychoanalysis is destructive and detrimental to the growth of the field. There is, or should be, room for many differences within the overall field of psychoanalytic psychiatry. However, it calls for a clarification of our underlying assumptions and for the freedom to expose dogma where it exists. The platform that underlies the conclusions drawn by these authors should, therefore, be examined.

In their judgement psychoanalysis transcends an awareness and modification of interpersonal processes as they unfold in the therapeutic relationship. The additional psychoanalytic dimension referred to by Zetzel and Meissner pertains to the reactivation of original conflicts that have been pushed out of awareness and repressed. What emerges is a resurfacing of the wishes and fantasies, which necessitated the formation of neurotic symptoms. Controlled regression aids the activation of a transference neurosis, the classical sine qua non of bringing old conflicts to the fore.

It seems that there are two basic inaccuracies in this attempted classical-interpersonal rapprochement to the problem of anxiety: (1) The term interpersonal is incorrectly conceived as a primary here and now transaction rather than as a historical, transactional approach. There are distinct roots to the developmental Self in its encounter with the environment. In fact, the interpersonal tenet of anxiety refers directly to formative relational experiences and their present-day emotional and cognitive extensions. (2) As has already been pointed out, there is genuine doubt about the literal aspects of repetitive compulsion, that is, that we are dealing with a stimulus-response system whereby we can relive or reconstruct original experiences in their original form. In our present state of knowledge we lack any kind of solid documentation that the classical "medicine of insight" is more than a placebo phenomenon. How are we to prove that alleged wishes and fantasies of early life are the primary building stones of neurotic symptoms? We cannot underrate the suggestive "hypnotic" power of interpretative, verbal constructs.

Verbal concretizations are often used as if they were an explanation for a basically obscure event. It may be comforting to some patients to be told that an acute anxiety attack is the result of an unresolved oedipal conflict, despite the fact that such a causal connection is a speculative assumption and beyond the realm of checking and verification. After all, people's anxieties respond or fail to respond to a wide range of logical and illogical approaches. We find here a gamut ranging from autogenic training to megavitamins, from religion to love, from sex therapy to primal screams and from the intervention of con artists to the concern of sincere practitioners.

A Clinical Illustration

Zetzel and Meissner most appropriately illustrate their conceptualization of traditional psychoanalytic compared to interpersonal formulation with a clinical case presentation. The case concerns a young man who undergoes an acute anxiety state that subsides during a relatively brief course of analytically based interpretive psychotherapy. The patient expressed the fear that he was about to have a nervous break-down and would require hospitalization in a mental institute. His mounting anxiety became intolerable when an acquaintance of his had suffered the very fate he feared most.

The anxiety attack coincided with new responsibilities (he recently assumed in the family business). In addition, he had taken on financial burdens by buying a new house for his own family — a wife and two little boys.

The patient's anxiety symptoms gradually diminished as he responded to an interpretation of his conflict; that is, he basically had the unconscious wish to be helpless and dependent. His anxiety about cracking up and possibly having to be institutionalized represented a disguised inner desire to avoid responsibility as husband, father, and provider. Consciously, he rejected his wishful fantasies and clung to his stated goals and ambitions. There was also some compulsive need to do what was expected of him rather than what he really wanted as well as a concealed rivalry with the oldest brother whom he overtly emulated.

We are then told that on an interpersonal basis the emphasis would be on predominantly environmental factors, such as dependency patterns and relationship between the patient and his brother. His anxiety would be interpreted as a chain reaction whereby every move toward independence arouses anxiety "because his inner feelings of inadequacy and dependency were threatened."

We are also given to understand that in interpersonal perspective the act of buying the house would be viewed as the main event in triggering off the acute anxiety attack. The purchase of the house is conceptualized as a symbolic gesture of the patient trying to stand on his own feet. Environmental factors threaten the patient's deeply ingrained passive-dependent patterns by leading him in the direction of greater self-reliance and autonomy. Under the pressure of present real circumstances, the patient has only one way of remaining passive and dependent, and that is by seeing himself as a helpless patient in a mental hospital. According to Zetzel and Meissner, the process described here represents the level of an interpersonal explanation pertaining to their clinical case report.

The authors make a distinction between the patient's reality problems in the adult world, including his intense rivalry and disappointment with his brother, and the intrapsychic components in his assuming greater responsibility. Regarding the situation with the brother, the stirring of aggression gives rise to a signal of an internal danger. A defensive retreat into passivity and apparent compliance are viewed as the patient's response to the danger signal. It is stated that "the unconscious meaning of aggression stemming from his childhood persisted and in terms of his original defenses remained unchanged."

Zetzel and Meissner refer to their case history (reported here in greatly abbreviated form) as a good illustration of the differences between intrapsychic and interpersonal dynamics. A review of the material by the author of this book does not confirm their assumption. Their interpersonal perspective is taken from a behavioristic model and is not in keeping with interpersonal conceptions.

Evaluation of Case Material

Rather than point out detailed theoretical and clinical differences, it will perhaps be more illustrative to describe the case in interpersonal terms.

Generally, direct observation and communication about what is observed is preferred to interpretation. The emerging observational data are viewed against the patient's developmental background. Comments are offered mainly for the purpose of hearing what response they evoke rather than interpretive statements of a preconceived theoretical nature. Much attention is given to security operations in the form of selective inattention, sterile bickering, apathy, lethargy, verbalisms, mutisms, and many other defensive maneuvers. Events under the impact of severe anxiety are not expected to be recalled by the patient.

The patient under discussion would be encouraged to tell how, to his way of thinking, he came to be the person he is today. At the end of this exploratory process, a feedback by the therapist is offered summarizing his understanding of the data presented by the patient. At the same time, an effort is made to formulate characteristic attitudes and patterns as they emerge.

The buying of the house would at best be looked upon as "the straw that broke the camel's back." Primary emphasis would be placed on learning the patient's areas of vulnerability in his personal transactions with other people, by observing the particular security operations emerging in the therapeutic situation. In each instance genetic connections are looked for pertaining to early interpersonal integrations indicative of anxiety-fraught patterns. The patient's anxiety attack would be explored along the lines of lowering of self-esteem inculcated very early in life and leading to potential maladaptations during the sequential developmental epochs. Attention is given to successes or failures in peer relations, sexual experimentations, social, professional activities, and so forth through the formative stages to the present. Experiences of tensions, lonliness, and potential intimacy are carefully examined in the collaborative, therapeutic process. In the case under discussion it is conceivable, for instance, that the patient had become increasingly isolated and lost his faculty for personally meaningful communication.

In other words, the interpersonal approach is not to be confused with an environmentally oriented cause-and-effect concept. It is rooted in a developmental point of view with emphasis on on-going interpersonal events harking back to the formative relational influences and pointing to anticipatory attitudes of future events.

An Interpersonal Conceptualization of Anxiety

Present-day psychotherapy tends to focus much attention on acute anxiety attacks. The emergence of crisis intervention centers, emergency units, and walk-in clinics has contributed a great deal to this development. Such a setup serves very real needs of people in acute distress and bears a resemblance to the lifesaving activities of an intensive care unit in a general hospital. At the same time, it fosters an overemphasis on dealing with the acute anxiety attack as a condition sui generis. The result of this type of intervention is often a desired calming down of the patient by means of chemicals, hypnotic suggestions, or workable common-sense approaches. In one way or another, the patient frequently feels reassured without getting anywhere close to the core of the underlying problem. At times the patient is offered an interpretation that often turns out to be a verbal placebo rather than a genuine understanding of his life-long conflict.

This concept will become more evident if we relegate the acute anxiety attack to the category of a broken down failsafe system. In other words, acute anxiety attacks do not necessarily have a particular cause of their own. They ordinarily are "short-circuits" in an inherently badly wired system.

There is considerable clinical merit in looking at anxiety as belonging to a different gender than an acute anxiety attack in spite of a complex genetic nexus or link between the two phenomena. Anxiety is a permanent, indelible interpersonal experience, whereas anxiety attacks are symptoms triggered off by malintegrations of on-going dealings with people who assume significance in one's life. Anxiety has always been there and consists of a warped Self image. It is implanted in the very early formative years. On the other hand, the anxiety attack is a cumulative interpersonal integration that centers on bringing to the fore major areas of low Self-esteem by mutually and unwittingly focussing on a person's defenses rather than on their areas of security.

Ordinarily, it is a basically well-functioning antianxiety system that obscures the degree of chronically defensive attitudes. There usually is no hint of the degree of looking the other way involved when it comes to a clear representation of the Self. A person's appraisal of himself in his own eyes as well as reflected to him through the eyes of other is chronically permeated with doubt, disapproval, and disdain. It is usually the failure of the anitanxiety system that leads to the acute anxiety attack whereby the Self is flooded with undigested experiences beyond its comprehension.

A few explanatory comments are required to outline this point of view.

Acute Anxiety Attack Versus Anxiety

Interpersonal theory distinguishes between two interrelated but inherently separate ecologic systems — man and his human environment. Anxiety as formulated in interpersonal terms relates exclusively to the world of people rather than to aspects of physical survival. It represents an experience of tension acquired very early in life and transmitted by one's fellow human beings. The assumption is that the mother is either the carrier of the anxiety or that she transmits anxiety stemming from her own interpersonal situtation. Whether the mother was a chronically anxious woman, or whether she was involved in a situational anxiety-fraught transaction connected with significant people in her life, the effect on the infant remains essentially the same.

An acute anxiety attack is the most obvious form of anxiety that confronts the clinician. It usually occurs as a state of acute tension which may render the victim totally helpless during the attack. At such moments the mind is frequently filled with thoughts of extreme distress and feelings of impending disaster. Most commonly, physiologic symptoms, such as violent palpitations, racing of the pulsebeat, profuse sweating, acute cramping of smooth or striped muscles, and a host of physical distress signals, overshadow all other experiences. There may be attacks of diarrhea, of migraine, of visual blurrings, of insomnia, as well as related conditions. On the other hand, the person may experience panic in the escalating and inescapable preoccupation with crippling or fatal illness, loss of control, going berserk, harming oneself or others, suffering a nervous breakdown, economic ruin, total isolation, or destructive actions pertaining to oneself or others.

It can be said that on a phenomenological basis the acute anxiety attack is not dissimilar to an acute schizophrenic attack (a state of losing perspective about real as compared to feared or imagined threats). At such a moment the person's state of relatedness to the world is in limbo. The term limbo is used here in its three traditional dictionary meanings: (1) a supposed region on the border of hell or heaven, the abode after death of unbaptized infants; (2) a place to which persons are relegated when cast aside, forgotten or out of jail; (3) prison, jail, or confinement.

This comparison of an acute anxiety attack to a state in limbo is based on the assumption that the acute anxiety victim has no reliable platform to orient himself in interpersonal time and space. He literally does not know what hits him, for there is no warning of an approaching danger. The first sensation is that of a person who has been hit by a bolt of lightning without first having perceived a single threatening cloud in the sky. The sensation of panic sets in without any conscious awarencess of an overwhelming menace coming near. Any experienced sailor learns to see ripples on the water as a sign of an impending wind or storm. The anxiety victim evidently sails through stormy water before realizing that he has hit a cyclone. Accordingly, it seems naive to assume that the sufferer of an acute anxiety attack is in any position to offer meaningful data about the origins of his acute distress. People who underwent such a harrowing experience are usually willing or even eager to accept almost any face-saving kind of rationalization on the part of others or based on their own imagination. Clinical evidence makes it abundantly clear, however, that they are in the dark about the origin of the attack, its direction, ramifications, and so forth. The patient is pleased with almost any plausible sounding explanation, because it indicates his return from the abyss of madness. Psychotherapists are pleased because they believe to have found the "medicine of insight" for an acute illness. Society is pleased because there is a way of explaining the unexplainable, which seemingly makes the world a safer place to live in. Nobody wants to consider the possibility that there may be a *folie en masse* without suspecting the "emperor's new clothing" as an illusion.

Classical Concept of Anxiety

It is generally known that Freud formulated two different theories of anxiety. In his initial scheme anxiety was basically the result of toxic substance that had been dammed up in the body because of inadequate sexual activity. This concept has been referred to as a physioneurosis in contrast to the psychoneurosis. For instance, Freud initially grouped neurasthenia, anxiety,neurosis, and hypochondriasis together under the collective term actual neurosis. He traced the symptoms in these disorders to physiologic alterations in the body chemistry caused by sexual abstinence or sexual misuse. In short, what later on came to be recognized as the symptom, initially was considered to be the cause of the anxiety.

Freud's second theory of anxiety has a distinctly psychological frame of reference and views this phenomenon as an intrapsychic process. The Ego is considered to be the exclusive seat of anxiety. Unconscious wishes and irrational Id impusles press for discharge. There is no faculty ascribed to the Id that enables it to experience anxiety. It is the function of the Ego to protect against danger. The anxiety in turn is responsible for causing repression. In the second theory it is clearly appreciated that the anxiety causes the repression rather than stemming from repressed libido. All symptom formation is a means of avoiding anxiety. Generally, symptom formation puts an end to the danger situation. At the same time, every danger situation corresponds to a stage of psychic development to which it appears appropriate. Anxiety represents a signal to the presence of old danger. The prototype of anxiety is the birth trauma and the resulting separation anxiety. It has four components:

1. Loss of the mother: that is, separation anxiety.
2. Castration anxiety, which includes the fear of losing the mother's love when the father is perceived as a rival. Combined with it are aggressive tendencies toward the father, sexual desire for the mother, and fears of retaliation.
3. Superego anxiety — fear of social ostracism.
4. Death anxiety.

In this scheme all neurotic individuals remain under the spell of the old causes of anxiety. The phenomena of repetition compulsion, and transference thus play a keynote.

Interpersonal Origin of Anxiety

Interpersonal theory offers the hypothesis that anxiety is an indelible experience that occurs very early in infancy. The concept is akin to the phenomenon of imprinting[2] as described by the ethologists Tinbergen and Lorenz. It must be appreciated that findings from lower animal species cannot be directly applied to the human situation. Imprinting is used here exclusively as a possible analogy to illustrate the principle under discussion. The reference is to an open developmental phase when certain experiences tend to take on an irreversible character. In interpersonal terms anxiety is conceptualized as an experience of an inherently irreversible nature.

Anxiety is a formative agent for the emerging Self of every individual. It is the direct outgrowth of the interpersonal situation that prevailed when the rudimentary outlines of Self awareness came into existence. Native endowment, temperamental characteristics, inherent individual potentials, and universally human capacities all combine with the particular field of human transaction to give rise to the emerging Self. The capacity for anxiety is there, but the actual experience is interpersonally acquired. The mode of transmitting anxiety at the early phases of infancy is obscure. It is assumed that an emotional pathway, referred to as empathy, is the "radar beam" that comes across and threatens feelings of personal security and well-being. Again, the infant is emotionally tied to the mother's experiential sphere. The mother can be a locus of anxiety in her own right. She can also respond to intrafamilial, intramarital, and other personal tensions that in turn she will transmit to the infant. Once anxiety has been inculcated, it is there to stay. A specific vulnerability to the core of this *locus minoris resistentiae* (the initial weak spot pertaining to feelings of personal security) remains a lifelong ingredient. It is for this reason that the primary goal in therapy is not the reduction of anxiety per se.

Here we need to make the commonly applied distinction between fear and anxiety.Fear traditionally represents an external threat. It produces a certain amount of learning from experience. Familiarity with the situation may lead to foresight, observational clarification, and conscious appropriate defenses. In the presence of external danger the principles of Cannon's law usually apply. Walter B. Cannon conceived of the phenomenon of "homeostasis" or balance to account for the organism's capacity to deal with externally threatening situations. The standard responses are fight, flight, or delayed reaction. In the first instance an adrenalin-induced state of combat readiness leads to a mobilization of the fighting stance. In the second instance the heightened response of the organism is used to escape from the danger. In delayed reaction there is a momentary cessation of defensive activity. It occurs at a later time, when the actual danger may have passed.

This offensive or reflectory defensive or delayed response is in sharp contrast to the experience of anxiety. An infant, for instance, has no capacity for relief of anxiety. The tension of anxiety aggravates all existing tensions and traps the person in an escapable tension vice. As a felt experience fear and tension are practically indistinguishable. The difference lies in the fact that external danger can be concretely identified and coped with in one form or another. But anxiety by its very nature is totally obscure and intangible, because it excludes from awareness the very factors that are responsible for its occurrence.

Anxiety in this formulation is not related to staying alive as such. It deals exclusively with the threat of isolating the person from his essential human environment, where personal interchange with people of significance takes place. Physical survival is concerned with the basic needs of the organic, physiologic substratum. It pertains to the needs of hunger, thirst, sleep, lust, and loneliness. The inclusion of loneliness in the realm of organic necessities implies an inherent gregarious nature of human beings. Total isolation from meaningful human contact may even, in extreme cases, constitute a threat to physical survival.

In other words, we are dealing with a phenomenon of interpersonal deprivation similar to the well-known concept of sensory deprivation. The problem, however, is not necessarily actual insulation from direct contact with other people. There may be an opportunity to be in touch with others that is neutralized or overshadowed by distance-making attitudes. People tend to hold appropriate partners at arms length while often falsely complaining that no one wants to have anything to do with them. Some people are capable of staying in touch with significant people while they physically are not in the picture. The result is often in the realm of missing somebody without experiencing undue anxiety in the process. Solitude, meditation, and focusing on a close person in absentia can be relatively free of distance-making components. Many people have a limited capacity for closeness without eye, physical, or sexual contact, whereas others are out of touch while overt contact takes place. They are often unable to take along something positive, and they grow anxious until the repetitive cycle is started again.

Generally, the human organism is equipped with specific channels for the transmission of particular sensations such as prepatterned physiologic pathways for sensory experiences. The only exception is anxiety that has no predictable pathway and usurps any or all of the prevailing sensory channels. The phenomenon of crossing over from one sensory channel to another is referred to as synesthesia, that is, to experience smell in colors or sound in a visual concept. In anxiety we have a "panysynesthesia," which suggests that it is acquired in the process of living with other people rather than representing an inherent human faculty.

Schematic Illustration of the Experience of Anxiety

The assumption of the theory under discussion, then, is that anxiety is an exclusively interpersonal manifestation which indicates a lack of feelings of personal worth, an absence of on-going human relatedness, and a resulting feeling of threat to being a bona fide member of human society. The hypothesis is that anxiety is acquired very early in life by means of empathy. Introjected personifications of eidetic people form an everlasting basis of hypersensitivity to real or imagined personal slight. The initial anxious identification centers on the first pair of maternal impressions, called the "good" or "bad mother." These are child-mother experiences that must not be confused with the qualities of the actual mother. The concept "bad mother" indicates anxiety-fraught experiences and is not a reflection of the person of the mother. The next link is postulated in connection with the emerging self-image referred to as "good-," "bad-" or "not me." The chart from Chapter 1 illustrates the conceptualizations outlined here with the field of relative anxiety-free transactions constituting a basically conflict-free sphere. "Good me," then, is a short hand for interpersonal situations capable of intimacy. "Bad me" reflects the sphere of moderate anxiety and shows areas of Self rejection and lack of affirming one's personal worth. The observational faculties still function marginally in "bad-me" or moderate anxiety-fraught interpersonal situations. In contrast, "not me" represents a sphere of almost total conflict and an inability to discern one's actual participation in dealing with other people.

The chart also illustrates how the anxiety gradient effects self-system activity, which in turn influences the integrating tendencies leading to minimal, moderate, or severe security operations and creating a polarity between potential intimacy or outright hostile integration.

Comparative Considerations

In the classical scheme anxiety is a signal of danger. There is a reactivation of internal, neurotic conflict which indicates an internal collision between Id impulses seeking discharge and Ego defenses opposing the overt discharge of the impulse or its conscious awareness. In oversimplified fashion, one could say that the classical notion of anxiety implies that where there is smoke there is fire. The anxiety is the signal pointing to a "smoldering conflict."

By contrast, the interpersonal formulation of anxiety conceives of the anxiety as the fire rather than as a signal of an internal conflict that needs to be remedied. Interpersonal anxiety is conceptualized as an experience that manipulates the content of consciousness. Anxiety runs counter to Self-awareness. The experience of "I," "my body," "myself" is almost totally blotted out by the tension of anxiety. At the height of an anxiety state the human mind is fully absorbed with a bombardment of psychosomatic sensations. There is no opportunity to maintain "an observing Ego" as a monitoring device capable of giving information about the interpersonal situation at hand. A further complication is brought about by anxiety's indiscriminate use of every available pathway, because it lacks a specific neuroanatomical underpinning of its own. Anxiety is viewed as the most powerful barrier to meaningful human integration. The interpersonal formulation has no room for existential, humanistic, or potentially constructive aspects of anxiety.

Assets and Limitations of Interpersonal Anxiety Concepts

Interpersonal theory, however, focuses so much attention on the phenomenon of anxiety that it loses sight of some significant details. Clinically speaking, there is merit in formulating anxiety as a man-made tension for which the human organism lacks adequate controls. Also, the distinction between acute anxiety and anxiety per se is of considerable value. Furthermore, the conceptualization of anxiety as the spark that gives rise to the birth of the Self is ingenious. It paves the way for a dynamic, evolutionary process whereby the Self forms the mirror as well as the matrix of interpersonal integrations. Central in this conceptualization of anxiety is the assumption that all anxiety is induced by direct contact with significant people, maintained by an indelible experience of truncated and warped Self awareness, and tributary to the congeries of more complex tensions later on in life. A major concern rests in the appreciation of anxiety operating for the better part inconspicuously but with grave effects. In most areas anxiety serves as a disruptive force that misinforms the individual about his most immediate needs by diverting the attention to distinctly unpleasant sensations. A rising feeling of tension interferes with the capacity of recognizing the need and taking appropriate action toward its potential relief. At the same time there is a closure of perception pertaining to relevant data about the precursors of the tension that led to a breakdown of informative observations. In other words, anxiety as defined here operates on two levels. It focuses central attention on peripheral aspects of the prevailing interpersonal situation, thus precluding an understanding of the threat to one's Self-esteem. The situation is then further complicated by the intervention of the anxiety system which brings a host of security operations into play. At the height of the tension the person lacks any meaningful awareness of how the anxiety was provoked and what concomitant need was pushed out of awareness.

Interpersonal theory holds that the original anxiety-fraught experience invariably goes back to an early tension-filled transaction with a significant person. We are dealing here with introjects (eidetic people or parataxic distortions, as Sullivan refers to them) that reach back to the initial experiential personification of what was felt as soothing (good mother) in contrast to what was felt as distressing (bad or evil mother). The term "good mother" refers to experiences of relaxation and well-being, whereas "bad mother" is indicative of anxiety. They do not represent a value judgement about the mother as a person.

The next link in the chain of events is the content of consciousness pertaining to the interpersonal Self. It is the degree of anxiety that controls the quality of one's Self image. Anxiety-free experiences ("good me") relate to feeling well and having a wide-angle observational horizon available for viewing oneself and others without undue distortions. The range of experiences in the presence of moderate to moderate-severe anxiety ("bad me") is the foundation for not feeling well, requiring considerable vigilance, and dealing with a constricted observational field. It is in this range that we find a host of antianxiety operations as mentioned previously.

Finally, we have uncanny experiences, crawling, chilly sensations (awe, dread, loathing, horror), indicative of "not me" or evil mother" phenomena that paralyze perception and lead to excitation, apathy, or profoundly disturbed behavior.

The theory presented here has the advantage of offering a longitudinal, evolutional concept of anxiety. It emphasizes the experiential quality of the tension of anxiety. Once again it burdens itself unnecessarily with the notion of energy transformations. The previously offered criticism of a carryover from Freud's mechanistic model is also appropriate for the interpersonal model of anxiety. Furthermore, the concept of imprinting as later developed by ethologists is rather prominent in Sullivan's formulation of the origin of anxiety.

Other theoretical blindspots or omissions worth mentioning in this connection are the vicissitudes of attachment-separation phenomena as outlined by Bowlby. Neither is there sufficient appreciation of retaliatory fears in connection with irrational thoughts or with aggressive impulses. For one thing, it must be appreciated that thoughts per se are always harmelss and should not be confused with actions. People have to be free to try on all kinds of thoughts "for size" without concern that this necessarily indicates an "evil core." The "bad me" concept or personification does not cover this aspect sufficiently. Furthermore, there is a wide field of self-assertive needs free of infringement on the rights of others that tend to cause anxiety because they are falsely associated with hurtful aggression. Usually, there is a distinct limitation in appreciating the meaning of anxiety if we recognize a low self-esteem as its one and only general foundation. We need to be more specific about a number of variables involved in the ingredients of self-esteem. It should be understood that these examples by no means cover the numerous nuances related to the experience of anxiety. The main point is to emphasize a conviction that certain shortcomings, blindspots, and incompleteness of the interpersonal theorem of anxiety do not detract from its novel approach or the multitude of its useful clinical applicability. The nature of the antianxiety or self system and the process of selective inattention as well as related security operations are discussed in the next chapter.

Clinical Considerations

At this point, there are some significant secondary aspects of anxiety that deserve consideration. In regard to secondary anxiety it needs to be said that it is experientially undistinguishable from basic anxiety. The key difference lies in its trigger mechanism. The phenomenon of secondary anxiety has for all practical purposes no bearing on dealing with a danger of the past or with specific internal conflicts. It is now the rigidity of the Self-system of antianxiety vigilance that gets in the way. In other words, the resistance to change, including change for the better, is experienced as the danger. The security operations have come to be second nature, the "neurotic shoe" fits while enhancing a feeling of familiarity with it. What causes major difficulty now is the fear of parting with well-acquainted defenses. In every successful therapy we reach a point of increased self-esteem, which the patient may be fearful to acknowledge. At that point he experiences difficulty in letting go of some deeply ingrained security operations.

This formulation bears some resemblance to the classical concept of Ego defenses, whereby the Ego employs the same measures against internal as well as against external threats. A major difference centers around the concept of repression. Anxiety in the Freudian scheme always harks back to the past, reproducing the initial affective state by reactivating the preexisting memory. All defenses are considered to result from unconscious wishes and include repression. There is no allowance made for here and now experiences having an impact of their own rather than being exclusively repetitive compulsive acts.

As for the interpersonal concept of anxiety, it is the sort of experience that keeps us from noticing things that would assist in coping with the situation at hand. By the same token, we cannot expect a person to have recall of earlier anxiety-fraught experiences. The presence of severe anxiety blunts the observational acumen and precludes conscious awareness of what went wrong in the interpersonal situation. It is akin to expecting a patient under the influence of a general anesthetic to recall what he experienced while his mind was in a "total fog."

Sudden, severe anxiety, or rapidly increasing anxiety gradients lead to "not me" experiences which may be described as dread, loathing, and horror. They are referred to as uncanny sensations of emotions. The occurrence of uncanny emotions leads to a morbid adaptation to the uncanny, to overt psychotic episodes or states of apathy.

For therapeutic purposes we are mainly concerned with the milder forms of anxiety or with a gradual increase in its intensity. In milder tensions of anxiety we may encounter a host of interpersonal difficulties. We find here many instances of complex misunderstandings between people. This refers to situations characterized by compulsive, communicative miscarriages. Either the sender of the information misinforms or the receiver mishears or any number of combinations occur, all designed to mismatch messages. A particular form of chronic miscommunication is the fine art of sterile bickering. People under such circumstances don't say what they really mean and don't hear clearly what has been said. The main purpose of this malintegration under the impact of anxiety is to engage in verbal fencing as a means of maintaining distance from each other. It is as if a legitimate affirmation of the partner's point of view or a clarification of his opinion would be tantamount to a confession of major inadequacy. There is a welter of techniques in the realm of disparaging performances, irrational prejudices, blind preferences, and related forms of acting out vestigial tensions of anxiety. The sudden ebbing of Self-esteem in being preoccupied with not being appreciated, thoughtlessly or evilly ignored, being put down, or outright rejected are cases in point. Experiences in the above-described category lead to resentment that is considered to be a significant aspect in many psychosomatic disorders. We find here the sensation of the chronically "tense belly," of chronic fatigue, hypochondriasis, and related substitutions for the experience of anxiety.

Then there are people who have a need to maintain a persistent high level of skeletal tension as a displacement of anxiety. This phenomenon is closely related to Wilhelm

Reich's formulation of a muscular "character armor." It is particularly found in people with major obsessional disorders, who are forever engaged in warding off experiences of anxiety. Their minds are preoccupied with thoughts, plans, and compulsive mental assignments of a hierarchy of tasks. The object of the preoccupation is the maintenance of a marginal feeling of security, a constant quest for recognition and prestige as a mask for their interpersonal lack of intimacy. Sullivan once coined a phrase that seems very apt in this respect — "If I am a molehill, there shall be no mountains." It sums up a feeling of being intensely driven upward and onward without a trace of conviction that one is made of the right stuff for it.

Anger, Rage, and Anxiety

Another emotional attempt at coping with anxiety is the emergence of anger. Culture, society, and family tend to misinform us about this complex phenomenon. We need not belabor the point that the inability to experience anger constitutes a severe personality problem. The other side of the same coin is the presence of chronic irritability, with the tendency to fly off the handle with little or no provocation. Then we have a form of extreme anger, which is referred to as rage. It can be said that blind anger deteriorates into rage and contains the component of hatred in its manifestation.

Within reason we may associate certain aspects of anger with the occurrence of fear or milder forms of anxiety, whereas rage invariably involves the presence of severe anxiety.

Anger is a basically legitimate response to being mistreated, disadvantaged, or injured in one form or another. Under ordinary circumstances anger leads to a raising of the level of consciousness with the capacity to choose among a number of appropriate options in coping with the anger-producing situation. This kind of rational anger is a prerequisite to Self-affirmation and essential in the maintenance of Self-esteem. Fear of aggression in oneself and others frequently leads to an unfortunate barrier of experiencing legitimate anger. A great deal of fear centers around the possibility of losing control over one's anger and exploding with violent rage. The other concern lies in the faulty perception of Self-assertion which is not directed against another person. Spontaneous affirmation of oneself even with thoughtful consideration of the needs of others may be misconstrued as being aggressive in nature and leading to fears of retaliation.

Also, we need to consider the manifestation of anger as a camouflage for anxiety. It is a widespread occurrence to react with irritation and anger to people who tend to make one anxious. There is usually little or no awareness of having been made anxious other than a feeling of chronic annoyance. This phenomenon is a very common clinical manifestation which every therapist encounters in his work. The problem may be a relatively minor or major focus in an on-going, interpersonal relationship. The dynamics involved may be compared to the principle of an unfortunate feedback that permeates the core of relating to one another. What makes the situation psychologically complex is that the so-called hateful integration becomes a necessary evil that has a tendency to perpetuate itself.

Malintegrations under the Impact of Anxiety

The reference here is to a situation in which people evoke in each other a great deal of frustrated anger through feeling evilly ignored, disliked, or outright hated. The difficulty usually starts when one partner or the other is made to feel anxious in a way that evokes distinct feelings of inadequacy and of lack of personal worth. It stands to reason that the prevailing emotional climate lowers the respective Self-esteem of the partners in a fashion that contributed to its formation early in life. In other words, the growing malintegration brings to the fore profound feelings of inescapable insecurity, which in turn feeds the emerging anger and irritation . What takes place next is usually the coming forth of a transactional field in which mutual blame prevails. Each partner comes to see in the eyes of the other a chronic negative appraisal. The relationship becomes geared toward mutual shortcomings, problems, and faults rather than toward respective areas of potential competence and strength. In such an unfortunate setting each finds his own self-doubt mirrored and aggravated in the attitude of the other. The outcome is a paralysis of mutually supportive actions, with a resulting fear of letting the destructive pattern go. There are at least two components involved in this kind of "Virginia Woolf" or *No Exit* situation. On the one hand, there is the fear of having exposed one's Achilles' heel. On the other, there may be an underlying concern that it takes a bad person to choose a bad person.

In this discussion of human malintegration under the impact of persistent anxiety it should be pointed out that not all difficulties are of a mutual nature. One partner may suffer from a much more severe anxiety than the other, as may be illustrated by a dream reported to me. The dreamer is a highly gifted woman — childless and married to a dependently controlling man. In her dream she is standing very close to her husband who is leaning heavily against her. At this point in the dream she realizes that he he has suffered a serious injury resulting in the loss of his right arm at the shoulder level. She has a powerful urge to move away, at least slightly, or obtain some mobility of her own when she recognizes that he would bleed to death if she made any move at all. For the record, it should be noted that he had a nightmare either the same or following night in which he attempted to strangle his wife.

This situation represents an extreme case of morbid, hateful dependency. The patient discontinued therapy, while her husband displayed one psychosomatic disorder after the other. As far as I know the marriage has prevailed without clarification of the severe anxiety underfoot and without appreciation of the symbolic "dance of death" as dramatized by Strindberg. There is no doubt in my mind, however, that the husband is by far the more crippled person in the relationship.

A special category in the realm of malignant integrations is the scapegoat transaction. Here one partner's anxiety manifests itself in a feeling of marginal worth. The person does not feel entirely without merit but is deeply preoccupied with his actual or real failings. He finds a partner whose chronically low self-esteem is such that it constantly evokes criticism. The first party tries to elevate his sagging self-regard by constantly criticizing the partner, who in turn communicates that it takes a "bastard" to kick a person in distress. In this process the mutual anxiety is fanned and has little chance to clear the field for an attitude of reciprocal regard and support.

It should be emphasized that these models should not be mistaken for the behavioristic model of game playing. The problem under discussion here is the underlying anxiety rather that the warped and distorted reactions to it.

Summary of Anxiety and Parataxis

The discussion offered in this chapter illustrates that anxiety covers like a giant tent a multitude of human transactions. No attempt has been made to show the endless nuances of anxiety-fraught relations and their manifestation in everyday life as well as in a welter of psychopathology. At the same time, we should caution against the tendency to make anxiety the core phenomenon underlying all human difficulties. Though interpersonal theory has moved us a big step ahead in understanding many tensions of anxiety, it has not been sufficiently discerning in its approach to this highly important topic. The theory has taken an almost global stance toward the problem of anxiety while ignoring or neglecting other aspects of anxiety such as the separation threat, the concern of aggression and of retaliation, as well as reality-related problems such as famine, severe economic distress, physical illness, political upheavals, and the fear of dying. There seems merit in considering the last-mentioned categories as anxiety rather than fear. The notion that we can face the world without undue trepidation as long as we feel relationally secure is appealing, meaningful, but not without distinct limitations. Reality is capable of undermining a person's self-esteem and undermining his on-going contact with significant others.

Now to sum up the salient points of anxiety in interpersonal terms:

Anxiety is an interpersonal scar, a vulnerable contactual area that has been acquired early in life. It reflects on-going unfortunate experience with a significant person leading to a malintegration in the developmental process. The experience as such is not reversible and restricts a person's self-awareness while keeping self-esteem at a low level. At the same time, the experience of anxiety controls focal awareness by obscuring the recognition of events triggering the distressing, anxious sensation.

The human organism requires a "fail-safe" antianxiety system (called the Self-system) as a means of survival. Failure of the Self-system leads to a state of panic (a breakdown of elementary security operations). A collapse of major defenses or security measures has occurred when we are confronted with an anxiety attack.

The interpersonal scheme of anxiety requires the formulation of two interlocking kinds of actual experience, the formative foundation and an activation of this dormant component by an on-going relational event. On the one hand, we have a developmental malintegration, which is the basis of a high level of vulnerability to feelings of "bad me" and "not me." The original events leading to a paper-thin layer of Self-esteem are beyond a person's recall because severe anxiety shuts down relevant observational faculties. What happens under the impact of anxiety is a phenomenon comparable to events taking place while a person is asleep, or is under the influence of an anesthetic or of some other toxic or traumatic agent.

On the other hand, we have an experiential trigger mechanism in the here and now. A chain of events locks the person into the area of his particular emotional Achilles' heel. A negative integration sets off the experience of anxiety without giving the victim an opportunity to pick up the telltales preceding the awareness of anxiety.

Therapeutic intervention is largely designed to alert the individual to the ripples prior to the storm. A distinct educational element is involved in recognizing the type of security operations that tend to camouflage an approaching anxiety experience.

In actual clinical work it is necessary to be more specific in dealing with anxiety-fraught situations. The first step consists of exploring in detail the known origins of excessive feelings of vulnerability. In some situations this approach is unsuccessful, at least when we do our initial probing. Our focus then shifts to here and now events when anxiety is experienced. It is of great importance to clarify the circumstances that prevail in anxiety-producing situations. What matters most is the appreciation of reality components and their respective hierarchy pertaining to evoking anxiety. Dream material, fantasies, and areas of preoccupations, together with a careful inventory of existing living and working relationships tend to be informative.

It may be argued that anxiety occurs only in the absence of an interpersonal Self. The acute distress results from a major isolation of the troubled individual. Marked vulnerabilities interfere with meaningful communication; there is a distinct fear of checking and verification out of concern that "bad me" and "not me" aspects will be uncovered or some compensatory grandiosity be revealed. We also have to consider the possibility that some people do not wish to acknowledge certain limitations or suffer legitimate, appropriate guilt feelings that have been blown up out of proportion.

Anxiety is the experience of a highly individualized predicament that precludes a feeling of commonality at the moment of its impact. Counterreactions to anxiety (including countertransference reactions in the therapeutic process) may generate feelings of being left out, cut off, not personally responded to, evilly ignored. In short, anxiety may lead to an interpersonal short-circuit with a stalemate between the interacting participants.

Sullivan probably overstressed the malignant aspects of anxiety. As a clinician I have deep respect for the destructive inroads of anxiety in human relations. I am opposed to the notion of anxiety as a potential source of creativity or as the source of any constructive endeavor. Nevertheless, I do not view anxiety as the mother of most evil among human beings.

I am also concerned about people who have gone through life with subliminal manifestations of anxiety. Such individuals tend to be psychopathic and show inadequate sensitivity to their fellow human beings.

General Definition of Transference

Transference, next to anxiety, is another key phenomena in psychiatric manifestations. At present, it is about the only clinical phenomena that has survived major changes from inside and outside the psychiatric profession. Nevertheless, there is much ambiguity about what transference is, how it originates, and how it operates under various conditions in life.

In its dictionary sense transference means to convey or remove from one place, person, or object to another. Implicit in the concept is the assumption that what is carried over or transferred is not changed in the process.

Psychologically, transference is widely conceptualized as an emotional displacement of early life — experiences that operate unconsciously in a variety of on-going contacts with other people.

Freud initially described this universal human manifestation in reporting the case of Dora. Since that time transference and countertransference have become a focal area of interest in the field of psychoanalysis and in most forms of psychotherapy.

It is of interest that, to the present, there has been a minimal amount of clarification in regard to the formative aspects of transference, particularly, of its potential metamorphosis in the process of living.

Generally, it seems a naive notion that the human organism contains a host of secret vaults that are sealed off from what goes on in daily life throughout the developmental epochs and beyond it. There is a question whether experiences retain a pristine character in the human mind that are imprinted on a cerebral videotape ready for replay whenever the particular experience is reactivated. It has been shown (Schachtel) that actual childhood events are transposed through an adult experiential mirror system with a host of sociocultural contaminants. The process of acculturation and socialization imposes a prescriptive point of view conflicting with the original open perception of childhood. In other words, the assumption that transference exclusively reflects the original memories of feelings, drives, attitudes, fantasies, and defenses is not tenable. For one thing, development is a dynamic process that involves the entire human organism. Another consideration is the undeniable impact of an expanding, contact-seeking, reaching out, native human component (the intentionality of the existentialists). Both a strictly deterministic view of human behavior and the notion of grooved, encapsulated memory imprints are not in keeping with modern concepts of man. The intrapsychic model of transference is due for a major revision.

Transference in the traditional sense still centers around the assumption that transference reactions are actual replays in the person's memory of early fantasies, wishful thoughts, or affectionate or angry feelings that have become unconscious. The transference as such has its roots in instinctual frustrations and resultant discharge opportunities. Furthermore, transference reactions are considered to be compulsive repetitions rather than ways of recalling past events. On this basis the transferential repetitions are the neurotic tracers par excellence. Analysis, then, is seen as a systematic interpretation of the transference reactions without any attempt to gratify or manipulate them. The transference neurosis is the prerequisite for a successful analysis. It means the acceptance of a regressive, dependent life situation for the duration of the analysis by making the analysis the center of one's existence. Much of the analytic ambience is designed to foster the transference neurosis by the atmosphere of intense familiarity with a person who retains a large measure of anonymity. As already pointed out, today a distinction is made between transference neurosis and therapeutic alliance. Efforts are made to recognize a larger dimension of the actual doctor-patient relationship. Nevertheless, transference is basically a repetitive process in the classical framework, a displacement in the nature of a "coathanger phenomenon." The patient blindly mistakes the analyst for a parental figure, and his memory relives his traumatic past.

Freudian Definition of Transference

Classic psychoanalytic technique centers around two specific forms of communication prescribed for the patient and analyst, respectively. The former must adhere to the method of free association, whereas the latter uses interpretation as his primary therapeutic instrument. A major reason for following this procedure is the firm conviction that it enhances the strong coming forth of transference reactions. Here it must be noted that the emergence of a full-blown transference neurosis is considered to be a sine qua non of the analytic process. It has been widely recognized among classic analysts in recent years that the so-called therapeutic alliance coexists with the transference neurosis in promoting a basic therapeutic momentum. The alliance consists of the patient having a relatively intact observing Ego that interacts with the actual person of the analyst in spite of his distinctly neutral or objective attitude.

In other words, there is a measure of health in the neurotic patient who has a desire to overcome his difficulties by submitting to acute infantile regression. The patient relives his childhood in memory, recognizes his compulsion to repeat unresolved conflicts from his early years, and gains mastery over his frustrated impulses. Interpretation by the analyst centers mainly around dreams, transference, and resistance. On this basis the transference neurosis is cured, and the more mature part of the person comes to the fore. Though this description covers the main theme of classic technique in capsule form, there are only minor variations of this technique, with no significant change of the basic pattern.

Every major psychoanalytic form of psychotherapy or modified psychoanalysis focuses attention on the manifestations of transference as well as countertransference. It is predominantly in the definition and degree of dealing with transference and countertransference that major differences exist. Generally, there has been a lessening of the need to overfocus on positive compared to negative transference. It is widely recognized that ambivalence is the rule and not the exception, and that one always has to deal with a measure of polarizing feelings. There has also been a tendency to look at countertransference from a dual point of view. One aspect reflects remnants of the analyst's neurosis that get in the way of useful therapy; the other looks at countertransference in a larger frame of reference. It is conceived as a fine tuning fork of the analyst's personality — a kind of an observing or monitoring countertransferential Ego that keeps the analyst informed about the nature of his own involvement. This broader view of countertransference has immeasurably contributed to therapeutic procedures. At the same time, it has constituted a potential risk by confusing necessary boundaries between patient and therapist. Excessive emotional detachment on the analyst's part is as much of a therapeutic handicap as misguided notions of openness and sharing. The mask of neutrality is an unfortunate artefact in any intimate human situation, including the analytic alliance. Likewise, the compulsive role of the friend, good parent, or benefactor has distinct limitations in its own right. We need to take care of where we stand in the therapeutic partnership lest neurotic participation substitutes for participant observation or another appropriate therapeutic stance. There is a distinct Scylla and Charybdis problem involved when it comes to being unrealistically objective as opposed to entering into a mutual acting out alliance in which the patient's difficulties are covered up. One thing seems clear, that analysis without limits is a relationship tending toward appeasement and toward placating the patient's neurosis.

Interpersonal View of Transference (Parataxis)

In comparing the clinical concept of transference with its interpersonal formulation we find obvious similarities. In the final analysis, however, the differences are more pronounced than the similarities. It is important that we do not show excessive sensitivity to the awkward terminology, but address ourselves primarily to the underlying dynamic concept. Sullivan shied away from the use of words like "transference" and "countertransference" since he was dealing with the transactional field concept, whereby the formulation of transference without the reciprocal formulation of countertransference did not seem relevant to him. His preference was for the term "parataxis," coined by Dom Thomas Vernon Moore. Sullivan had become disenchanted with "neurosis" as a reference to neurons and to an underlying organic image of interpersonal relations. To him "parataxis avoided this pitfall and addressed itself to universal human behavior above and beyond psychopathological warpings. In particular, the term parataxic concomitance, or parataxic distortion, refers to cognitive phenomena that occur in a great variety of interpersonal situations. In contrast to transference, parataxic distortions require the intervention of anxiety. Involved in the process are relatively primitive parataxic symbols that persist through life.

According to Sullivan, (*Clinical Studies in Psychiatry* pp. 200-202, Crowley #125) "any patient manifests toward the analyst a series of parataxic distortions which are wholly to be understood on the basis of past experience and the morbid experiences of this patient." The distortions under discussion include basic personality warps that color much of the person's life and need to be dealt with directly if a patient is to improve in therapy.

To some degree parataxic distortions are akin to introjects — internalized experiences with one's fellow man under the impact of anxiety. The difference from the classcal formulation of introjects as rigid fixtures is modified in Sullivan's thinking by his insistence that such introjects or "parataxic distortions" do not and could not exist in utter separation from each other. In other words, the imaginary people introjected into a person's way of thinking and the concomitant cognitive distortions are subjected to life experiences; thus, they do not follow the principle of repetitive compulsion and are modified by a number of variables. What matters most, however, is the initial warp, that is, the underlying parataxic distortion which leaves a person vulnerable to human integrations which take place under the impact of anxiety.

In a note on the implications of psychiatry, "The Study of Interpersonal Relations For Investigation in the Social Sciences" (*The Fusion of Psychiatry and the Social Sciences,* pp. 23-24) Sullivan speaks of the complexity of parataxic situations. He refers to sudden shifts of communicative processes from a number of warped integrations that may occur frequently or only occasionally. He found in particular that parataxic situations represent a play of cross purposes in which consensual validation is often difficult or impossible to achieve.

Anxiety and Transference

Transference in the interpersonal sense is the outgrowth of anxiety-fraught early experiences that failed to produce anything like clear and useful guides about oneself and others. They are related to the organization of uncanny emotions of "not me" or "very bad me" feelings — on the one side — and "bad" or "evil mother" personifications on the other. The transference or parataxic distortion then occurs as a Self-system activity or antianxiety measure. More simply, the parataxic concomitant is a referential process based on misinformation about oneself and one's formative interpersonal environment. In the interpersonal concept transference is a cognitive screen that operates to a large degree through the principle of selective inattention. As a result of this distorting process we find the person's thinking to contain many stereotyped conceptualizations about himself and others with an excessive readiness toward experiences of disparagement and derrogation pertaining to one's own and the other person's feelings of personal worth. Furthermore, parataxic distortions include a reaction to the requirements of the ongoing interpersonal situation.

In essence we can say, then, that the interpersonal formulation of transference covers a wider territory than the classical concept; first, it addresses itself to the genesis of the phenomenon in a particular transactional field; then, it emphasizes the cognitive distortion resulting from a specific kind of malintegration. Finally, it deals with the response-counterresponse pattern in which selective inattention prevails and includes a component of countertransfernece in the transferenetial process.

Clinically it is clear from the foregoing that in interpersonal practice a transference neurosis would be minimized rather than reinforced. The method of fostering regression would take a back seat in favor of consensual validation based on careful developmental exploration. There would be less concern with the patient's neurosis and greater attention focused on recurrent areas of miscommunication, misunderstandings, and other apparent distortions in the therapeutic field. Stated differently, the individual patient and his particular neurotic problems are secondary considerations to the emergence of the complex processes involving analyst and patient. The emphasis is always on improving communication, on verbalizing complicated experiences, in expanding one's observational horizon and the relatively conflict free sphere of the self.

Evaluative Comments

At this point some additional comments on the classical and interpersonal conceptualization of transference should be added, for, although the latter formulation is a distinctly broader point of view of transferential reactions, it does not go far enough.

We have seen that in the Freudian theory transference is a predominantly intrapsychic process that constitutes blind, repetitive behavior rather than a recall of infantile wishes. Repression obscures early instinctual frustrations within the framework of a two-way, and — in the oedipal phase — a three-way interfamilial pattern. The path of transferential regression leads to reactivation of early memories. Aided by the therapeutic alliance, it brings about potential mastery over immature striving.

Interpersonal formulations of transference rely on a

somewhat similar frame of reference, except that they high-light different aspects. In both theories we are dealing with past experiences that become reactivated under certain conditions and assume a central position in the therapeutic situation. One major difference, however, lies in the attitude toward transference neurosis. In contrast to classical technique the transference-neurosis or parataxic concomitant is viewed as the basic warp of personality — the key problem causing major difficulties in living. Accordingly, it is dealt with as a necessary evil, and a powerful contaminant toward the potential achievement of intimacy. In oversimplified form it can be said that classical theory looks at the transference neurosis as a potential ally. It serves a purpose similar to that of a fever that physiologically aids in the cure of an infectious disease by attempting to drive out the noxious agent. On the other hand, interpersonal theory looks at the transference neurosis or parataxic distortion as a cognitive defect that works like a psychopathic principle, excluding meaningful learning from new experience. The problem here is seen as residing in an observational blindspot that controls the content of a person's awareness. What we are able to notice in this process is the functioning of selective inattention. Under the impact of parataxic distortions the mind is cluttered with perceptions that do not truly reflect what is going on between oneself and others. Hence the formulation that "one achieves mental health to the extent to which one becomes aware of one's interpersonal relationships" (*Conceptions of Modern Psychiatry*, p. 207). Anticipatory conviction of difficulties leads to attitudes which tend to affirm one's underlying negative expectations (self fulfilling prophecy). It is clear, then, that the parataxic distortion transcends what has been directly transferred from the past. It involves a measure of interpersonal programing based on morbid experience of the past as well as a reaction to the requirements of the on-going relationship and the way in which it becomes integrated. The resolution of the original parataxic warp lies in the possibility of experience in the syntaxic mode by intricate, personal verbalization of the difficulty and the opportunity for sensitive checking and verification (consensual validation). On this basis the Self as the focal instrument of experiencing oneself in interpersonal relationships expands its horizon and registers an increasing number of distorting prejudices in oneself as well as in others.

Interpersonal theory does not confine transference to the intrapsychic sphere; it does include a larger degree of here and now interpersonal components. It also stresses the heightened sensitivity to the presence of countertransferential reactions by strongly overreacting to concealed or unconscious attitudes of the partner. In addition, transference responds to some kind of empathic linkage between the parties involved and does not entirely operate in a vacuum. This is another way of saying that total neutrality in the presence of transference is probably an illusion. Involved in this phenomenon is the emergence of implicit and explicit roles, as was pointed out by John Spiegel.

Nevertheless, as already suggested, the interpersonal formulation of transference does not go far enough. There is insuffucient allowance made for potential parataxic modifications in the process of growing up and living with and among other people. The application of an epigenetic principle is missing, that is, a process whereby modifications evolve leading to novel constellations as formations which were not there in the beginning. It is useful to conceive of a transferential development in its own right, for transference reactions are not predominantly distorting experiences in the earliest years of life. It stands to reason that the transferential patterns become modified at each and every developmental phase in one form or the other. The interpersonal concept of transference still contains too much rigidity in regard to the antianxiety, or Self-system as if attitudes were poured into concrete except for the period of preadolescence. There has also been insufficient emphasis on the way in which society and culture tend to contribute as well as maintain a host of transferential distortions.

Summary of Transference

Our traditional definition of transference is too restrictive and is no longer applicable to a host of transactional phenomena. Transferential manifestations in a group setting, for instance, are not merely a replica of a one-to-one relationship. Furthermore, no family lives in a total cultural vacuum, and transference does not originate exclusively within one's "four walls." There is evidence that transference is not simply molded in some vague way; it is also transformed and perpetuated in a higly complex fashion.

There is no doubt that progress has been made since transference and countertransference have been accorded focal significance in most forms of psychotherapy. Up to the present, however, little or inadequate attention has been given to transference outside the realm of psychopathology and psychotherapy. In particular, the role of transference and countertransference as specific mediums for transmitting individual, familial, as well as sociocultural ideologies has been grossly neglected.

To a certain degree, this point was already appreciated by Freud, who worte in the "Introduction to Group Psychology and the Analysis of the Ego" as follows: "Only rarely, and under certain exceptional conditions is individual psychology in a position to disregard the relations of this individual to others. In the individual's mental life somebody else is invariably involved as a model, as an object, as a helper, as an opponent and so from the very first, individual psychology is at the same time social psychology — in this extended but entirely justifiable sense of the word."

Another manifestation of the individual's mental life may be found in the phenomenon of transference. Freud initially described this universal human manifestation in the case of Dora. Since that time transference and counter-transference have monopolized the field of psychoanalysis and most forms of psychotherapy. In the narrow sense transference reactions are considered to be actual replays of early experiences, fantasies, or wishful thoughts without any relation to the here and now experiences. On a larger scale there is increasing evidence that transference covers, like a tent, a multitude of reactions that have undergone significant modifications in the process of living. In other words, we do not necessarily deal with the initial experiences per se, but rather with variations on a basic theme.

Implicit in this formulation is the assumption that transference follows a developmental scheme, that is, transference reactions are of an evolving (epigenetic) nature. The suggestion is that transference includes experiences from all phases of the life cycle, rather than early, formative events to the exclusion of all others.

Transference transcends the phenomenon of imprinting during a specific developmental phase and is viewed as an on-going process that is constantly modified in the process of living. In this frame of reference, transference reactions are influenced by a variety of life situations above and beyond the sphere of troublesome, formative encounters. Also, transference incorporates certain aspects of the prevailing cultural value system as is discussed later. As a final consideration, most experienced clinicians have become aware of the hypersensitive radar system of certain patients. Such patients tend to tune in focally to remnants of defenses, security operations, and value judgements on the part of the analyst. This heightened sensitivity to the existence of countertransference is an integral part of transference reactions.

In brief, then, transference evolves from early interpersonal encounters with significant people in the particular cultural setting in which the person grew up. It is not a purely intrapsychic process of introjected, formative events but a more open-ended developmental process. Transference is modified by the life experiences at all phases of human development. The phenomenon of transference includes an overfocused awareness of countertransference occurring in the relational partner. It leads to an excessive emphasis of the "you" in a "me-you" interpersonal situation.

At this point an illustration of a transferential flight into socially acceptable behavior may be helpful. It deals with a clinical description which I discussed in a paper called "Treatment of Asocial Attitudes in Ambulatory Schizophrenic Patients." In the text, my discussion centers around the kind of schizophrenic remissions that lead to sociopathic adaptations. Patients in this category achieve a "social cure" by a type of "I will be as you desire me." The result is a chameleonlike blending in with the more warped societal attitudes. In the sociopathic adaptation, the patient is relatively free of suffering, his sensitive feelings are dulled and attenuated, or they are pushed out of awareness. This phenomenon may be illustrated by a dramatic dream of a patient in this group. He dreamt he had a fatal illness as a child and actually died in the dream. By some miraculous event he was reborn, and found himself standing in front of a full-length mirror. To his great surpirse he noticed that in the place where his heart had been, there now appeared a triangular, empty space which extended sagitally through the body so that the light would shine through.

The dream speaks of the patient having died in childhood and having been "reborn" as a "heartless person." In actual life, this patient had been a sensitive child with a vivid imagination. He became increasingly withdrawn and antisocial during his adolescence until he suffered an acute, paranoid schizophrenic episode. Eventually, he adopted a new personality, including a change of name when he took on a distinctly sociopathic life style.

This patient found a measure of societal approval by exclusively using his head rather than his heart. His high native intelligence permitted him to manipulate people and avoid any kind of emotional involvement. Conventionally, he became a "useful member of society" by conforming to a socially acceptable image, even if he was literally hollow inside as the dream indicates.

This patient illustrates one aspect of cultural transference. He managed to turn a profound tragedy into an artificial success by his capacity to pick up implicit societal recommendations. A pathway was needed to the intricate ambiguities of the prevailing social order. His "solution" for his misery was the aspiration "to be as you desire me." He spoke frequently of wanting "a heart of steel" so that guilt and consideration for others no longer mattered. It is my firm conviction that his masterplan to become a Skinnerian model beyond freedom was the direct result of cultural transference. There probably are a sizable number of refugees from madness who escape from their turmoil by wearing an acceptable social or political hat. They have a certain empathy for cultural phenomena related to suppressing feelings and shying away from spontaneous emotions. The end result is a pragmatic collusion with societal forces whereby both parties look the other way in their conspirational scheme. Again, I want to stress the point that the patient's ability to turn to sociopathy as a way out of his dilemma requires an unwitting familiarity with how to join the system. This intuitive knowledge on his part is what I consider to be transfreential in nature.

Doubtless, not every sociopathy is a flight into social approval from the traumatic experience of schizophrenic turmoil. There are a large number of psychopathic and sociopathic individuals who do not show evidence of such a connection. Nevertheless, the psychopathic escape from severe mental disorder occurs and deserves to be clinically appreciated. On the other hand, borderline states usually differ from sociopathy, except in those cases in which there is much overlapping with character disorders and certain narcissistic states. It may be helpful to make a distinction between borderline states and sociopathy based on the nature of transferential manifestations. Borderline states have a penchant toward intense transference experiences on a one-to-one basis. Sociopathic individuals may have fleeting transferential flareups without any capacity for a sustained, durable emotional involvement with another person.

I have addressed myself to the transferential impact of society on the formation of borderline symptoms. In this connection, I should like to state categorically that my aim is not to blame society for most human maladaptations and maladjustments. My approach is not based on a direct cause-and-effect sequence but on a complex transaction between individual, society, and family in the formative process as well as in the process of living. To my way of thinking, the systematic exploration of transference and countertransference is a prerequisite in that respect. My recommendation is to postulate transference as an epigenetic phenomenon with particular reference to group, familial, and cultural aspects. The formulation of transference as an exclusively dyadic process narrows the field of our psychotherapeutic practice and research.

Usually, it is not difficult to point out obvious correlations between inauthentic precepts of the social structure and psychopathological reflections in the symptoms of certain mental disorders. This does not answer the question why some people adopt the above symptoms while others do not. It would be folly in our present state of knowledge to look for a definitive answer. At the same time, a clearer understanding of transference in general and cultural transference in particular could do a great deal to increase that knowledge.

CHAPTER 3

Uniqueness, Self and Self-System

A Historical Sketch

The term Self has had a relatively short psychological existence. However, there have been a number of statements about the Self in the fields of philosophy, the social sciences, religion, and related disciplines for some time.

In nontechnical language, the word Self is a person or thing referred to with respect to individuality. It is used in terms of one's own Self, one's nature, character, identity, self-image, self-regard, self-awareness and so forth. But a complex problem arises when we attempt to define a measure of constancy, continuity, and sameness in terms of the Self. I am in certain respects the same person I was one or more years ago, while at the same time I recognizably and unrecognizably change. What is persistent in the maintenance of identity and individuality cannot be specified with accuracy.

Philosophically there are two major traditions in the concept of the Self. One conceptualization, exemplified by the thinking of Leibniz, views the Self as part of an infinite variety of individual beings, each with an independent core rather than modifications of one basic ·element. By contrast, the British empiricists Locke and Hume looked at a permanent, stable Self as an illusion and stressed a kaleidoscopic point of view, that is, a series of changing impressions. Also implied is an essentially unchartered or pristine territory that acquires its characteristic aspects in the process of living. They argued that the Self starts out as a tabula rasa and later is in a state of constant flux.

In the field of psychology, William James was among the pioneers who looked at the Self as one of the most significant psychological considerations. He made an important distinction between the Self as known and the Self as a knower, leading to the formulation of an I and a me. The Self as a knower he also referred to as the "empirical Self" — the forerunner of the social Self which incorporates approval by one's fellow men. According to James, a person has as many social selves as there are distinct groups of persons about whose opinion he cares. James' social Self can claim a legitimate ancestry to Sullivan's Self.

It was predominantly the field of social psychology that was centrally concerned with the way in which the human Self originates. In particular, George Herbert Mead dealt with evidence pointing to the way in which the individual Self represents a reflection of a societal group. Mead was among the first to recognize that the unique individual person could never be isolated as such and always had to be seen within a complex, transactional process involving the individual in relation to others. Mead addresses the genesis of the Self and the nature of "human psyche" or mind. In this frame of reference the primary emphasis is on the intimate field of contact between organism and environment. It seems that Mead also thought, independently of the early existentialists, about the essentially active nature of the human organism, a concept that has led to the coining of the term intentionality by Brentano. It became an important consideration in existential formulations as well as in the field of Ego psychology. The interplay between "role taking" and evolution first was emphasized by Mead in connection with his well-known term the generalized other.

All conceptualizations of the Self constitute abstractions in one form or another. Mead was able to recognize that we must include an observational platform in order to make sense out of our observations. The notion of a Self as an inherently self-sustaining, self-defining, and self-motivating unit is not viable. In no way can we transcend the human frame of reference in creating this human abstraction. We are confronted here with the ancient truism that we cannot be actor on stage and audience at the same time. The observing Self of the observer would have to leave his universe in order to observe accurately another Self in the world in which both have their existence. At the same time, any individual Self requires the presence of another individual Self in a relational transaction before the characteristics of the respective Selves can emerge. Inherent in the point of view presented here is the conceptualization of the Self as a dynamic, transactional process rather than an object with relatively static boundaries, outlines and qualities.

Psychoanalytic Definitions of the Self

It is particularly in this area that a rapprochement between the Self as object and process has been attempted. Fairbairn attempted a synthesis between endopsychic and interpersonal conceptualizations of the Self in his well-known object relations theory of the personality. The core of his formulations centers on an Ego psychology revolving on object relations, that is, internalized objects. R. D. Laing, a Scottish psychoanalyst with an existential point of view, objects to Fairbairn's reference of objects rather than persons in object relations theory (*Practice and Theory: The Present Situation, Proceedings 6th International Congress of Psychotherapy*, Pines & Spoerri, Eds., New York and Basel, Karger, 1965).

Guntrip, a major advocate of object relations theory admits that the term objects is awkward. It reminds Guntrip of Freud's "sexual object" formulation, with its reference to an instinctual attribute rahter than to a two-way human interrelatedness. Nevertheless, Guntrip defends the term object as long as it means an experiential process whereby the Ego-object encounters the object in another Ego. Only then, Guntrip believes, do we have the full reality of personal experience and personal relations.

The object relation theorists acknowledge their indebtedness to the metapsychology of Melanie Klein, who introduced a new conception of endopsychic structure. The Kleinian introjects are not related to actual or external experiences.

They are postulated as internal operations of a biological factor.

All the proponents of object relations theory conceive of the Self as a distinctly observable configuration. This is in sharp contrast to interpersonal theory, which considers the uniqueness of individual personality to be a mythological concept. For Sullivan, unique individuality is a psychiatric phantom problem, because it defies all valid methodology for its study.

Classical Formulations of Self

Here the term was introduced by Hartman in 1950 (a year after Sullivan's death). Hartman applies the concept to the whole person of an individual, including the body and the body parts as well as all aspects of the psychic organization. Used in this way, the term may be appropriate by its reference to body, self, or physical self or psyche self and similar descriptive terms.

Edith Jacobson, another outstanding classical psychoanalyst, assures us in her book (*The Self and the Object World,* International Universities Press, Inc., New York, 1964) that "the meaning of the concepts of the self and self representations, as distinct from that of the ego, becomes clear when we remember that the establishment of the system ego sets in with the discovery of the object world and the growing distinction between it and one's own physical and mental self. From the ever-increasing memory traces of pleasurable and unpleasurable, instinctual, emotional, ideational, and functional experiences and of perceptions with which they become associated, images of the love objects as well as those of the bodily and psychic self emerge. Vague and variable at first, they gradually expand and develop into consistent and more or less realistic endopsychic representations of the object world and of the self." We observe here an attempt to bring about a rapprochement by the structures that are both inside and outside of the person — and an attempt to bring under a

common denominator continuous and discontinuous processes. Be that as it may, the terms endopsychic and intrapsychic
need to be contrasted. We suggest that intrapsychic refers to
the overall boundaries of psychical phenomena that take
place within the conceptual framework of the psyche, whereas
endopsychic means a process that comes from within the
psyche but operates without the aid of the sense organs. In
short, intrapsychic concerns itself with a region, and endopsychic addresses itself to the origin of an event. In practice,
the terms are often used interchangeably, and there is considerable overlapping between them.

Still another prominent analyst, Heinz Kohut, made a
major contribution to the classical understanding of narcissistic personality structure and the treatment of narcissistic disorders. In his highly respected work, *The Analysis of the Self*
(International Universities Press, New York, 1974), he refers
to the Self as "a comparatively experience-near, psychoanalytic abstraction, as a content of the mental apparatus." He
rejects the Self as an agency of the mind but refers to it as a
structure within the mind. To Kohut, the Self as a psychic
structure is cathected with instinctual energy and is enduring
by means of having continuity in time. He also postulates a
psychic location for the Self, that is, a representation within a
single agency of the mind aside from experience-distant Self-
representations in the structural units of Id, Ego, and
Superego. In Kohut's summary "The Self then, quite analog-
ous to the representations of objects, is a content of the mental
apparatus but it is not one of its constituents i.e. not one of the
agencies of the mind."

We can appreciate now the basic differences that emerge
in the conceptualization of the Self in classical compared to
interpersonal formulations. The classical point of view looks
at experience as a potential surface phenomenon with a postulated deeper level of hidden psychological aspects. An a
priori status is accorded to hypothetical constructs which
serve as a quasi reality. The abstractions of Id, Ego, and
Superego as well as of psychic apparatus are given an excessively concrete meaning.

As has been pointed out, modern classical theory considers abstractions of an experience-distant nature (Id, Ego, and

Superego) to be constitutional, fundamental, or elementary aspects of the psychic apparatus. By contrast it views comparatively experience-close abstractions (the Self) not to be an integral part of the human mind. In other words, concepts only remotely connnected with experience are given primacy over experience related ones. It also illustrates that the psychoanalytic construct of a psychic apparatus is treated as if it were concerned with concrete agencies of the mind rather than with abstractions. On the other hand, the Self as an observable, experiential phenomenon is relegated to a lower conceptual level. It is depicted as being psychically energized, as having both a certain permanence and psychic location. The classical Self has emancipated itself in many significant respects without so far transcending some of the cumbersome classical metaphors.

Sullivan's Formulation of Self and Self-system

The Self and Self-system are interpersonal constructs of a complex and at times contradictory nature. Inherent in the constructs is an attempt to establish an explanatory basis for a number of key psychological concepts. The principle of connotation is involved here, which deals with the set of attributes constituting a term and thus determining the range of objects to which the term may be applied. The terms Ego, Self, Individuality, Uniqueness, Identity, and Consciousness largely represent abstractions or metaphors without connotative clarification. Many are used loosely or in a dogmatic fashion. Often they tend to be viewed as "realities" and assume a static rather than dynamic quality.

Sullivan had an unflagging conviction that the language of psychiatry had to be altered in the direction of generally verifiable terms. He was greatly concerned with defining appropriate data of psychiatry and forging a clinically viable language designed to improve the range of checking and verification pertaining to clinical material.

In this connection, Sullivan submitted much psychiatric

and psychoanalytic vocabulary to his particular kind of scrutiny. Sullivan's model was strongly influenced by P.W. Bridgeman's epistemology, with its emphasis on verbal terms as operational tools.

Sullivan groped for psychiatrically viable terms that would serve as sensitive instruments in enlarging the observational field of the practicing psychiatrist. In particular, he sought removal of certain generic terms from metapsychological speculations and their replacement by epistemological considerations. One of the key terms of Sullivan's interpersonal psychiatry is, of course, Self.

Sullivan's formulation of Self underwent many changes, and it is difficult to construct a cohesive picture out of the mixture of terms used by him over the years. Initially, Sullivan included the Freudian terminology of Ego, Superego, and Id with minimal differentiation between the terms Self and Ego. Later he introduced the notion of a dynamic process of dynamism by speaking of a Self-dynamism. He tells us in a footnote (page 142, *Conceptions of Modern Psychiatry*) that he did not find the classical structural triad of Ego, Superego, and Id useful. To Sullivan the terms were metaphors with a mechanical, hydraulic system connotation. At a later point he replaced the term Self-dynamism with Self-system. The change coincided with his disenchantment over an earlier emphasis on dissociation as an explanatory phenomenon. He employed the dissociative principle a great deal in connection with his concept of Self. (This shift is mentioned in his introductory remarks to the *Conceptions of Modern Psychiatry,* dated December 31, 1931). Actually dissociation is a quantitative term without a longitudinal, developmental background. It suggests that its presence or absence is not integrated in the entire personality. Sullivan shifted his explanations of the vicissitudes of Self increasingly to the security operation he called selective inattention, that is, an observational field highlighted much like headlights of an automobile at night illuminating what is in their beam while leaving the rest of the landscape in darkness. Dissociation, similar to repression, is based on a mechanistic model that simply pushes distressing thoughts underground. By contrast, selective inattention is a scanning operation that includes the entire observational field

but focuses exclusively on events with a low-anxiety component. In this case the Self is the circumscribed observational
area of the ongoing interpersonal situation.

In Sullivan's scheme, the Self-system has an exclusively
interpersonal origin. It is an organization of experiences designed to avoid increasing amounts of anxiety in connection
with the process of education and acculturation.

The Self-system is referred to as a secondary dynamism
arising from the anxiety encountered in the pursuit of the
satisfaction of general and zonal needs.

The general idea centers around forbidding or disapprov-
ing gestures of the mothering person that tend to organize the
infant's experiences of itself along tender cooperation or its
absence. It must be appreciated that the "bad mother" is not to
be confused with a bad person, but with an individual posses-
sing the capacity to induce distressing experiences of anxiety
in the infant. As such, the forbidding gestures are extensions
or refinements of the "bad mother experience." They are
clearly distinguished from an incorporation or introjection of
a bad mother. The notion is that the perception of the mother,
and the reciprocal self-awareness of the infant are both distorted. Accordingly, it is unlikely that the infant can set up an
inner picture of a person who is poorly and inaccurately
perceived. Confusion thus results about the "I," "me" and
"myself" representation within the infant's mind.

Foremost in the discussion of the Self-system is the appreciation that we are dealing with an exploratory conception,
not a thing, a region, or a structure like the Ego, Superego, or
Id. Though he feels that "there is some noticeable relationship between the interpersonal personification of the self and
the psychoanalytic ego," (*Conceptions of Modern Psychiatry* p.
167), Sullivan does not recommend that we make such a
comparison.

Sullivan considers the Self-system to be an essential ingredient for every conceivable human society. The origin of the
Self-system in our particular culture and society is attributed
to misleading prescriptions for human behavior, motivations,
and value systems that are frequently at odds with the conditions that prevail. Furthermore, family and culture are frequently in collusion with each other, because many families

indulge in a double-bind communication[1] whereby they practice one thing and preach another. In our particular civilization parental groups do not tend to reflect the essence of the
social organization in which the young are trained to live.

Even in an ideal culture the Self-system would make its
appearance but develop in a different direction. The self-
system pertains to that part of the I which is the personification of the Self. On this basis it is clear that the Self-system is an
essential organization of experiences that permits people to
integrate information and develop even in the presence of
moderate to moderately severe anxiety. It can be said that the
Self-system is essential for growth and survival, while at the
same time representing the most obstinate barrier in overcoming distorted perceptions.

The distinction between the term Self and Self-system is
highly complicated in Sullivan's terminology, and we cannot
find a clear-cut line of demarcation. Both terms refer to the
organization of experiences triggered off by the intervention
of anxiety, and both represent a process rather than an entity.
Indeed, Sullivan considers the Self as an entity of little service
as a general explanatory principle in the study of interpersonal relations. ("Data of Psychiatry," p. 35 in *The Fusion of
Psychiatry and Social Sciences*). It is the pronoun I that refers to
one's Self, which includes only conscious aspects of self-
awareness. The Self is a much less inclusive entity than personality ("the relatively enduring pattern of recurrent interpersonal situations which characterize a human life"), three
aspects of which pertain to the Self: first, the waking and
thoroughly active; second, the part of the personality that is
not readily accessible to awareness — the rest of the personality, which in another context can be considered as the whole
personality with the Self as the eccentric part: and third, the
state of sleep in which the Self does not have a very active part.

The Evolution of the Concept Self
in Sullivan's Thinking

Sullivan's development of the concept Self can be traced
from his early writings, in *Personal Psychopathology* published

posthumously in 1972, (Crowley #128), where he speaks of
Self consciousness activities, including an approving reference system called Self (p. 30). This he traces to primitive,
early experience referred to as sentience, that is, the crude
material of undifferentiated events impinging on our sense
organs. (In later definitions this earliest mode of cognition is
referred to as prototaxic.) We then read (p. 38) of the person
"as a nexus of processes in communal existence with a
physiochemical, social and culture world." From there we
come to a definition (p. 64) whereby "each of us constructs
from the perceived reactions of others to us a body of beliefs
as to our personality, this going to make up the Self." Sullivan
continues (p. 74) that "the Individual is at one moment a
Self-conscious person, at another a quite different person
engaged in activity intolerable to the Self."

Later we find a reference to a dichotomy between an
observing and a dissociated Self. The latter is based on the
nonincorporation of experiences into the Self in the early
phases of development. We are informed that the term unconscious refers to inaccessible aspects of experience, which is
in contrast to the Freudian unconscious as the intrapsychic
manifestation of primary process.

Still another concept of Self is introduced (p. 101) when
Sullivan speaks of sentiment of self and the objects of this
sentiment as the Ego. Here we run into a distinct confusion
between Self and Ego: "We come now to the more direct
investigation, the formulation of Self or Ego, the ideal systems
or Superego and of the repressed and the totally refracted
tendency system, the Id." Later in the book (see p. 337), the
confusion is even more pronounced, but here Sullivan goes
on to offer three formulations of experience incorporated in
the Self.

1. The person as he wishes and has wished to be.
2. As he has suspected and now suspects that he actually
is.
3. As his "enemies" have seen and now see him.

If this array of statements is confusing, it is at least clear that
Sullivan was greatly concerned about the origin and stability
of the Self. The former is traced to the initial exposure to
anxiety and its high level of sensitivity as a potential deroga-

tory and hateful system that leads to major distortions in the personality and the range of interpersonal integrations. But of equally great concern in Sullivan's thinking about the Self are his therapeutic considerations. In a footnote (p. 98, footnote n, *Conceptions of Modern Psychiatry*) he emphasizes that "therapeutic results are the expansion of the Self dynamism and the simplification of living which results from it."

Sullivan's final concepts about the Self are to be found in "The Illusion of Personal Individuality" based on a paper presented in May 1944 at the New York Academy of Medicine. In it he refers to the Self as a system within the personality built up from innumerable experiences from early life. Here the Self is that part of the personality which is central in the experience of anxiety, and it is not to be confused with the classical concept of Ego nor with the formulations of the Ego psychologists. The Self is the content of consciousness, the direct awareness of oneself and one's reflected appraisal of oneself in the eyes of others. The Self represents an experiential matrix, a cumulative Self-image based on the central notion "that we satisfy the people that matter to us and therefore satisfy ourselves, and are spared the experience of anxiety." In other words, the range of self-awareness, the content of the self are what reflects a person's conscious, ideational content. The Self appears in total awareness only when there is no anxiety.

Experience as an Organizing Component of the Self

From its beginning, interpersonal theory has stressed the intimate relationship between an individual's behavior and the conditions under which the behavior occurs. Sullivan's emphasis on interpersonal processes as the appropriate unit for therapeutic exploration has provided a powerful stimulus for psychiatric research and practice. In the same vein his rejection of individual uniqueness as a viable area for psychotherapeutic investigation has been the foundation for genuine clinical progress. It can be said that uniqueness is a suitable focus of interest for collectors who are interested in a one-of-a-kind specimen. Its psychiatric applicability cannot be supported or documented by any meaningful evidence. Sullivan's one genus postulate is the leitmotif of this theory. His interest is in human identities rather than in human differences, and his quest is to study what is ubiquitously human. Sullivan's theoretical and clinical considerations convinced him that personal individuality is beyond the reach of scientific analysis. It can never be detached from its interpersonal network, which is an integral part of the unit under study. In other words, elements external or outside of the individual person interpenetrate with internal components. Experience is the individualizing factor, because experience is a particular instance of personally encountering or undergoing something. However, experience as the foundation of cognition still requires another person as a sounding board for purposes of checking and verifying the nature of the experience (consensual validation).

Psychological terms connnected with the field of psychotherapy and psychoanalysis have been excessively rooted in metapsychological speculations. The difficulty is that whatever level of supplementary construct we employ — Id, Ego, Identity, or Individuality — we cannot explain the correlation between psychological assumptions and clinical phenomena. Our terms must be open-ended, free of dogma, and as close to actual experience as possible.

The Interpersonal Concept of Self

The interpersonal formulation of Self largely represents the content of a person's consciouness, or what can be said to be within the scope of direct awareness. The Self is also conceptualized as that part of the personality that is central in the experience of anxiety. In other words, focal awareness of one's Self in this scheme depends on the relative absence of anxiety, which in turn is controlled by the Self-system or antianxiety system.

Thus the construct of Self in interpersonal theory is best understood when we explore it within the interconnecting framework of Self, anxiety, and Self-system. In essence, the

Self-system is considered to be a dynamic safety valve against the destructive inroads of severe anxiety. It permits a measure of growth, of learning from experience, and it maintains a level of functioning in spite of certain pernicious effects of anxiety. As is often the case in life, there is a price to be paid for such benefits. The Self-system provides a potential lightning rod and offers some protection against the thunder bolts of severe anxiety. In doing its job, though, the Self-system develops a homeostatic system, an equilibrium, and a certain rigidity of its own and is thus largely responsible for resisting change, which includes change for the better.

A high level of vigilance is employed by the Self-system in regard to the conscious awareness of moderate to severe anxiety. In this connection the Self-system is intimately linked to the gamut of defensive or security operations. At its disposal are the familiar phenomena of selective inattention, somnolent detachment, apathy, lethargy, irrational anger, sterile bickering, belittling, and disparaging operations, as well as a host of other activities designed to promote feelings of security. The intervention of antianxiety or Self-system maneuvers misinform the individual about the nature of the on-going interpersonal situation. At the same time, these interventions complicate or hinder positive relational integrations. They tend to isolate the person and stand in the way of more intimate dealings with other people. The Self-system, therefore, restricts the field of personal observation and constricts the content of consciousness.

Self, Self-System, and Anxiety

The operational interplay between Self, Self-system, and anxiety may be illustrated by analogy to the function of the eye, pupil, and retina in perception, although it is admittedly a highly simplified scheme.

It is the function of the pupil to adjust the amount of light that is permitted to impinge on the retina. The aperture of the opening is related to the intensity of light. Intense light constricts the aperture, and dim light produces an optimal opening. This principle can be applied to an operational concep-

tualization between Self, Self-system and anxiety in the following manner. What can be "seen" by the Self (i.e., the content of
consciousness) is controlled by the amount of light the Self-
system permits to be shed on the awareness of the prevailing
interpersonal situation. This, in turn, depends on the intensity of anxiety in the picture. It should be emphasized once
more that the anxiety is not a primarily intrapsychic
phenomenon. The scanning process or the nature of the
cognitive experience is highly sensitized by a person's basic
level of Self-esteem. This dormant component must be activated by the quality of the on-going interpersonal situation in
order to unleash the emergence of sudden anxiety. In other
words, the anxiety is neither inside nor outside of the person.
It permeates the field in which the respective personalities
encounter one another. The intensity of the anxiety (light in
the analogy) is a complex series of happenings consisting of a
blending of past, current, and future events.

In a discussion of the Self and Self-system in interpersonal
terms, care should be taken not to rigidify these formulations
or view them as fixed entities. They are, instead, explanatory
conceptions and not "things," "regions" or particular
"aspects" of the human psyche. There is no justification for
linkingthe Id, Ego, and Superego to organic structures; certainly no documentation along these lines has been provided.

The open-ended interpersonal conceptions of Self and
Self-system represent a significant step ahead in our
psychological explorations of human relations. Nevertheless,
in the field of scientific inquiry, even faulty theories have led
to important discoveries. Navigation, for instance, made considerable strides at a time when the theory prevailed that the
earth was a flat disc. In a similar vein, we are not necessarily
doomed to sterile preoccupations if we adhere to outmoded
theories. As long as we consider the Ego to be an explanatory
concept rather than an entity, it does not particularly matter
whether we speak of an Ego or of a personified Self. After all,
both interpersonal psychiatry and so-called Ego psychology
have gained valuable insights into certain aspects of human
behavior notwithstanding oppositional formulations and
basic points of view.

The Psychological Roots of the Self

The term Self should not be viewed as a static entity or a singular unit. The Self, in interpersonal language, consists of a broad spectrum of lifetime experiences that have been incorporated into a dynamic field of self-perception. The horizons of the field are largely determined by the way in which the initial communicative network has evolved. Fleeting images pertaining to I, me, my body become organized into more durable impressions of the Self. Again, what is central in the evolution of the Self (the content of conscious awareness), is the experience of anxiety. Information relating to oneself thus depends on the level of anxiety surrounding the observational field. A chronically anxious mother will affect significant aspects of the infant's self-awareness. The mother's muscle tone, the way she holds the infant, the soothing or distressing quality of her voice, her gestures, her facial expressions, and related communications, all transmit the level of her anxiety. It may have no direct relation to the infant and may be the result of disturbances in her own life. However, once anxiety permeates the mother-child contact, regardless of its origin, complications in the infant's self-awareness arise. Experiences become tinged with unpleasant sensations, which gradually become organized into a feeling of "good me," "bad me," or outright "not me." What enters the content of consciousness, or the Self, begins to acquire a value orientation that forms the foundations of a person's self-esteem. It is at the point when anxiety first intervenes that a new kind of self-awareness comes into existence — the Self-system. Its purpose is to provide a warning, anticipation, and foresight of approaching or increasing anxiety. It permits an inflow of information, a measure of learning, and a potential capacity for satisfaction in spite of the presence of anxiety. However, the type of learning and self-observation that takes place under the defensive umbrella of the Self-system constricts what is represented in the Self. Accordingly the Self-system is a safety valve, a type of character defense designed to permit a certain modus vivendi while setting up an excessive self-defeating security system.

We can see, then, how the Self and Self-system are the shutter and the lens of an experimental recording system. What is reflected on the screen of the Self is intimately related to a person's Self-esteem which in turn is related to the operations of the Self-system. There is a basic reservoir of Self-esteem resulting from the sum total of life experiences and depending on the degree of anxiety inculcated early in life. It is the basic level of anxiety that calls into operation the antianxiety self-system, or the security operations. In turn, the rigidity of the Self-system impedes the raising of a person's self-esteem. It follows that the term Self as used here is intimately related to a person's self-esteem and to the extent of the Self-system intervention. Included in the concept Self are preconceived notions about oneself and people of significance in one's life. This is coupled with familial and sociocultural value orientations. Last but not least we find in the Self a full range of transferential phenomena.

Looked upon from this vantage point, the Self emerges as a phenomenological representation composed of developmental, on-going, and anticipatory experiences. It manifests itself in reciprocal relation to the Self-system, which provides a dynamic screen against intense anxiety. The Self-system contains many attributes assigned to the Freudian Ego and includes the "conflict-free sphere" posited by Ego psychologists, as well as a host of "character defenses."

Further Comments on Sullivan's Description of Self

In the "Data of Psychiatry" (*Psychiatry;* 1938; vol. 1 pp. 131-134), reprinted in *The Fusion of Psychiatry and Social Science* we find one of Sullivan's recurrent definitions of Self. He states: "Psychiatry concerns itself with the way in which each of us comes to be possessed of a Self which he esteems and cherishes, shelters from questioning, and criticism and expands by commendation." He emphasizes that the Self has little regard for objectively observable performances, and includes many contradictions and inconsistencies. The vicissitudes of the Self in a severe psychosis point to the fact that "the Self has been acquired in the life of the person, chiefly by communication with others. Much of the praise and some of the blame that has come from parents, friends and others with whom one has been significantly related have been organized into the content of the Self."

In the "Illustration of Personal Individuality" (*Psychiatry;* 1950, vol. 13 pp. 317-332), also reprinted in the *Fusion of Psychiatry and Social Science,* Sullivan stresses that his notion of the Self differs distinctly from the Ego formulation of Freud or that of the Ego psychologists. Rather, he conceives of the Self as the content of consciousness under conditions of favorable self-esteem, that is, minimal anxiety. We find some additional comments by Sullivan in the discussion of his paper on the "Illusion of Personal Individuality" which appear following its reprint in the *Fusion of Psychiatry and Social Science.* Here he points out that individuality does not mean genuine autonomy of freedom of behavior. His argument centers around his observation that even in total privacy people usually act as if someone else were present. Thus it makes little sense to think of ourselves as "individual," "separate," or capable of anything like definite identity in isolation. Sullivan leaves no doubt that he considers the notion of a "real Self" to be a verbal artefact.

A Comparative Evaluation of the Self and Self-System

A Comparative evaluation of the Freudian and interpersonal formulation of the Self can be found in a chapter by Clara Thompson on Sullivan and Psychoanalysis, which appears in *The Contributions of Harry Stack Sullivan,* edited by Patrick Mullahy, Hermitage House, New York 1952. Thompson stresses similarities and differences between Freud and Sullivan. She compares transference and

parataxis, highlights Sullivan's original concept of preadolescence, discusses the connection between Self-system and
character structure, and points to Sullivans view of secondary
anxiety.

However, certain additional aspects deserve to be mentioned. In the classic frame of reference, the individual person and his intrapsychic mechanisms are the primary focus of
exploration. An integral part of character formation is related
to the impact of instinctual drives and to the vicissitudes of the
libido. The process of acculturation in the classic scheme
centers around the formation of Superego functions which
largely represent cultural introjects, particularly as transmitted by the parents.

By contrast, interpersonal theory emphasizes the powerful impact of the world of significant people as a matrix on
which we come to organize experiences about ourselves and
our immediate interpersonal milieu. There is a notion of a
relational arena or sphere leading to a merging of nature and
nurture in the forging of the self-image, self-esteem, and
personality structure. Approval or disapproval by maternal,
parental, and cultural attitudes represent guidelines for the
quality and clarity of the infant's growing self-awareness. Personality in the interpersonal frame of reference is an action
potential rather than an intrinsic commodity. Variations in
the personality come to the fore depending on the particular
interpersonal integrations and their developmental implications. Anxiety is not a signal of danger but the danger itself,
because it is the manifestation of a profound lack of self-
esteem. The content of consciousness is at all times controlled
by the experience of anxiety which, through the intervention
of the Self- system, restricts what one is able to observe about
oneself and others.

Evaluation of the Self in Interpersonal Terms

Sullivan's definition of the Self has remained among the
most controversial aspects of interpersonal formulations.
Even Clara Thompson ("Concepts of the Self in Interpersonal

Theory"; *American Journal of Psychotherapy,* Vol. XII, No. 1, January 1958), one of the staunchest supporters of Sullivan's conceptions, finds his presentation of the Self inconsistent. According to Thompson there is an inconsistency between Sullivan's views of the Self as a dynamic, interactional process, and as a subject lying outside of his sphere of interest.

Thompson's discussion, however, is limited in a number of respects. Nowhere does she refer to the principle of ecology as a concept of interpenetrating entities. She fails to appreciate the fact that the Self requires another Self in order to be definable. Sullivan's Self is an action bound process that cannot be defined in a static way. The Self in interpersonal terms ceases to be a Self once it is separated from its necessary environment. The Self cannot be detached from its network of interpersonal integrations in which it has its moorings.

So far we have discussed Sullivan's various formulations of the Self from his earlier to his later thoughts on the subject. Included in the comments has been a critical exploration of Sullivan's psychology of Self.

One final point should be added here. The Self has been described as an observational screen that is controlled by the prevailing degree of anxiety in a given interpersonal situation. Sullivan's basic theme is that human commonality prevails over human individuality (see similarity principle and one genus postulate in Chapter 1). He insists that the basic characteristics of the human species are dominant over the multitude of deviations in people's behavior. What is represented in the Self reflects an experiential matrix related to self-esteem and resulting from specific interpersonal situations in the past, here and now, and in the near future. It covers an individual's entire life space while controlling the content of consciousness and the quality of self-awareness.

Changing Concepts of Self

In a previously published paper ("The Changing Language of Self" in *Contemporary Psychoanalysis,* Vol. 7, No. 2, Spring, 1971), I commented on literary representations of

Self and how they relate to Freud's and Sullivan's formulations.

For instance, we find Dostoevsky's creation of an underground man to be a person who is both sentimental and cynical. He constantly watches himself in a self-reflecting mirror and assumes to some degree the dual role of actor and observer. Much of his energy is invested in posturing as an observer without having a reliable platform for his observations. Dostoevsky's underground man suffers from "the disease of consciousness." He is a strongly romantic character with a tendency toward rebellion. Central in his personality is a particular form of narcissim expressed in his never-ending desire to view himself as the center of his universe. The Self depicted here is inherently heroic. At the same time, the Self is afflicted with the burden of residing in a mortal body that is incapable of successfully resisting corruption. The result is disillusionment and romantic despair.

Dostoevsky's underground man is a conceptualization of Self against the background of man's dualistic nature. Man's basic striving to fulfill himself within the boundaries of a biologically corruptible system creates an insurmountable polarization and antithesis. Similar to the theme in Goethe's Faust poem, the Self is split in a schizophrenic-like division between God and the devil. Against this background of religious symbolism, the Self is unable to bring about a successful resolution.

We find here the familiar image of Freud's underground man who is at the mercy of his inbridled libido while pursuing his humanistic goals. The Self in Freud's concept is held captive between the forces of destructiveness and noble ambitions. His metaphor of the Unconscious is largely the force of darkness related to the symbolism of the devil. In contrast, the abstraction of the Superego represents a predominantly benign, rational. humanistic counterforce. The Self is powerless to run its own life and is caught between the forces of darkness and light. Freud's basic concept of Self is characterized by his famous reference to the image of an iceberg — only a small part rises above the surface while its mass is submerged and hidden from view. Freud's Self is externally vigilant against visualizing what is kept out of awareness and is highly resistive to bringing the light of reality (secondary process phenomena) in contact with the darkness of the unconscious (primary process).

To some degree Freud's concept of Self has undergone modificatons. In addition, the advent of Ego psychology with its notion of a conflict-free sphere of the Self has placed the entire concept in a potentially different setting. Nevertheless, modern Ego psychology with its concept of the Self and object relations has not transcended the inherent symbolism conflicts related to Dostoevsky's model of the underground man. The classical Self even in its liberated form is rooted in an outmoded metapsychology rather than a modern epistemology.

By contrast, Sullivan's underground man has exposed himself in many respects. Sullivan feels that the part of the personality that is totally hidden from consciousness has little or no significance in human relations. He considers Freud's notions of dangerous, subterranean destructiveness, of impulsivity and unchannelled sexual energy to be a phantomproblem. To him the immutably private aspect of Self, that is, the part unaccessible to awareness, is entirely subjected to speculative thought and permanently excluded from being made visible. Sullivan considers a person's innermost Self to be virtually irrelevant for communicative purposes because it is action-bound and can never be captured without intersecting with another person.

Sullivan's Self exists exclusively in the process of defining itself. The only way the Self can do so is by making contact with another human being. There is no room for conceptualizing a Self removed from its essential interpersonal milieu. Such a Self would be nonrepresentative because it reflects a dead or morbid specimen that has been removed from its natural habitat. Sullivan's underground man has no cave to hide in; he is always out in the open displaying various and variant aspects of his basically human quality.

The underground man, as Sullivan conceives him, is a complementary aspect of the person kept out of awareness at a given time and under certain circumstances, rather than a substance that does, or does not, have an independent existence. Sullivan's Self lives for the purpose of asking questions with the understanding that there are no final answers. This concept has a certain similarity with Beckett's notion in asking

"What was God doing with himself before the Creation?" or "Why may man identify himself if he is to die?" Beckett has the conviction that one must go on without knowing why. As he expresses it in *End Game* : "It is forbidden to give up or even stop for an instant, so I wait jogging along for the bell to say 'Molloy, one last effort. It is the end.' " To Beckett, man is that "creature that cannot come forth from himself, who knows others only in himself, and if he asserts the contrary, lies."

This concept of human existence based on the duality of being, separate yet compelled to have an awareness of the presence of others, characterizes much of Sullivan's thinking. He views the Self as always lonely, yet always hopeful that some form of contact can be made with others. The main spring in life then is conceptualized as man's everpresent need to reach out for his fellow man despite an all-powerfull anxiety that he may fail or be rejected.

Freud, in keeping with the spirit of his time, took refuge in metapsychological extrapolations as a means of explaining uncertainties in his frame of reference. He relied on allegorical language and had a masterful literary style. In contrast, Sullivan, who was greatly concerned with precision and mistrustful of jargon, so asserts himself linguistically that occasionally he seems neologistic. To Sullivan, language is always culture in action and, as such, it is constantly engaged in the process of defining itself. Sullivan uses language as an epistemological tool designed to probe the intricacies of human thought and behavior, particularly in the therapeutic relationship.

Change in the Nature of the Self

Along with changes from metaphysics to epistemology, there has been a change in our concept of the nature of the Self. The psychological Self of Freud had a hysterical, righteous, moralistic quality. It was constantly preoccupied with denying unconscious libidinal drives and uncontrolled sexual impulses. Freud's underground man tended to be furtive about his sexuality, his aggression, and his pleasure-directed "instinct." He was inclined to wear the garment of Victorian inhibitions. The Self in Freud's conception, within the zeitgeist of the Freudian era, was constantly bombarded with dramatic demands in the sexual sphere, ranging from incest to homosexuality, as well as encompassing socially forbidden heterosexual desires.

It is evident that the modern Self is emancipated to a large degree from its sexual vulnerability and has assumed a role of greater self-expression and self-indulgence, particularly in the sexual realm. There is an increasing freedom toward the awareness of and the pursuit of sexual desires that previously were considered perverse or pathological. Sexuality has taken on a conscious, if not compulsively self-conscious, component in modern existence rather than its former puritanical, clandestine preoccupation.

This leaves little room for metapsychological inquiry into sexual meaning, because the climate today encourages sexual acting out and ordinarily does not drive it underground. Sex has shifted rapidly from a private to a public mode of manifesting itself. Once more we are confronted with an epistemological inquiry into the modern sexual Self, stripped of its old symbolism and compensatory activities.

The number of people who seek psychoanalytic assistance because of repressed sexual desires is becoming small. There is, on the other hand, an increasing group of people who are engaged in meaningless sexual activities in the absence of genuine human encounters. It is in this area that a shift in the nature of the Self has taken place, permeating literary and psychoanalytic writing as well as daily life.

The language of the Self in the literary productions of the 1970s is more clearly in the realm of consciousness and the dialectic exploration of goals, meanings, or their absence. The dialogue of the modern Self takes place in an atmosphere outside the anchorage of the devil and Christ and is divorced from a metapsychological conceptualization of sexuality. Rhetoric has shifted its focus from content and causality to skepticism, questioning, and honest doubt.

Part II
THE
THERAPEUTIC PROCESS
AND THE
EMERGENCE
OF AN
INTERPERSONAL SELF

CHAPTER 4

Goals and Methods of Therapy

The preceding chapters addressed themselves to an overview and critical exposition of the basic tenets underlying Sullivanian psychiatry, that is, the study of interpersonal relations. In the following pages focal attention turns to the emergence of an interpersonal Self as an extension of Sullivanian psychiatry. The primary concern here is on enlarging the scope of clinical applicability. Particular consideration is given to the redefinition of individual personality as an open-ended system, the fuller application of the ecological principle, a redefinition of participant observation, the transcending of energetic considerations, and the clarification of the Self as an experience-close term for observational and therapeutic purposes.

Sullivan's denouncement of personal individuality as an illusion represents a courageous attack on a long-cherished metaphor. He buttressed his interpersonal theory by rejecting atomistic constructs of the Self, of personal identity, and individual personality, and by recognizing the fallacy of looking at the Self as a God-given indivisible core of man. Sullivan appreciated the interpenetrating aspects of life as the most appropriate areas of psychological study, that is, interpersonal relations as the mirror reflecting particular characteristics of two or more individuals within the field of their transactions in the social, economic and cultural setting that prevails. To essentially human is embedded in a required process of man to man contact. Man cut off from the network of his existential and experiential roots is a basically inhuman specimen.

Inherently human characteristics rest neither inside nor outside of the person. They are part of an ecologic unit that can never be divided.

Up to this point Sullivan's formulations stand on sound foundations. Then he weakens his position unnecessarily by taking a strong position against a construct of individuality per se; for though the concept of a "real Self" is unnecessary and misleading, it is doubtful that "individuality" and "real Self" belong in the same category.

Sullivan rationalizes his opposition to individual personality by invoking a pragmatic argument. He claims that the concept of personal individuality hampers technological advances in psychiatry and the social sciences. Sullivan's aim was to forge operationally viable terms capable of serving as observational and therapeutic tools. There is considerable merit in this approach as long as it is kept flexible. Nothing is gained, however, by dispensing with one metaphor at the expense of another. For instance, Sullivan was content to deal with hypothetical constructs as a means of explaining certain interpersonal events. He constructed an abstract, which he called the Self-system (a hypothetical antianxiety device) in order to explain the phenomenon of an inauthentic Self. The latter is perceived by Sullivan as a faulty cognitive pattern — the root of much parataxic distortion, that is, "the most empathic and conspicuous and troublesome influence on awareness."

Sullivan attempted to transcend Freud's mechanistic and metapsychological model with one mechanistic in its own right as well as having an unduly operational point of view. Sullivan's overemphasis on the observable truncated his psychological point of view by leading him to look excessively at instrumental aspects. At the same time, he advocated hypothetical bridges, heuristic formulations, and related methodology as a necessary exploratory procedure. There is an ironic similarity between Freud's denouncement of free will as a fallacy and Sullivan's attack on personal individuality as an illusion. Both men are guilty of "overkill" in their respective dogma.

Freud forged his psychoanalytic postulates of human behavior on bold speculative assumptions. His superb rhetoric gave force to those metaphors designed to underline an inherently instinct controlled image of man. In Freud's concept, man's Self is predominantly determined by biological forces and a socially controlled stimulus-response system. Freud's intrapsychic Self is a captive of drives and the conflicting external conditional attempts to tame the instinctually controlled energies. This model has essentially been retained by the Ego psychologists who changed the superstructure but left the core untouched by reifying the metapsychological basis of the Self.

The way things are, Self, Ego, personality, identity, and individuality are all descriptive attempts to conceptualize some aspects of human beings. Each construct represents a part or a device of a larger configuration. It is not of major importance which term we prefer, as long as we recognize the hypothetical nature of each and appreciate that none can ever be all-inclusive. The purpose of the term, whichever it may be, is to provide additional information about vaguely or inaccurately chartered territory. Hopefully, the term will serve as a vantage ground for viewing the individual and his existential network in better perspective.

In the overall field of psychotherapy, there is merit in selecting a term that is relatively close to experience rather than a predominantly theoretical concept. At present, terms such as Ego, personality, identity, and individuality each have assumed a biased meaning, whereas construct Self has maintained a more open-ended stance.

Self and Self-Esteem

Sullivan gave much thought to the genesis of the Self and its dynamic transactions in interpersonal situations. His basic model centers on the organization of experience; he stays relatively clear of psychic structures and avoids an adherence to closed systems. Nevertheless, his Self is at the mercy of anxiety and lacks a continuity in its own right. Sullivan's construct of Self is a system forever caught in operational anonymity. To a large degree, self-esteem is the major characteristic commodity that pertains to the Self. A person's basic level of self-esteem is inculcated early in life and is a cross to be carried from then on. According to Sullivan, it is doubtful that the core level of self-esteem can be raised much beyond the developmental epoch of preadolescence. At that time, the basic, underlying self-image is fairly well engraved. It does not mean that the future is totally bleak if the self-esteem has not been shored up at that level. However, favorable changes will be more difficult to achieve, and they will not be as solidly anchored as they are in people who inherently have come to think more highly of themselves.

Clinical Illustration of Self-Esteem

A brief clinical reference will illustrate this point. The case pertains to a young professional woman of outstanding intellectual endowment. Her family was unable to cope with her free-wheeling formative years. The parents were deeply troubled people who found a tranquilizing effect in applying themselves to compulsive, routinized work. A younger sibling was pressed into the same mold and grew up in the parental image by repeating their life-social, and performance patterns.

The patient was an outstanding student until she entered college, where she acted out sexually, scholastically, and socially. Her postgraduate work was stormy, ill-organized, and led to a number of difficulties. She obtained a professional position in a highly prestigious setting and managed to get fired from her job because of persistent absence and an inability to get her work done in spite of her acknowledged high level of competence. The patient went through several jobs, often working with distinction, but also with increasing unreliability. She suffered two severe psychotic episodes requiring hospitalization of medium duration. Her overt psychosis manifested itself both times while she was in analytic therapy. The episodes were characterized by a complete break with reality, by overt paranoid ideation, morbid sexual fantasies, and a wide range of major psychopathology. Her postpsychotic adjustment was very good and she can serve as an illustration of a number of patients who emerge stronger and humanly more intact from the ordeal. There were indications that her self-esteem had risen after she had overcome her collapse and temporary disintegration. Gradually a great deal fell in line for the patient, and she was able to organize her personal and professional life with increasing satisfaction. There were fleeting, shaky moments, but her basic stability was of a high order. Two problems remained: her excessive sensitivity to the disturbance of others and her profound difficulty in maintaining her own boundaries in that respect, and her persistent unreliability about time routine and routine work requirements. She was highly appreciated at work and treated with respect and consideration. Nevertheless, her excessive absenteeism (staying in bed and doing nothing) and lack of follow through once more backed her into a corner where she had to show up, complete assignments, or be dismissed. In that latest crisis, the patient reported a series of highly significant dreams. One key dream made it appear that she and her father (a man who undermined her self-esteem particularly during her juvenile and preadolescent period) were working on the same job. It was announced that in order to stay on the same job, she was required to obtain a divorce from her father (both parents are living and are active in their own right). After this dream, which greatly startled her, she had a nightmare reminiscent of her last psychotic episode. (The dream was about a girl who had a nervous breakdown on the job and had to leave followed by bizarre events involving an "eye bank" and eyes floating around). There are many ways of interpreting her dream, with the traditional Oedipal theme coming to mind first. In that respect it did not matter whether she had to separate from her actual father or another father surrogate in the form of the analyst or what have you. In the therapeutic situation it was suggested to her that she ask herself precisely what the metaphor of divorcing her father meant to her. In the meantime, a working hypothesis was pursued whereby the divorce from the father, whatever its particular significance may have been, was intimately tied to her self-esteem. The question arose then as to what were the foundations of her self-esteem and what affected it most directly in the here and now. This illustrates the difficulty of working with a global concept like self-esteem, its genesis, and its on-going maintenance operations.

Low self-esteem, like insecurity, is a ubiquitous characteristic of legions of people. Probably the majority of mankind
suffers from it in one form or another. But there is considerable difficulty in quantifying feelings of worthlessness and
deciding at which level they become morbid manifestations.

Let us assume, however, that we can establish a clinically
workable yardstick for neurotic self-esteem; how do we go
about raising self-confidence and promoting a better self-
image? It clearly does not suffice to tell a person "you are
really a much better person than you think you are." Neither
does it sufficiently help to encourage positive aspects while
showing less interest in liabilities. Our work centers on the
detailed exploration of a given individual's highly individualized and personalized value system, his reasonable and
unreasonable expectations of himself, as well as the familial,
socioculture guidelines. In many instances we find discrepancies between native endowment, inherent talent, and over or
underexpectations of what is legitimately available to a person. A measure of objectivity can be achieved mainly in a
setting of relational mutuality whereby personal data emerge
with increasing clarity from the interchange of transferential
and countertransferential experiences.

The above illustration shows that some people grow up
with a persistent Achilles heel, that is, a vulnerable, thinly covered area of low self-esteem. This clinical reality can be more
effectively dealt with by ascribing to the Self a personalized
form and shape rather than treating it as an amorphous
phenomenon. A detailed exploration of the Self in its developmental, interpersonal manifestations has much to offer
as a broader therapeutic platform.

Characteristics of the Interpersonal Self

The term interpersonal Self avoids some of the pitfalls
inherent in the notion of either a predetermined personal
individuality or a state of amorphism. The suggested con-

struct represents an open-ended system for the coding and integration of personalized, individual experiences. What is in the interpersonal Self reflects a cumulative storage of interpersonal experiences with the stamp of personal perception. In other words, the scope of the Self is determined by the degree of prevailing anxiety in past and on-going relations with significant people. At all times, however, we have a highly individualized data process that is modified by life experiences in the formative years as well as present-day living. There is no legitimate basis for outlawing personal individuality or denouncing it as an operational anachronism. Accepting individuality as a postulate, and as a reality beyond the scope of our observational methods, does not invalidate an ecologic psychological model with all of its conceptual and therapeutic implications. An open-minded attitude toward individuality does not force us into the unfortunate dichotomy of a "true Self" compared to a "false Self." Individuation need not be confused with the idle search for a pristine Self — for a permanent, atomistic core, isolated from the process of living and unaffected by human experiences. There is no need to dispense with the "uniqueness" of the person one loves, even if this concept has no particular psychiatric significance. The interpersonal Self we study is not a love object or an appropriate medium for our idealized projections. We are entitled to dislike relatively unique aspects of a patient's personality without losing therapeutic perspective. Therapeutically we can safely transcend the role of an observing while participating Ego, for there is considerable latitude in our transactional therapeutic range as long as we adhere to the concept of an interpersonal Self and the model of an ecological process.

Accordingly, the emergence of an interpersonal Self promotes a sounder platform for therapeutic explorations. We are no longer burdened by confronting a "generalized other" by a generalized Self. Individuality comes into the picture by focusing on the way in which experiences are personalized. The interpersonal Self has a solid longitudinal axis that goes beyond the restrictive awareness dictated by anxiety. A stable continuum of individually coded events interacts with other individuals who are part of the interpersonal field. The exchange of communication, rational and irrational feelings does not depend primarily on energetic factors. A minimum of energy is required for information to be transmitted from one person to another.

These factors have yet to be incorporated into much of psychoanalytic practice and theory. In spite of profound changes in our field, psychiatry and psychoanalysis are still entrenched in conflicting ideologies without workable bridges between them. Professionals in the field and the public at large lack meaningful guidelines in this particular area. A discussion of Sullivanian Psychiatry and its extension into present-day practical application, therefore, requires at least a cursory review of the way in which basic concepts and prevailing practice have changed.

Changing Directions of Psychoanalysis and Psychoanalytic Psychotherapy

In the course of events psychoanalysis in its classical and neoclassical form became the preferred model of American psychotherapy. There was a period in the 1930s when the American culture contained strong socialistic currents. The sociopolitical climate of that era lent itself to the emergence of a psychological philosophy that wanted to rescue the individual person from society's dehumanizing thralldom. It was a time when the cultural schools of psychoanalysis came to the fore and promised to assist people against oppressive, alienating working and living conditions. Psychological emancipation, increased individuation, and independence represented highly desireable goals. New schools of psychoanalysis emerged in increasing number, side by side with the growth of traditional psychoanalysis. Sullivan, who for a while was part of the establishment, branched out on his own. The events of World War II brought about significant changes, which already have been alluded to. After the war, classical, neo-Freudian, and other forms of psychoanalysis reached a high level of popularity. It was more and more a basically psychoanalytic point of view that permeated the field of psychotherapy, regardless of the different schools of thought. The tide reached its height with the Kennedy Mental Health Act in the early 1960s when it began to take a turn. From then on the psychoanalytic method and its derivative psychotherapies came under increasing attack from within and without the field. The mounting wave of criticism has attacked the core of psychoanalytic tenets and has questioned the inherent therapeutic usefulness of method, procedure, process — in short, all aspects.

The attacks have taken place against the background of profound and rapid changes in the entire field of mental health. In the process of reevaluating the foundations of psychotherapy it became increasingly clear to some thoughtful practitioners that neither the larger mental health compound nor any of its component parts have arrived at a clear-cut definition of themselves in a fashion capable of providing useful guidelines as the nature of mental disorders, their genesis, and the most effective ways of coping with their manifestations. In addition, the problems of having sufficient competent practitioners where needed most, of appropriate training facilities, distribution of professional manpower, availability, and cost of necessary services all began to emerge. Clearly, there is a necessity for interdisciplinary, transcultural, transpolitical alliances in the mental health field. This change of direction places psychoanalysis and psychoanalytic forms of psychotherapy in the midst of a network of sociocultural, economic, political, humanistic currents. It forces the entire field to give up its socially detached position and to reexamine many of its reified psychological conceptions. This shift in orientation has pointed to the awareness that psychoanalytic therapies outside of their Zeitgeist and Weltgeist tend to be sterile, intellectual instruments. The psychoanalytic approach cannot afford to insulate itself, for closed systems are doomed to disintegrate.

The indiscriminate application of psychotherapy, the irrational expectations of its benefits, the proliferation of unqualified,, overzealous and unethical practitioners have all contributed to producing a credibility gap for the entire field of psychotherapy. An increased polarization between organic and psychological approaches has also been hurtful. In addition, there has been an unhealthy commercialization and destructive psychopolitical ideology, which have undermined the foundations of psychiatry.

My thesis is that the lack of rigor in defining the limits and methods of psychotherapy has done a great deal of harm. Psychotherapy can never be dispensed with regardless of the range of physiochemical, behavioristic, and social advances. Accordingly, the necessity arises to improve interprofessional communication, to delineate the boundaries and appropriate methods of psychiatry, and to distinguish between social and psychological roots of maladaptations in a setting of mutual respect for ubiquitously useful therapeutic procedures.

Psychoanalysis as the Paradigm of Psychotherapy

As stated previously, the psychoanalytic approach was for many years the undisputed model for most psychotherapeutic interventions. The focus of the analytic method rests on the pivotal assumption that transference is the sine qua non for overcoming resistances. This basic tenet has been maintained in spite of changes pertaining to the genesis, nature and modification of transferential phenomena.

Almost all other tenets of psychoanalytic theory and practice have been challenged with increasing intensity by both supporters and detractors of the analytic method. The only exception is a qualified acceptance of unconscious processes, that is, the qualification pertains to rejecting the notion of a sealed or underground cave which has not been affected by on-going life experiences. On the other hand the validity of a dual instinct theory, the notion of psychic energies, the prescribed form of dreamwork and of primary and secondary process are all metapsychological constructs that have stood in the way of progress.

In the realm of technical procedures such old standbys as free association, insight, and interpretation have become stereotyped formulas often unrelated to the patient's problems. Accordingly, an ivory-tower atmosphere has been created within the psychoanalytic situation that is far removed from where and how life is lived.

Psychoanalysis is still in the process of emancipating itself from unnecessary dogma as a theory of human nature and as an explanatory model of human motivations, dogma that has led to a host of contradictions and undocumented causal connections. Though there have been many efforts in the direction of an interdisciplinary integration with an openness to epistemological advances in other fields (the advent of system theory has done much to promote this concept), progress in this direction is slow, and psychoanalysis still has a good distance to go in keeping with the march of time and in cultivating a greater awareness of its social, economic, political, and scientific surroundings. As a clinical procedure the psychoanalytic method can no longer perpetuate itself exclusively on basic trust of its foundations. It must expose itself to the prevailing ecological conditions and abandon its conservative, isolationist spirit.

One may wish to ask why anyone would want to continue with an inherently psychoanalytic approach when the core of its methodology is considered faulty. Is there any point in giving artificial respiration to psychoanalysis when it is either on its death bed, has already expired, or needs a total transfusion?

In my judgement the psychoanalytic mystique and its related metapsychology deserve a long overdue burial. They do not have a legitimate place in the modern world as potential remedies for many forms of human suffering. It is by no means necessary that the name psychoanalysis be enshrined as the one and only true psychotherapeutic model. No science can claim a monopoly of inherently human manifestations. The important consideration, however, is to transcend clinically valid observations rather than to discard them. In that respect transference, resistance, and experiences outside of conscious awareness form a heuristic, clinical foundation for psychotherapeutic work. They do stem from the psychoanalytic approach and need not be dispensed with in spite of major changes in the way we understand these phenomena; they can still be used to clinical advantage.

These comments are intended to recommend an adherence to a psychoanalytic point of view that is truly open-ended. We do not have a humanly more appropriate and clearly more effective alternate method so far, in spite of a host of shortcomings which call for revision and modification. Psychoanalysis cannot be fashioned after the Zeitgeist of Freud, Sullivan, and other pioneers. The field must advance in a clearly solid fashion by incorporating newer concepts without discarding workable aspects of the initial model.

The Clinical Approach

The word clinical is basically a medical term that pertains to a clinic, that is, a procedure used in a sickroom. It is the act or mode of treating a patient who is in need of medical attention. In a clinical sense both psychoanalysis and psychotherapy are viewed as psychological procedures capable of treating a variety of mental disorders, but there has been considerable criticism to the use of a medical model for the psychotherapeutic procedure. The point might have validity if psychotherapy, like medicine, dealt predominantly with organic disorders of known and unknown origin. Furthermore, the medical model does not in any way justify a potential monopoly for medical psychotherapists or medical psychoanalysts. People working in this specialty should have a thorough training in the biological, social, and psychiatric specialties without being card-carrying medical doctors.

The term clinical is only meaningful in a psychological sense if its reference is to dealing remedially with patients who are psychologically handicapped. Many attacks on the myth of mental illness are primarily directed against the metapsychological and pseudomedical formulations of mental disorders. By their very nature disorders are disarrangements, irregularities, or derangements that cannot logically rest on any kind of metapsychology.

At present, we lack even a basic understanding how mental disorders originate in most cases. We have a wealth of theoretical assumptions rather than hard-core data capable of explaining how people acquire their particular emotional handicaps and problems.

It is remarkable that psychoanalysis and psychotherapy have been able to cope successfully with a number of maladaptations, malfunctionings, and disturbances in spite of inadequate clarity as to the nature and specific genesis of psychiatric disorders. Over the years a body of empirical data has accumulated that becomes increasingly difficult to integrate with a host of theoretical constructs. In addition, the empirically founded data have not been sufficiently checked, verified, or compared with data arrived at from other disciplines. Accordingly the foundation for an up-to-date applicable clinical methodology is missing.

In this connection it should be appreciated that every psychotherapeutic thoery has an element of a built in self-fulfilling prophesy. It stands to reason that the therapist's theory of therapy contains a measure of prejudice, for he will want to confirm his basic tenets or hypothesis. For instance, people who believe in the universality of the Oedipus complex will find proof of its general applicability if that is what they are specifically looking for. The same can be said about adherence of a libido theory, an Ego-centered theory, a primal scene theory, and what have you. The prejudice of the observer does not permit him to make entirely neutral observations.

An Internal Reevaluation of Psychoanalytic Tenets

Classical psychoanalysis has gone through an initial period of reevaluating its basic premises. There is increasing internal and external criticism of the reification of psychoanalytic metaphors. We hear an increasing reference to a crisis in present-day psychoanalysis. Leo Stone, a loyal and dedicated psychoanalyst of high caliber, puts his finger on a number of core problems pertaining to each major part as well as to the entire structure of the psychoanalytic method. Among other issues he is critical of the "analytic mystique," its elitism, group narcissism, and phobia of contamination with other points of view. (L. Stone, *Psychoanalytic Quarterly,* No. 3, 1975).

In a symposium on "The Ego and the Id After Fifty Years" (*Psychoanalytic Quarterly,* 1975, Vol. 4), Emanuel Peterfreund states uncategorically that the time is ripe for a fundamentally new psychoanalytic model: "The basic frame of reference — the ego, the psychic energies, the dreamwork, primary and secondary process, and so on must now — I believe, be abandoned." In the same issue Robert R. Holt casts doubt at the inherent changes in Freud's structural over his topographic theory because, according to Holt, the later theory failed to remedy its gravest methodological faults. Holt goes on the say that Ego-psychology was doomed because its foundation rested on metapsychology, and predicts that the concept of Ego will not survive the general collapse of psychoanalytic metapsycholgy.

These comments are relevant to a discussion of the interpersonal Self in a clinical context. At present we have a metapsychologically based theory of therapy with a therapeutic model of inherently intrapsychic conflicts. It is essentially a nature-nurture antithesis with a polarization of Id and Ego demands. The dark regions of the unconscious are to be explored exclusively by means of free association so that infantile wishes can be revealed against the background of the transference neurosis. This classical model does not address itself to the conditions that prevail in the here and now. There is no allowance made for the great variety of living conditions, of social and economic opportunities, of political structures, of ecological considerations, and so forth. Early experiences — important, significant and formative as they are — do not qualify as the exclusive foundation for all human behavior, and repetitive compulsion is not the one and only basis for the maintenance of symptoms.

The second major psychotherapeutic model is to be found in the realm of Ego psychology, which includes an increasing reference to the term Self without changing its fundamental metapsychological point of view. This model is bound to the abstract of a psychological structure called Ego. Freud's earlier theory pertained to regions of the mind (topographic) that were largely determined by their closeness or distance from conscious awareness. His later theory (1923) focused on structures of the mind (Id, Ego, and Superego). Some analysts are of the opinion that the structural theory invalidates the earlier topographic formulation, while others reject this assumption. The fact is that the initial metapsychological scaffolding was reified in the later revision and incorporated in psychoanalytic theory as a dogma.

Ego Psychology

It is the structural reformulation which forms the foundation of so-called Ego psychology. The notion of a conflict free sphere (Hartman), the defenses of the Ego (A. Freud), and many modern exemplifications have been hailed widely as bringing psychoanalysis more in tune with social, cultural, and interpersonal aspects. Nevertheless Ego psychology is in a tight cul de sac in view of is adherence to an outmoded, experience-distant metapsychology that precludes the incorporation of ongoing empirical data.

Ego psychology relies on the concept of a psychic appartus, of an agency of the mind. Ego, Id, and Superego are mental structures in contrast to the Self, which is not a mental structure in classical formulation, but rather an auxiliary, descriptive term pointing to the person as a subject. (E. Jacobsen).

By contrast the interpersonal Self does not have any metapsychological foundation and is not an auxiliary, descriptive term. It represents an open-ended, transactional system that is predominantly shaped by experience. Experience gives events a distinctly individual component. We no longer have to focus our exclusive attention on the unique individual person.

Ego psychology reinvests the body with some properties that had been placed outside of its sphere previously. However, the Ego psychological Self remains an experience-distant abstraction that defies direct clinical observation.

Nowhere does Ego psychology abandon the original doctrine based on articles of faith which have turned into dogma.

The intrapsychic Self and its derivative Self as viewed in Ego psychology are both built on the construct of a psychic apparatus — an imaginary agency of the human mind that is beyond the possibility of checking and verification. This is not to deny that both the older and the renovated psychoanalytic theories have led to some valuable clinical discoveries. Aside from the key concepts of transference, resistance, and unconscious phenomena, other clinically useful data have been uncovered, such as the emphasis on the role of the will in human relations. An element of intentionality (reaching out from the inside) has brought about a reevaluation of certain predetermined considerations. There have been other clinical benefits from intrapsychic and Ego psychologic constructs without producing an improved methodology specifically geared to the task at hand.

Permeation of the American Culture with Psychoanalytic Slogans

When it comes to an overview of psychoanalytic therapy we find that the Americanization of Sigmund Freud has been a revolutionary event with far-reaching consequences. Nowhere else in the world has an entire culture been permeated to such a degree with psychoanalytic slogans, metaphors, and speculations, all treated as if they represented factual knowledge. From childrearing to education at large, from criminality to legality, from medicine to psychology, psychoanalytic dogma has been applied, often with unfortunate results. Our daily language has been polluted with psychological lingo so that everything is pschologized. People are forever insecure, defensive, show displaced emotions, hate their parents and siblings, and what have you. The news media tend to reinforce this unproductive pseudopsychology.

The way things are, no American criminal is granted the inherent human privilege to be an ordinary criminal, or given the benefit of the doubt in being just mean, cruel, or insensitive. His behavior is artificially pressed into a psychological scheme that places blame on society, family, and environment indiscriminately. No doubt people are *not infrequently* victims of circumstances beyond their control. They are criminals whose behavior cannot be explained in terms of our present psychological knowledge. For instance, we do not have proof that children who have been abused are automatically turned into criminals or that specific psychological traumas necessarily produce antisocial, destructive behavior.

American psychoanalysis has to contend with a dual problem. On the one hand it has to gain perspective on psychoanalytic mystique and dogma. It means that it must have the courage to reevaluate every single aspect of the psychoanalytic method and its clinical application. (See Leo Stone "Some Problems and Potentialities of Present-Day Psychoanalysis," *Psycholanlytic Quarterly,* 1975, No. 3).

On the other hand, it has to deal with the cultural permeation of psychoanalysis in the United States — for instance, the analytic method turned into a conservative tool of a particular establishment (middle-class value systems steeped in the prevailing sociopolitical-economic order). Here, there is a risk of expecting psychiatric patients to conform with specific modalities of behavior. Carrying this to the extreme, psychiatrists would become the judges and enforcers of "mental health." Be that as it may, psychoanalysis has pronounced itself the standard bearer of the one and only true form of depth psychology. All other methods are declared to be psychologically inferior.

At the same time, psychoanalysis has been symbolically placed on the Detroit assembly line, and has fallen victim to the sales pitch of the automobile industry. Instead of two cars for every family, it recommends at least two couches for them as symbols of "being with it" or it favors an oversized psychological station wagon to hold the entire family. Psychological technology is supposed to revitalize every nuclear family, every marital unit, lead to intimacy, growth, creativity, and what have you. All we have to do is to tinker a little bit with emotional tools here and there, and things will improve in one form or another, yet favorable changes based on such a simplistic prescriptive formula are nowhere in evidence.

Another problem of American psychotherapy is the principle of overindividuation, that is, the preoccupation with *uniqueness* in people. In my judgement uniqueness is the domain of the collector who looks for one-of-a-kind specimens. This is in sharp contrast to our previous definition of individuality, which concerns itself with an on-going continuum even if we are unable to observe the individual in toto.

Traditionally psychotherapy is the United States has been divided into two groups; the so-called insight directed therapies and the supportive approaches. The distinction may even have some clinical justification as long as it does not overemphasize the element of insight. In many instances, insight is based on interpretation, which often means a preconceived theoretical point of view. Furthermore, insight per se is not necessarily protective. The proverbial road to hell is paved with the most insightful intentions. The rebirth of hypnosis in the United States, the mushrooming of behavior therapies including the new sex therapies a la Master and Johnson, and many other procedures are to a large degree an attack on the principle of insight therapy. There are still a few diehards left who agree with Ralph Greenson that interpretation administered in judicious dosage is the ultimate medicine of the analyst, but generally there has been a shift away from analytic mystique and a beginning inquiry into the conceptual core and its clinical application.

I consider the psychoanalytic approach to be a medium concerned with individual dignity, integrity, self-expression, and appreciation of the destructive inroads of crippling anxiety. In no way can I accept the view that psychoanalytic ideology can be an answer to all of life's problems. The exclusive preoccupation with internal processes insulated from the conditions and events of daily life is a cul de sac. Furthermore, there are social, economic, political, and organic situations that affect the practitioner and patient at the same time.

Psychoanalysis has great merit in its particular domain of individual human development, in the realm of personal maladaptations, and in the understanding of tensions that promote destructive and disruptive behavior. However, I consider it ill-advised and highly naive to look at psychoanalysis as an overall applicable model for the improvement of all of mankind. Many problems in daily life and in the world at large are not psychological in nature as pointed out previously.

Changing Directions

The changing directions in the psychoanalytic approach point in a number of significant areas.

1. Psychoanalytic cultism with its rites and ceremonies needs to be abandoned. There is no longer room in our modern world for a veneration of a person or a method in a devotional sense when it comes to the field of psychotherapy. We need to bring an end to an exclusively sacred psychological ideology and a series of rituals centering around its symbols and metaphors.

2. The cornerstones of psychoanalytic theory and practice require a novel, up-to-date reassessment. This includes the conceptual core from the unconscious to free association, from transference and countertransference to resistance, and so forth. The principle is not an either-or consideration, but a way of transcending the old metaphors. For instance, the unconscious can be a useful concept if it is not fixed into an a priori structure. Transference and countertransference retain their clinical usefulness as long as they are placed in an on-going, open system setting. Free association has merit up to a point, but does not represent the exclusive prescribed method of communication. Insight and interpretation need to be opened up in concept and in application. Flexibility in the number of hours, in the lying down or in sitting up, in using appropriate behavioristic and other useful parameters, all need to be approached with an open mind and a spirit of clinical freedom.

3. Analytic training, institutionalization, and unionization of the field are another big area where changes are called for. Different analytic schools tend to promote their concept of analysis as the best. Institutionalization leads to regimenta-

tion in the type of supervision and promotion system that plagues a large number of institutional settings. Candidates in analysis are often trained more specifically in the rules of the game of their particular institute rather than in the spirit of being psychoanalytic practitioners. Furthermore, we also find a potential exploitation of institutional transference that traditionally goes under the name of loyalty or family support. There is a danger in fostering dependency and promoting skillful self-promoting ladder climbing that complicates the task of appropriate teaching of psychoanalytic tenets. By the same token, unionization refers to people who become card-carrying members of a particular group that sets them apart from other groups. (see "On the Complexities of Teaching and Learning Psychotherpy" by E.T. Dannevig, H.V. Brazil, G. Chrzanowski in *Contemporary Psychoanalysis,* Vol. II, No. 2, 1975).

A New Model of Growth

Above all, we need to reevaluate the goals of psychotherapy and psychoanalysis. In this connection, a particular area of consideration suggests itself — the psychological concept of growth. In the world at large there is considerable gloom about its limits (see Rene Dubos a microbiologist, "On Growth," *New York Times,* Nov. 11, 1975), but this misapprehension is based on the conception that growth means predominantly production of an ever-expanding nature: bigger, stronger, richer in terms of onward, outward, and upward. In technology, this kind of growth means the exploitation of materials stored in the earth and the consumption of products converted for human purposes. It has become increasingly clear in science and technology that growth cannot be measured exclusively in quantitative terms. History has demonstrated that each era rechannels social activities in the direction of resources that are essential to its needs. At present we witness a thoughtful reappraisal and changing attitude toward the sources and use of energy.

The meaning of growth is also undergoing radical changes with regard to human existence and human relation. Strictly quantitative human growth interferes in many ways with the growth of others and threatens the quality of human ecology.

Accordingly, if we in psychoanalysis use the modern model of growth among adults, we need not be unduly concerned with the expansion of inner space and outer dimensions. We do not have to focus on energy levels, quantitative dimensions, or related concepts of limits to growth in that respect. In developmental child psychology the element of cognition has removed some of the quantitative considerations. This principle has not been sufficiently applied to adults so far.

Our modern model of growth emphasizes the sensitivity and awareness of the quality of life in terms of a good environment. It means that essential resources are not only outside of the individual — they are embedded in man's "inalienable needs" as related to man's "inalienable environment." The individual's human and technological resources form an indivisible unit that is in a state of flux and evolution. It is this kind of growth that increasingly interests me as an analyst.

In today's world growth is still seen as power-oriented expansion that tends to disadvantage the environment in one form or another. This unfortunate concept of growth has also gained a foothold in the field of psychoanalysis, where it has acquired a political significance. We must not be misled by propagandistic agitation outside as well as inside the field. A great danger lies in the possibility that the advocates and the enemies of psychoanalysis unwittingly join forces in killing off what is most valuable about it.

As stated repeatedly in this text, psychoanalysis, like many human institutions, can be misused or be improved and can lead to beneficial results. The fact, that there are possible risks, dangers, and misapplications does not entitle us to declare the field obsolete and dismiss it as not having intrinsic value. In science, to paraphrase Bertrand Russell once more, old ideas are not thrown away or disposed of like obsolete machinery; they are to be transcended, improved and revitalized rather than "killed off."

The psychoanalytic method is a sensitive instrument capable of enhancing authenticity in people, in enlarging their observational acumen about themselves and others, and in fine tuning cognitive experiences pertaining to the past, present, and future. For that reason constructs and abstractions closely related to experience are preferable to theoretical experience-distant postulates.

Psychoanalysis is a free enterprise that should not be excessively contaminated by political party loyalties. The method must remain open-ended and not irrationally exclude parameters from the behavioral and social sciences. There is a strong need for analysts of all persuasions to work together toward a common goal, rather than weaken the field by unproductive infighting. A partisan spirit is appropriate to sports, politics, and religion. It has no place in the field of psychoanalysis.

Psychoanalysis stands an excellent chance to emerge as a stronger and more effective psychotherapeutic method if it can reevaluate its foundations, its expectations, and its methods. The changing directions in the field provide an excellent opportunity to broaden, strengthen, and deepen the entire field of psychotherapy.

Psychoanalysis and the Interpersonal Self

The practice and teaching of psychoanalysis remains a highly complex task. On the one hand we are dealing with a rather amorphous field that has attempted to cover all of human behavior with one theoretical umbrella. On the other hand, a body of clinical data has accumulated without a methodologically sound platform. Accordingly, we are burdened by a multitude of theorems that defy constructive utilization.

Psychoanalysis has been helpful to many troubled people. It has also failed in many instances for a variety of reasons. Some psychoanalytic failures can be logically explained, but others remain obscure and defy adequate explanation. Aside from the basic requirements of first-rate training, genuine dedication to the work, respect for the troubled person, and a host of other legitimate expectations there is always a problem in acutally hearing the patient on his own terms above and beyond psychoanalytic metapsychology. Another problem concerns the selection of appropriate patients for psychoanalysis. In recent years the psychoanalytic approach has been increasingly applied to narcissistic disorders, so-called borderline disorders, and even outright psychotic conditions. I consider the distinction between psychoanalysis and psychoanalytic psychotherapy to have some legitimate didactic foundation. However, the dividing line may clinically be arbitrary in many cases and have little or no practical significance. The distinction does not entirely depend on the number of visits or the tangible manifestation of a therapeutic alliance. Some failures of the psychoanalytic approach rest with the analyst, others with the method of psychoanalysis, still others may be external factors transcending the analytic situation. In addition, we find patients who are unwilling or unable to collaborate on their own behalf, and patients who cannot relate successfully to one analyst while having much less difficulty with another. Finally, there is serious doubt in my mind that any psychoanalyst can be of lasting help to a patient in an area where his own difficulties have not been worked through. Nevertheless, some analysts do well with very difficult patients, whereas others are distinctly less successful.

Areas of Therapeutic Modifications

There are numerous issues related to success and failure that go far beyond the scope of this book. Psychoanalysis is a field with a number of imponderables that defy any kind of prescriptive therapeutic formula. There are complex technical considerations involved pertaining to the nature of the mental disorder to be dealt with, the method most appropriate to the condition at hand, the quality of the therapeutic alliance, the clarity about mutually appropriate and viable goals, and a host of other factors. Our primary concern is with the elucidation of potential limitations, blindspots, and misdirections of some prevailing approaches in psychoanalysis and psychoanalytic psychotherapy. The shift of emphasis under discussion here moves from intrapsychic to interpersonal considerations. It stresses epistemology over metapsychology and favors a psychology of Self over Ego psychology. Pivotal in the scheme to be outlined is the emergence of an intersonal Self with highly individual components and characteristics. Our outline is a rough sketch of potential therapeutic interventions. It covers some of the following points.

1. The individual person is no longer the exclusive focus of psychoanalytic exploration, but rather his entire network of past and present human integrations under the conditions that prevail. Personal experiences assume a pivotal position in the formation of relational and integrational patterns. Childhood experiences cast a shadow on future events, without necessarily determining the constellation of evolving human contacts. Every new phase of development opens the door to modifications and potential changes. In addition, the quality of interpersonal encounters has remedial possibilities that can shape the patterns of future living with and among other people.

It follows that there is no longer major concern about the speculative construct of an individual's psyche. Cultural, social, and economic factors come to the fore, as well as a host of other components, such as native endowment and familial, communal, dyadic, and group experiences.

What emerges is an interpersonal Self, a transactional, experiential matrix against the background of the me-you analytic relationship. Individual aspects pertaining to analysand and analyst, respectively, transpire above and beyond parataxic manifestations. In a successful analysis the patient as a person makes relatively uncomplicated contact with the analyst as a fellow person. It becomes necessary for patient and analyst to transcend respective parataxic distortions in order to experience an actual me-you encounter.

2. There is less concern with internal conflict per se and

greater emphasis on actual events that have left their mark on the individual's self-esteem, his estimation of others, and his anticipation of the quality of his personal environment.

Numerous areas of reality conflicts associated with value systems, decision making, and prevailing living conditions are scrutinized. We have no legitimate basis for assuming that all conflicts hark back to internalization, introjection, projection, and the vicissitudes of the human psyche. A clearer distinction has to be made between socially and psychologically induced conflicts. Many difficulties and therapeutic failures arise from the need to view the root of all conflicts as a function of the human psyche. Biologic, hereditary, constitutional aspects combined with sociocultural, economic, and related environmental conditions deserve full consideration in their own right. Among a host of other factors attention should be paid to clusters of a basically nonpsychological nature compared to predominantly psychological components. Consideration should be given to:

(a) Temperamental, intellectual endowment as a possible foundation for conflict prone personalities compared to relatively conflict low character attitudes. We find a wide range of parental tolerance or intolerance toward a variety of temperaments in their offspring. Some mothers respond very well to an active, demanding child, but experience major distress with a placid infant or the other way around. In some instances we find the same mother behaving as a "good mother" with the child of compatible temperament to her and taking on the role of "bad mother" with a temperamentally anxiety-producing child.

The significance of countertransferential reactions to the hypersensitive transference of such patients plays a major part in analytic therapy. Much therapeutic benefit can be gained from recognizing conflict-prone personalities and dealing thoughtfully with them in the category of difficult patients (G. Chrzanowski, "Interpersonal Treatment Method with the Difficult Patient" in B. Wolman, Ed., *International Encyclopedia of Neurology, Psychiatry, Psychoanalysis, and Psychology*, in press).

(b) Environmental deprivations, socioeconomic factors, life opportunities, career possibilities, physical health, and general living conditions. Reference has already been made to reality factors, which deserve specific consideration in the therapeutic process.

3. Conflicts between aspirations and endowment. There may be a wide gap between ambitions,, and inherent talent, and this can give rise to unrealistic competitiveness and unwarranted expectations of success. Related are conflicts associated with the need for power, domination, and manipulation. Conflicts of this kind may lead to a dual problem. One relates to the damage caused by suppressing, exploiting, and dehumanizing people. The other has to do with the increasing isolation from other people whereby others lose their human significance.

These conflicts are of a primarily nonpsychological nature; the following are mainly psychological:

(a) Developmental miscarriages, that is, unfortunate interpersonal experiences at the threshold of new capacities and opportunities. This includes forbidding, discouraging, truncating environmental responses to reaching out, exploring, and expanding behavior.

(b) Complexities of family dynamics leading to hostile, self-negating integrations. Included here are the quality of the parental relationship, the sibling situation, relations to maternal and paternal families, as well as the family's sociocultural integration or malintegration, their aspirations, successes, failures, and range of opportunities.

(c) The sociocultural expectations in contrast to individual and familial wishes. Different expectations are inculcated by prevailing systems of reward and punishment, by educational methodology, by forms of indoctrination, as well as by a hierarchy of value systems. One may want to include here the available range of workable models in the environment and the range of reciprocal roles recommended by the social order.

4. Confrontation plays a more significant part in the therapeutic endeavor than interpretation. The method of confronting the patient consists of offering the analyst's reflected appraisal of the patient using as many of the patient's own words as possible. He is confronted now with the way the analyst has understood the communication and the impres-

sion he has formed of it. This type of confrontation includes a good measure of countertransference phenomena and has a different connotation than interpretation that rests largely on a clinical observation within the framework of a theoretical concept. Combined with this type of confrontation is the analyst's offer of feedback and a personal impression as to how he responds to interpersonal data reported by the patient. The principle of both forms of confrontation centers around an effort to bring about consensual validation. It must be appreciated here that consensual validation is a calculated risk, because there is always the possibility of a *folie-a-deux*. The confrontational procedure correlates data to developmental periods as well as to particular ongoing interpersonal situations.

5. A major therapeutic instrument lies in the judicious sharing with the patient of countertransferential experiences. Countertransference is used here in the larger sense as the sum total of the analyst's personal reactions to the patient rather than in the narrow sense as an indication of unresolved conflicts on the analyst's part. In the previously mentioned technique of confrontation a certain amount of countertransference was acknowledged. In the procedure under discussion now there is greater emphasis on bringing the analyst's peripheral thoughts to the fore and asking the patient for comments on the material that is relevant to the particular topic under discussion.

6. The analyst does not administer insight as medicine. Comments are offered with the specific request that one wishes to hear what thoughts and feelings they evoke on the patient's part. But insight is a complicated and dangerous process; "I will see things as you want to" can become a particular form of resistance and a barrier to communication. Many troubled patients have learned to read between the lines, and say what they are expected to say rather than what actually comes to mind spontaneously. We encouner a good number of troubled people who have a highly developed "radar system" that enables them to a tune in in much the same way that a prize pupil gives the teacher the "right answer."

7. Dreamwork takes up an important part of the

therapeutic task. The tendency here is to minimize or discourage reference to standard symbols. The manifest content of the dream is considered alongside its concealed or coded message. In general, the dream is viewed as an integral part of the overall mode of communication. Here are two brief examples of how this works.

A patient dreams that she is driving a car downhill when she finds that the brakes are out of order. In this case the discussion centers around the patient's fear of losing control and exploring this feeling in its developmental and present setting. It was learned how the patient's parents had a great capacity to push her to a point wher she would lose her temper. At that point she would become defiant or rebellious and do something hurtful to herself or others, thus evoking a temporary feeling of coping with her parents. This, however, would turn out to be a pyrrhic victory (i.e., winning the battle and losing the war). The other result would be one of compliance in doing something, often against her better judgement, that frequently would disadvantage her, while the freedom to act on her own accord was distinctly hampered.

Another brief illustration of dreamwork deals with a patient who has three consecutive dreams on three consecutive nights. In the first dream he is playing an instrument that he has mastered quite well. He is very upset when he cannot play a familiar tune and feels stuck in the situation. The second night he dreams he is on a stage and expected to deliver a line he had carefully rehearsed. Stage fright prevented him from performing the task. Finally, in the third dream, he sees himself as a 5-year-old boy who, to his great surprise, has his penis attached to the side of his hip and is urinating with this anatomical artefact.

In the discussion about these dreams the thought was developed that after two obvious failures in dreams one and two, he then concluded in dream three that the difficulty was an organic malformation rather than a psychological problem. In other words, he felt he was inherently defective from early childhood on and did not see his present difficulties as an outgrowth of anxieties and personal problems.

8. No attempt is made to draw a sharp line of demarcation between primary and secondary process. There is no valid evidence that primary process always reflects irrational

phenomena and that secondary process is predominantly the domain of rationality. For one thing, it is a mistake to consider polar concepts to be inherently oppositional to each other. Under certain conditions the irrational can contain a constructive component while the Rational may have been contaminated by sociocultural value systems (See G. Chrzanowski, "The Rational Id and the Irrational Ego," *Journal of the American Academy of Psychoanalysis,* Vol. 1, No. 3, pp. 231-241, 1973)

9. Role definitions in the therapeutic situation constitute another important dimension. The analyst is conceived as the collaborative participant. Particular attention is given to the evolution of role reciprocities inside and outside of the therapeutic situation.

10. Transference represents a key consideration. It is explored in its developmental setting as well as in the therapeutic collaboration and in the outside world. The focus of attention rests on transferential modifications above and beyond "parataxic distortions," "introjects," eidetic figures, and related warpings of the relational field.

11. Defenses or security operations are to be explored in regard to the patient's attitude as well as pertaining to the analyst's attitude when and where such phenomena occur (another aspect of countertransference).

12. The main topic is the encouragement of the patient to elaborate his personal experiences in communicable terms. The I, the cognitive patterns, and their elaboration are key factors in that respect. Particular emphasis is placed on the patient's ability to translate ill-defined feelings into personal verbal communications. Many patients experience a feeling of relief when they can find words to describe feelings and experiences that until now had eluded verbalization.

13. A particular point is made of discussing the quality of past and present interpersonal integrations. The emphasis here is placed on the concept of "growth" as discussed previously, that is, a qualitative improvement of relational ties and personal satisfactions rather than an expansion, a greater power, or greater magnitude. The quality of growth is studied through the manifestation of dreams, through the nature of the therapeutic relationship and environmental integrations in personal and professional contacts.

This outline suggests a model that has a minimum of theoretical structure. It relies mainly on direct observation of oneself and of one's patient in a collaborative field of exploration. The purpose of the therapeutic encounter is for the patient to gain some appreciation of how he came to be who he is today. It also is designed to assist him in seeing more clearly how distortions and warpings in his Self concept affect his impression of other people. The increased awareness of how anxiety works as a means of suffering from "tunnel vision," selective inattention, and a host of other security operations becomes a significant area of experience. There is also a growing sensitivity to how the patient overreacts to trends or attitudes in others that he dislikes strongly in himself. The therapeutic relationship forms a bridge to the past as well as a guideline to the quality of on-going interpersonal integrations. The constructive use of countertransference forms a significant accumulation of data as to how the patient affects his environment and what impact he has on others.

Furthermore, considerable attention is given to external life situations, including existing, on-going family dynamics, friendships, reality problems, work-related difficulties, and economic considerations. These topics are not merely explored as extensions of the past, as repetitive compulsions or related psychological constructs. They are firmly explored in terms of here and now situations, with full appreciation of the circumstances under which they occur.

The interpersonal Self constitutes an ecological unit with roots deep into the developmental epochs, their experiential modifications, and the totality of the person's here and now existence. There is an ever-present concern about the quality of the environment in the formative years as well as under the prevailing conditions. Uniqueness and internal conflict come to be peripheral considerations compared to the many faces of Self in the particular interpersonal setting that brings them to the fore. The ultimate success of an analysis based on this model can be judged by the person's ability to be relatively comfortable with himself and to pursue the goal of improving the quality of his human environment in harmony with his basic needs and requirements.

CHAPTER 5

The Psychiatric Process,
Role Definition of the Practicing Psychiatrist,
Case Illustrations

The Accuracy of Case Illustrations

The discussion of psycho-therapeutic procedures has a number of inherent pitfalls. There are limitations to the degree of accuracy that can be achieved in describing the complexities of an on-going clinical process. A lack of clarity surrounds the specific role and task of the psychiatrist. His particular function, the nature of his relationship with the patient, and the goals of therapy are not clearly spelled out. There are also limiting factors involved in convincingly documenting cause-and-effect phenomena pertaining to therapeutically helpful procedures. Only in rare instances can we point to specific strategic interventions leading to durable improvement for the patient.

Among the difficulties encountered in accurate reporting is the essential requirement of maintaining the patient's anonymity. It calls for a fictionalization of many case histories by necessitating the omission, distortion, or qualification of much salient data. To protect the patient's identity his age, sex, or occupation are frequently changed. Other situations lead to a falsification of time and place or sequential events for the same reason. Children may be added or deleted, parents, siblings, spouses may be cast in a different light — whatever may be required to conceal the patient's identity.

In addition, every therapist wittingly or unwittingly takes some liberties in his choice of the material. Material may be presented out of context, significant preceding events or important sequelae may not be mentioned. Focal attention may be placed on a peripheral aspect of therapy or of the patient's history, or peripheral events may be projected in a central light. The element of elipsis may prevail (Freud's term for omitting a pivotal word in a sentence), or selective inattention may be operative (Sullivan's term for blindspots in the observational field).

Distortions, omissions, or fictionalization may occur because the therapist has a vested interest in illustrating a point of particular interest to him. In other situations certain facets may be lifted out of context by the therapist because they represent his theoretical ideology and indicate to him a significant therapeutic implication. Other data may fall victim to the therapist's covert "pruning shears" as reflections of his loyalty to his theory of therapy or the data may reveal embarrassing aspects of his own personality. It follows that most case histories, even when reported by the most honest and reliable clinician, tend to contain a distinct element of fiction or distortion.

The situation is not essentially different, even with a verbatim report, a tape recording or an audio-visual presentation. To a certain degree the therapeutic situation is infiltrated by an instrument that effects the observed data in one form or the other. The above-mentioned phenomenon does not invalidate the usefulness of verbatim reports, tape recordings, videotapes or one-way screens. Our task is mainly to be aware of the instrumental intrusiveness, rather than labor under the illusion of having obtained distortion-free data.

Case reports have been the essential staples of clinical teaching in psychiatry and psychoanalysis. This procedure has been helpful in many respects and has undoubtedly aided in the advancement as well as refinement of therapeutic practice. Nevertheless, it is notorious that modern psychoanalytic literature abounds with case histories that are not truly representative of what transpires between analyst and patient. Furthermore, even relatively untampered reports are not necessarily authentic reflections of transactional, therapeutic events because no therapist is capable of avoiding a measure of selective inattention. This point is often vividly illustrated in the supervisory process, when a superviser reports a case from memory and then plays a tape recording of the same interview. Needless to say, what is recorded and what is replayed to the supervisor usually contain witting or unwitting screening processes.

The Role of the Psychiatrist

Psychiatry and psychotherpay always pertain to the process of living with untold complexities rather than to the treatment or cure of specific mental disorders. In Sullivan's interpersonal scheme, mental disorders are valid but variant aspects of human existence: they are always basically human manifestations that occur out of context or as highly exaggerated general behavior patterns. According to Sullivan, there is nothing in the attitude or experience even of the most severely disturbed person that is not an aspect of inherently human phenomena. On the one hand, we are dealing with diverse complications that arise in living with and among one's fellow human beings. On the other hand, we must recognize characteristic patterns of maladaptations that form more-or-less consistent patterns and fall into nosological categories, that is, diagnostic entities. Diagnosis serves a dual function: facilitating therapeutic intervention and judging the prognosis of the particular mode of malfuntioning or maladapting. In addition, interprofessional communication depends on generally acceptable diagnostic criteria.

It has been pointed out by many investigators in the field that the model of organic, physical illness has major limitations when it comes to categorizing, understanding, and ameliorating mental disorders. The trouble is only that we run into other difficulties once we dispense with the medical model. There are limitations in one form or the other whether we use a physical, social, or any other frame of reference. Nevertheless, we do require a structure outside of the biologic one as well as a reliable, systematic approach to mental disorders, lest we lose the possibility of communication, teaching, learning, and practicing a speciality *sui generis*. Sullivan was aware of these difficulties and made numerous efforts to cope with them. His definition of psychiatry as the study of interpersonal relations is by far the most comprehensive endeavor in that respect, particularly when he introduced the ecologic principle. At the same time, it still does not suffice in delimiting with clarity the special boundaries of the field of psychiatry and the psychiatrist as the practitioner of the specialty.

Sullivan's View of the Psychiatrist's Role

Sullivan defined the role of the psychiatrist in predominantly operational terms. He coined the term participant observation as a psychiatric methodology, that is, an expert-client siituation based on the epistemological principle of observing as a means of modifying what is being observed.

It is clear that no one term can cover the entire role repertory of the psychiatrist, who is neither a healer nor an adjuster. His essential task is of a humanitiarian nature and embraces a multitude of functions and attitudes. The psychiatrist touches on an exceedingly broad range of roles. Some of his functions are educational, parental, and to a certain degree advisory. He indirectly transmits value judgements as a representative of his society and culture. There are philosophical, theological, economic, and political connotations woven into his transaction with the patient. We need no longer belabor the illusion of the mirror analyst, catalytic agent, neutral judge, or a surgeon's detachment in speaking of the psychiatrist's role. Neither do we dwell unnecessarily on the risk of the magical helper, the overseer of mental health, or the collusive partner in humanly disruptive or destructive enterprises.

There is persuasive evidence that Sullivan was a highly intuitive and empathic therapist, particularly with severely disturbed patients. Clara Thompson (personal communication) frequently commented on Sullivan's respect for the patient and what she called his "sweetness" in dealing with schizophrenic patients. (To many people who knew Sullivan very well on a personal basis, the term sweetness seems misapplied to him.) Be that as it may, Sullivan had an uncanny way of asking the kind of helpful questions that would encourage the patient to give meaningful information. His own personality, his way of coining a phrase, his nonthreatening, supportive stance, and a whimsical kind of self-mockery all contributed to his role as a psychiatrist and his skill as a highly sensitive listener.

Sullivan had a distinctly personal style which he cultivated in many respects. It is doubtful that his innovative stance as a clinician fits the model of the participant observer, in asmuch as Sullivan was a keenly active observer. Nevertheless, he advocated the principle of participant observation as a universally applicable procedure of the psychiatrist's position in the therapeutic process. He coined the term participant observation as a functional and descriptive methodology for all forms of psychotherapy. His own, highly personal method proved to be successful for him with the type of patients he preferred to work with. This does not necessarily qualify his method as actually being participant observation. Nor does it stamp participant observation as the therapeutic procedure of choice.

Participant Observation

Participant observation is a distinct improvement over the construct of the mirror analyst or the image of neutrality in the analytic role. It is based on a transactional model that places the therapist in a basically nonauthoritarian position and makes him an essential part of the therapeutic alliance. It is a far cry from the original "Papa knows best" with his analytic-parental wisdom. Participant observation no longer focuses on the individual patient as the primary object of therapeutic study, but rather on the evolving relational field between patient and therapist. The element of a particular form of participation is a clinically useful consideration that opens the way to widening the therapeutic field in many directions. The reliance on free association, insight, and interpretation is diminished, because participant observation stresses a form of dyadic encounter with a number of novel avenues to explore.

Participant observation is also a methodology that assigns to the analyst the role of an expert observer in the study of interpersonal relations. As such, the analyst is expected to function predominantly in the syntaxic mode of cognition, that is, his observations are more-or-less objective and are offered to the patient for the purpose of consensual validation. The analyst's participant observation also offers him a measure of detachment that serves as a protection against an alliance with the patient's neurosis or psychosis.

Reference to viewing the psychiatrist as participant observer has been made previously in this text. At this point I wish to affirm the historical significance of this formulation while calling attention to modifications in defining the psychiatrist's role today.

First, it should be understood that participant observation is a tautology, because observation always includes the observer in what he observes. The observer as the instrument of observation is invariably in the same field with his object of observation, whereby objects and instrument of observation form an indivisible unit. Furthermore, observation is not to be confused with a passive or neutral process, because it invariably brings about some alteration in the observed object.

The model of participant observation has clinical limitations in view of its distinctly instrumental quality. To a certain degree, it still harks back to Freud's psychoanalytic model with its mechanistic, energetic connotations.

It is difficult to include the phenomenon of countertransference into the formulation of participant observation because the term does not address itself to emotional components. Yet it is sophisticated countertransference in its broadest meaning that provides us with our primary therapeutic tool. Participant observation remains a mechanistic procedure and thus is not a sufficiently open-ended term to include the judicious sharing of personal responses (countertransference) with the patient. The emotional components of rational and irrational responses to the patient's transferential and actual attitudes to the analyst require a broader representation than is possible within the instrumental model of participant observation.

My clinical preference is for a different role definition of the analyst, which emphasizes the role reciprocity between patient and analyst while focusing on the analyst's self-monitoring and self-revealing attitudes. If the term were modified to therapeutic self-monitoring or self participating therapeutic partnership, it would be more expressive of the therapist's role in the analytic process.

As stated previously, one of the most important therapeutic tasks lies in raising the patient's self-esteem. There is nothing in the model of participant observation that lends itself to boosting a patient's morale. It does not contain a particular channel for clinically useful encouragement of the patient nor of a specific way of legitimately affirming the patient's genuine assets.

In keeping with the tradition, some case material is presented in this text hand in hand with some explanatory comments.

For instance, a 20-year-old girl who had a brief psychotic episode made noticeable progress in our therapeutic work. She had previously made a serious suicidal attempt leading to psychiatric hospitalization. It was following this episode that she first came to see me. It took her considerable time to be actively involved in the therapeutic process, and two major areas of difficulty remained in spite of a rather remarkable degree of improvement. One area centered around her inability to give vent to rational as well as to irrational anger. The other problem is the polarization between deep-seated suspiciousness and compensatory gullibility.

The patient's first love affair was with a profoundly disturbed man who burdened her excessively with his own major maladaptations and lacked sensitivity for her legitimate needs. I felt torn in my analytic role by wanting to communicate to her that I consider him to be a liability and potential danger for her, and by finding myself in a protective, parental role. The patient brought in dreams which indicated that she feared him and that she had detected a sadistic streak in his nature. We made the connection to her father's attitude to her — a man who was capable of lashing out at her without provocation. This did not change the patient's conviction that she was in love with the man who gave her a very bad time. She developed sexual and somatic symptoms without wanting to see them as signals of conflict in her. Finally he pushed the situation too far, and she brought in two dreams. In the first dream she had turned into a cannibal who devoured her brother's head. In the second dream she noticed that I had small metal pincers, and she suddenly realized that I used them to torment patients. At that point in the dream I assured her that she need not be concerned, because I would not use the torture instruments on her. Her associations to the first dream were plain horror, for she felt that she had carried her lover's role as a sadist into the therapeutic situation. My response to her comments was a shuddering gesture in hearing the cannibal dream, which I associated to her repression of rage turning her into a dangerous infrahuman creature. When it came to the second dream I was aware of fleeting feelings of hurt that she would not trust me. I casually communicated this to her with the clear mutual understanding that it flattered me somewhat, but that I clearly did not need or really want her reassurance. Furthermore, I indicated that I was probably capable of retaliatory thoughts if I felt that my feelings had been hurt. However, she could have given me in her dream worse torture instruments The fact remains that she considered me capable of sadism, and we both had to live with this attitude of hers at least for the time being.

This illustration does not fit the concept of participant observation. My role has several facets that basically respond to the patient's direct communication. On the one hand, her interpersonal Self emerges, particularly in the way in which she makes contact with men. My rational and irrational responses to her attitude made up a great deal of material that was shared with her. In other words, I consider the direct emotional interchange as outlined here to be a dimension that goes beyond the definition of participant observation.

Another objection to the clinical usefulness of participant observation is its implicit designation of the patient as an object of study. It underplays the significant element of the alliance or collaboration. There is also a limit to what degree any actor on stage can simultaneously be part of the audience.

Historically, Sullivan's construct of participant observation is a milestone in analytic therapy. The principle has found almost universal acceptance without credit to Sullivan's innovative contribution. The myth of the analyst's anonymity or catalytic role in the analytic process was dispelled by the newer definition of the analyst's role.

Nevertheless, Sullivan's model retained an excessive instrumental quality and overemphasized principles taken from the field of the natural sciences without sufficient allowance for emotional transactions. Actually, patient and analyst affect each other emotionally in the analytic encounter of their respective personalities. The analyst brings to his task his total life experiences, his individual responses to the patient's attitude toward him, and his repertory of cognitive processes within the realm of the therapeutic field. It means that prototaxic and parataxic experience of the analyst may serve as sensitive communicative bridges between patient and analyst. In particular, the quality of the analyst's responses to irrational thoughts, attitudes, and behavior of the patient form a significant therapeutic parameter.

Expansion of Clinical Tenets

In chapter 4 I presented a highly condensed and schematized outline of how the concept of the interpersonal Self can be applied in a clinical setting. What follows is an elaboration of that basic scheme and an illustration of the transactions on hand of case material.

Sullivanian psychiatry is a predominantly interpersonal formulation without sufficient emphasis on transactional phenomena. The illusion of personal individuality assigns an anonymous role to the Self. It highlights the communal aspects of the Self without paying adequate attention to the highly individualized, personalized coding of experience. In clinical terms a more open-ended, personally centered model of therapy lends itself to certain modifications in therapeutic method and therapeutic goals.

Each numbered point corresponds with those in the primary scheme.

1. The emphasis in point one is on the "interface," transaction or ecology of the patient's interpersonal network within his present setting against the background of his individual developmental vicissitudes.

The observational field includes the verbal and nonverbal expressions of the patient in conjunction with the particular response of the analyst to rational, irrational, distorted, and realistic observations. This should not be confused with a right or wrong response on the part of the analyst for the patient should be free to enter into the gamut of emotional and intellectual reaction within the therapeutic process. There is a continuum in the relational pattern between patient and analyst that is bound by respective individual formative experiences in both. Both parties in the therapeutic alliance share their common humanity above and beyond their individual foibles, peculiarities, and maladaptations. It means that a great deal of deference is paid to the variety of responses that people evoke in the patient, as well as the observational impact the patient has on others, including the analyst, and that every meaningful interpersonal situation has a developmental imprint from the past. However, the past behavior is not viewed as a rigid pattern, but as a dynamically flexible envelope that takes on shape and form, depending on the nature of the on-going interpersonal situation.

Here is a brief illustration of point one.

A young professional woman, who is a highly gifted and substantial person, takes the consistent attitude that nothing ever goes her way and that she is utterly incapable of taking any kind of corrective action. She has been an academic achiever of solid caliber who suffers from morbid feelings of helplessness. Her interpersonal Self is that of a "woman for all seasons" who then resents deeply experiences of exploitation, largely in response to "tell me what I can do for you," while initially communicating that her own needs are minimal.

The patient is a desired and desirable person, who has

assumed the role as ex-officio head of her nuclear family. Whatever is pointed out to her in every direction is invariably countered with an angrily tearful response of "I know but there is absolutely nothing I can do about it." Her transference is strong but easily denied by her when directly confronted with it. The countertransference is difficult, because she is basically appealing and rewarding but takes the role of a sharp, prickly pear. She loves to do battle with me and gets a measure of satisfaction when I rise to the bait from time to time.

Our therapeutic focus rests on her interpersonal network, which tends to be complicated. We deal with her depressive component, with her compensatory grandiosity, and reciprocal extreme helplessness. Her anger, its causes, ramification, and the highly personal coloring of other emotions in her are stressed. She is one of those patients who makes visible progress in spite of her loud protestations to the contrary.

The patient had a highly traumatic experience in childhood which in not relevant to repeat here for reasons of required anonymity. Her response to it is still intellectual.

The patient is in reanalysis with me, and some of the above-mentioned procedures are significantly different from what she had experienced previously. Many of the factors mentioned in point one are applied in this therapeutic situation, and the prognosis of this case is favorable. This clinical vignette can also serve as an illustration of point two, because the emphasis of conflict per se is minimized while me-you encounters outside and inside of the analysis are stressed with particular attention to the emergence of her interpersonal Self.

2. In view of minimizing the individual person as the primary area of psychological interest, it follows that conflict is not seen as having its center of gravity inside of the person. Ambivalence, Id-Ego clashes, nature and nurture incompatibilities, all are seen in a different light. Past events are explored side by side with on-going situations in life and therapy. Conflicts are, strictly speaking, neither internal nor external, but are action bound in terms of their developmental preshaping. Disturbances in developmental experiences lead to vulnerabilities that tend to contaminate present inter-

personal integrations. In one way, past experiences inject potentially faulty expectations into novel human situations. There is a lack of freedom in permitting the evolution of an unbiased field of contact between the participating parties. The process of bringing two or more people together toward a mutually desired collaboration is hampered, and faulty expectations on either side lead to difficulties. In response to a distorted anticipatory attitude something happens that interferes with an uncomplicated human transaction. Conflicts exists when there is a potential intermeshing of distortions and counterdistortions. In other words, the internal nature of a conflict is much less significant than the conflict when and where it manifests itself. We are not dealing with a focal, delimited disorder like a tumor, a gall bladder stone, or an endocrine deficiency. Our focus rest more clearly on the prevailing interpersonal situation and the overall background at the time conflicts come to the fore. As an analogy, there is less concern whether a person has asthma per se. It will not tell us what tends to trigger off asthmatic attacks and what can possibly be done to alleviate or prevent them. We need to know a great deal about allergies, immunological, environmental, and emotional factors in order to deal with "the conflict." In the analogy used the problem or conflict is not so much the "internal" asthma, but rather the circumstances that tend to set off asthmatic difficulties. What takes place in the abstract called the human mind is speculative and unavailable for direct observation. It requires a host of metaphors with shaky foundations that can only build an equally shaky theoretical structure. By contrast, the interpersonal Self as an observable field offers greater opportunity to study conflicts in terms of on-going human relations and their constructive, unproductive, or negative integrations.

3. Confrontation in preference to interpretation serves a dual purpose. On the one hand, it represents more of a feedback process whereby the patient has an opportunity to see himself reflected through the eyes of a specially trained observer. At the same time, it enables him to appreciate the fact that the patient himself is alway the primary source of data. It aids in the awareness that one needs to give information in psychotherapy in order to obtain information about

oneself. On the other hand, the playback principle of confrontation deals predominantly with on-going processes that can be observed. It does not unduly concern itself with causes and explanations. Accordingly, there is a greater element of spontaneity involved and a larger opportunity for checking and verification.

Last but not least, the method of confrontation has a less authoritarian and less parental connotation than interpretation. The latter procedure always has the implicit element of telling the patient why he is thinking, behaving, or acting in a particular way. In essence, interpretation represents a hypothesis, a theoretical assumption rather than a factual explanatory bridge linking past and present. By contrast, confrontation lends itself to historical explorations in a more flexible field of investigation. The method of confrontation is also useful in dealing with the content of conscious thought and the restrictive observational horizon caused by the intervention of anxiety.

Point three may be illustrated by a brief sketch of a therapeutic transaction. A basically conservative postgraduate student is a childless, divorced young woman. She comes from a prominent family and excessively plays down her social connections. The patient is an attractive person, endowed with a high degree of intelligence she denies by "talking silly" much of the time. Her interpersonal Self can be said to consist of a misleading role for most occasions. Recently she has been involved with three men "simultaneously" and has caught on to the fact that it is her way of presenting an inauthentic Self.

A number of events led to direct confrontation with her present behavior, which goes back to unfinished business at an earlier time in her life. We had an emotionally charged session just prior to my vacation that led to a clarification on her part. In essence, she debated the possibility of reducing her sessions with me after I had raised the question previously as to whether she wanted to increase, decrease, or keep a status quo with her sessions. Her main consideration was to determine the minimum number of times she could see me without getting into difficulties. My reply was that I saw the situation differently; my view was how much she avail herself of what was offered rather than how fine she could cut it. In other words, I saw no point in having her come more often than she could constructively utilize. My comment upset her a great deal and pointed to the predicament of a person who always had a great deal available in life without necessarily recognizing it or taking advantage of it.

About one hour after the session she called my office. With a frantic voice she explained that she had an automobile accident and had run a person over while turning a corner. (She saw herself as an expert driver who never had a driving mishap.) It turned out that the person was not seriously hurt, but this did not stop the patient from having excessive guilt feelings. The facts of the accident as reconstructed by police and others absolved her of all negligence in the situation.

The therapeutic task was twofold. On the one hand it was important not to psychologize the accident on a cause-and effect basis. At the same time it became necessary to discuss the psychological aspects preceding the accident without placing them in a focal causative position. A host of historical data came to the fore, including an almost fatal accident with the patient as the victim and somebody else driving.

Several aspects mentioned in point three are relevant to the technique under discussion. There is no need for illustrating point four here, because the use of countertransference has been illustrated on previous occasions.

4. Frequent reference has already been made to the judicious application of countertransference in its broadest sense as the sum total of the analyst's reactions to the patient. We are dealing here with the process of self-monitoring whereby impressions, central as well as peripheral thoughts, appropriate fantasies, and related material are brought to the patient's attention. The attitude described here transcends the instrumental role of the analyst and focuses on his ability to give a wide range of thoughts, feelings, and reveries to the patient in an informative fashion. It goes without saying that withholding a certain amount of data is necessary and essential. The degree and scope of what is shared with the patient depends on the severity of the patient's disorder and the analyst's judgement as to what is therapeutically useful. Openness should not be mistaken for a free for all that is

therapeutically counterindicated and tends to foster neurotic and psychotic manifestations. As stated previously, every therapist must be able to maintain a certain distance from the disturbance he and his patient are attempting to deal with. The freedom to share a wide range of information requires considerable sensitivity and security on the part of the analyst.

5. Interpretation and insight are used most sparingly and predominiantly as a means of encouraging self-expression on the part of the patient rather than telling him "as it is." Many situations become clear to the patient and do not require a specific interpretation or an appeal for insight. A lonely, self-conscious man has a long history of trouble in dating girls. He is distinctly attractive and well-endowed person in his mid-thirties who has a total score of three dating situations. The first girl had a one-track mind about marriage, and she found a husband when he could not be pressured into matrimony at that time. The relationship remained platonic. His second encounter included fleeting sexual contact and came to an end when he did not sufficiently respond to the girl's basic needs. The third contact with a girl was of an extended nature and had a distinct on-again, off-again pattern. She wanted him more as a friend than a lover. In the midst of it he had a revealing dream in which his mother took a central role. This coincided with the mother's verbal statement that she had always "loved him so much that it hurt. "There was no point in telling him the obvious, which he knew in his own way anyhow. The fact is that the awareness of his mother's stranglehold over his love life had little effect on him. Instead we addressed ourselves to practical aspects of his life, to available dating situations, and to expectations, fears, and anxieties in that respect.

6. Some details of dreamwork have already been reported in the previous chapter. What needs to be added is a distinct effort to demystify dream work by placing dream content as much possible within the framework of overall communication.

The dreamer is usually presented with options in understanding his dreams. The patient's thoughts about the dream material have primary consideration. One may encourage the patient to try on for size every single character that has appeared in his dream. Developmental considerations go hand in hand with representations of on-going relationships and life situations. In general, the principle of confrontation in terms of observable phenomena takes preference over interpretative comments.

7. Freud's ingenious constructs of primary and secondary process have not been helpful in the long run, for these constructs have an antithetical quality and are defined in terms of polar opposites. We are dealing here with a cognitive hierarchy whereby primary process as the phylogenetically earlier mode of thinking is considered to be primitive, undifferentiated, and outside the realm of rationality. By contrast, secondary process is controlled by rational or reality considerations. The trouble with this formulation is its black-and-white quality. An excessive fear of the irrational can be a retarding force in the direction of human progress. We are aware that certain familial, social, and political "reality considerations" may at times be more dangerous than the dangers against which they are evoked. There is a distinct risk in a worship of reality (secondary process) as the ultimate norm and irrationality (primary process) as an ever-lurking danger. Clinically we must deal with irrationality in all of its ideational aspects with the clear understanding that thoughts and actions are not to be confused.

Primary process is considered to be the domain of psychosis with its disregard for logic, reality, and sensibility. To a certain degree this is a viable assumption, as long as we do not confuse the phenomenon with a universal truth. The fact is that oppositional terms do not necessarily qualify as being appropriate counterparts. There is often an excessive fear of irrationality. In some instances the fear of "primary process" manifestation is a greater danger that the phenomenon per se. We need not be unduly concerned with a reversal of human order by appreciating some nondestructive aspects of "crazy ways of thinking." It is possible to recognize some "primary process" activities as serving a useful purpose, and it is helpful not to be unduly seduced by the logic and rationality of secondary process which has its own pitfalls. (See "The Rational Id and the Irrational Ego", Gerard Chrzanowski, *Journal of the American Academy of Psychoanalysis*, Vol. 1, No. 3, pp. 231-241, 1973).

Many patients are afraid to pursue irrational thoughts because they experience them as the pointers to action. It needs to be made clear to many patients that actions and thoughts are not in the same category.

For instance, a patient reported to me that he saw vaginas all day long in his fantasies. He had a vivid fascination with their imagery, linked it to exciting sexual fantasies, and then was disturbed by the phenomena. His life situation was that of a bachelor in his late 30s who had never lived with a girl at any time. He had some preoccupation with homosexuality and had done some occasional acting out. In his case it was easy to establish the defensive nature of his homosexual thoughts, since they occured with some regularity when he was seriously involved with a girl. At present he is having a basically reward-ing contact with a girl whom he experiences as rejecting him. The fact is that he has a deep-seated ambivalence about set-tling down with this girl and has a need to make excessive distance from her while consistently blaming her for turning him down.

Anyhow, his fantasia-like images of vaginas are primitive prototaxic phenomena or primary process functions that serve the purpose of depersonalizing his love object and using concretization. The process in itself is not pathological and lends itself well to clarification.

On the other hand, I am seeing a highly obsessional man who, through excessive reliance on secondary process ("What else is there in life other than pure reality?"), resembles a programed computer. He is capable of even distorting facts by overfactualizing them. His reality sense is so highly over-developed that he misses vital emotional dimensions in his perception of events.

8. The concept of collaboration is enhanced by the use of the social role model. Central is the inherent reciprocity of all roles whereby the role of the parent requires a child, the role of a husband requires a wife, and so forth. In addition, the principle of role commitment assumes a specific meaning in the therapeutic process. It is intended as an open-ended goal that is to be pursued beyond the therapeutic process and hopefully does not come to an end when therapy is termi-nated. Role commitment constitutes a potential structure of a desired mode of integration based on realities of a person's

life situation and other developmental history. The analyst's clarity about his own role commitment serves as a stimulus and encouragement for the patient.

Role playing has become a technique in various forms of individual, group, and family therapy. My concern is not related to that technique. I am addressing myself to the specific role reciprocity between analyst and patient — with particular emphasis on locking oneself into a consistent position, i.e., role commitment. A patient may expect the analyst to assume the father's, mother's lover's role, or what have you. The response to this implicit or explicit demand is not merely to stand on the principle of neutrality. Neither does it suffice to deal with the demand exclusively on a transference-countertransference level. What matters most is the analyst's ability to stick to his appropriate role and discuss in detail with the patient the evolving transaction.

A young woman in her early 20s came to see me about one month after her father had died. Her mother had been a chronically disturbed lady who was utterly incapable of giving the patient support. It soon became obvious that the patient wanted and needed somebody to offer her sympathy and understanding following the father's death. There was no doubt that her expectation was legitimate, and no difficulty on the part of the analyst to offer it. After more than a year's time it was pointed out to her that the period of mourning was over now and though she needed to express her feelings to the fullest about the loss of her father, life's tasks had to be resumed. She agreed fully at this point of view, only to act out in protest. Her competence and reliability at work had always been outstanding. Suddenly she quit her job and set things up in a fashion that did not permit her to stay in therapy any longer. She had become acutely negativistic and hostile in view of my desire to modify the therapeutic relationship slightly. Anyhow, I kept on seeing her in spite of her need to punish herself and me for not fully maintaining my initial role. We went through some very difficult times, and the final outcome is still in doubt.

The illustration points to a particular problem in shifting roles after an initial pattern was established.

There is no need to discuss transference and counter-transference once more. Both phenomena have been discussed and illustrated throughout the text.

9. Transferential distortions are a major area of therapeutic exploration and always pertain to both participants in the therapeutic endeavor and the respective impact of the outside world on both of them. The emotional components of transference are explored in terms of introjects, eidetic figures, parataxic distortions, and other forms of relational warpings. A determined effort is made to draw a line of demarcation between components of transference related to individual, familial, and interpersonal experiences in contrast to transferential phenomena brought to the fore by economic, social, political, and cultural factors. In this connection the role of the therapist as a proponent or opponent of the prevailing sociocultural order assumes major significance. In many parts of the world analysts had to live through major political upheavals that required a clarification as to where both patient and analyst stood in terms of the external upheaval.

(Points 10-12 have also been covered in some detail and do not call for more discussion here).

Clinical Case Illustration and Discussion

This man, in his early 40s, was referred by the analyst of his girl friend with the following introduction: "This is an extremely difficult man who can be very hard on other people and who is having a number of difficulties. He may or may not call you." I heard from the patient approximately 3 months after my colleague had contacted me and it took another 6 weeks or so before we actually managed to get together.

It turned out that the patient came to see me mainly because of intense eye symptoms. He had consulted a large number of outstanding eye specialists because he suffered from an almost unbearable pressure "behind his eyes." Each eye specialist had independently assured him that he did not suffer from an eye condition, and the consensus was that he was a very tense person whose tension manifested itself in a psychosomatic fashion. It was suggested to him by several of the eye specialists that he take tension-relieving medication which he did (Valium). The medication helped him for a short periods of time, but did not basically alleviate his distress.

I inquired what he thought I could do for him in my capacity as a psychoanalyst. He made it clear that he wanted me to free him from his eye symptoms. My reply was that I was not in a position to do anything about his eyes as such, but would be glad to hear something about his feelings of tension. He did not have much to say on the subject except that his girl friend and her analyst (he saw the latter only once) both felt that he could benefit from seeing a psychiatrist.

At this point I encouraged him to tell me something about his personal background. I found that he was the only son of immigrant parents. His father had always been a hard worker earning his livelihood as a manual laborer. There was no room in the home for lightheartedness of any kind, and performance and achievement were stressed without a letup. The mother had been on the stout side as far back as the patient remembered. She never did any outside work and was overly involved in her maternal role, frequently complaining that she did not receive sufficient attention. Both parents had the faculty to make their son feel guilty. The patient was always an outstanding, all "A" student. However, the father reacted with dismay and actual despair when a single mark did not reach the top of the scale. All through his childhood the patient was a model boy who never made any waves and who never got into any kind of trouble. Adolescence, college, and young adult life were recalled as having been uneventful.

The patient obtained a good job in an academic field and did well in it. He married a pleasant, thoughtful, and attractive woman when he was in his 20s. They had one child, who stayed with the mother after a divorce at the wife's instigation. His wife's complaints were that he was cold, humanly unresponsive, and unable to relate on a personal basis. His detachment and withdrawal, combined with overinvolvement in his work, became more pronounced. He acknowledged his wife's observation and allegations without being much bothered by them. The patient did not overtly experience their divorce as a painful event. He maintained a friendly attitude toward his former wife, who in turn maintained an interest in him even after she remarried.

The patient's subsequent bachelor life was predominantly work oriented. He had no interest in ever taking a vacation, which he could well afford workwise and moneywise. There were no personal friends in his life, and he was very much of a loner. His mind was filled with endless details of his daily schedule, and there was no break of his routine on weekends or holidays. He maintained telephone contact with his parents in a dutiful manner, saw his teenaged daughter at regular intervals, and took an interest in her intellectual and social development. Much of his time was spent away from his apartment, involved in professional trips, lecture assignments, teaching, and conferences. There was one girl friend who became very much involved with him and made it clear that she would like to be married to him. He had an inherently high opinion of her, but tended to be compulsively critical. It was an-on again, off-again situation in which he did most of the rejecting. It seemed to bother him that she was genuinely devoted to him and cared for him deeply. His attitude was that of a critical parent. For instance, he may have been out of town for several days. Upon returning to his apartment where she would wait for him, he ruminated about her domestic sloppiness (he was preoccupied with petty details about putting things away or minor aspects of surface orderliness). In his mind, he would already convict her before a blue-ribbon jury by the time he inserted the key to open the apartment door. For instance, he imagined that he would find her watching T.V. rather than cleaning up the place which he admitted did not have to be cleaned up. Anyhow, he went through a self-fulfilling prophecy by finding her waiting for him in front of the television and grew angry out of all proportion. In addition, he complained that she did not turn him on intellectually or sexually, but was unable to document his highly subjective statements. He had a few sporadic sexual involvements on his travels and a more involved affair with a married woman. Somehow, he possessed an awareness of his own difficulty in commiting himself. He was lonely, and he claimed that he would like to "settle down" while running away from any kind of binding commitment at the same time. It is characteristic of this man that practically nothing in life gave him real satisfaction. He was ungenerous with himself and took the role of a harsh task master toward his own and other people's needs. Performance was the driving force, and human relations reflected themselves as distant, dim, and unrewarding. Male companions played no part in his life, and women were attracted to him in spite of his aloofness, his problems in giving of himself, and his tendency to make distance. One clearly gets the impression of a man who had sensitivities, feelings of duty and obligation, as well as feelings of guilt. There was something naively boyish about him, in spite of his strong blinders that shut out the world of human enjoyment.

The primary and almost exclusive topic on his mind was the awareness of his eye sensations. His recurrent comments each hour consisted of statements like "my eyes are killing me" or "my eyes feel just terrible" or "they hurt a lot." He barely managed to keep his mind on anything else; a few words about his childhood, his present life (mainly his professional activities) and his mind would go back to his compulsive preoccupation with the discomfort centering around his eyes. In my role as a psychological listener, I carefully avoided reference to the notion of "psychosomatic symptoms," "conversion phenomena," or other explanatory concepts. Instead, I suggested that he focus his attention on when, where, and with whom his eyes hurt. In particular, he was encouraged to tune in to this thoughts and feelings before the eye symptoms began to occupy his focal attention. His obsessional character was utilized in keeping a detailed diary in connection with his symptoms. The result was that the field of his human contacts was explored in detail, including the emerging relationship with the analyst. What emerged was a series of recurrent situations that in one form or another occupied his attention above and beyond his preoccupation with his eyes. We learned of his excessive concern about fearing rejection in situations where the evidence pointed clearly in his favor; that is, there was every indication of his being persona grata. The question was raised with him to what degree he experienced negative feelings toward others before he felt or feared their rejection. The chain of events was traced to his childhood, where according to him his acceptance by his parents was strictly performance bound. In this connection we learned something about his profound difficulty to state or even know what he actually wanted in a given situation. He also found it exceedingly difficult to say no when there was a clear option available to him.

It increasingly became evident to both of us that he tended to be suspicious of himself and others. He also was hypersensitive, even to the mildest criticism and insatiable in his desire for praise.

The preoccupation with his eyes continued as his observational field steadily grew. He frequently reported eye symptoms on his way to my office, and he began to relate some of his sensations to the analytic situation. For instance, he felt free to express irritation in hearing my secretary use her typewriter, complaining that is deflected his attention. However, I learned that he concentrated well elsewhere within the sound of typewriters. His eye symptoms remained central in his focal field of attention for about one year while he kept seeing me. There was never a reference to feeling better until the typewriter incident, and his reasons for continuing his contact with me were not elaborated on by him. Things changed distinctly after about one year's time, when he more or less stopped mentioning his eyes. Instead he began to discuss thoughts of a more personal nature. Now he mentioned three areas of recurrent concern to him: (1) a preoccupation about being impotent; (2) a pronounced self-consciousness in having to urinate in a public urinal; (3) an intense fear about being confronted with the sight of blood. At the same time, he also started to recall a few dream fragments. The first concerned itself with his position as an academic teacher. In it, he rushed to class in order to teach his course. A professor friend of his was in the classroom as well as a very pretty girl. Suddenly, to his dismay, he discovered that he was dressed in an undershirt and nothing else. His comment was somewhat vague, but he emphasized his feeling that he had a great need to impress his audience. He identified me as his "professor friend" whose approval he sought together with the admiration of the prettiest girl in his class.

His comments were tentative, and when I inquired "how about you being in an undershirt?" he replied that it told him he was insecure and felt ill equipped. His associations centered around all the praise he received as a teacher and his awareness of his competence, whereupon I commented that I wondered whether *he* was ever satisfied with *himself*. There was no reply on his part, and I queried him, "do you ever feel arrogant or superior in your quest for perfectionism?" In one form or another it came to his mind that his teenaged daughter accused him recently of wanting to kill her when she felt that he was wrong about something. At a later point there was also some discussion about his previously mentioned problems pertaining to a fear of impotence, urination in front of other men, and his panic at the sight of blood. It turned out that by impotence he meant an initial inhibition with a new sexual partner. His short-lived difficulty always disappeared once a feeling of familiarity was established. I did not show a strong interest in the above-described phenomenon and let it go with the the understanding that there was not much to explore from my point of view unless he felt genuinely troubled by it. The urination problem in front of others proved to have been a very long standing and was attributed by the patient to a powerful feeling of competitiveness. A discussion of his sight of blood reaction brought a fear of violence to the fore on his own part as well as on the part of others in retaliation.

This brief clinical vignette is not to be mistaken for a protocol of a psychotherapeutic process. It may correctly be argued that much of what has been presented is in the realm of ordinary good clinical sense. Nevertheless, the purpose of the case presentation is to document the sparing use of theoretical structure. There is minimal or limited reference to metaphors and no particular need for metapsychological considerations.

The patient accepted the assignment of becoming a thoughtful observer of his thoughts, actions, and deliberations. Much attention was placed on the conditions that prevailed at the time of his observations in order to explore the network of his human relations.

Conflicts were discussed within their historical setting as

well as in here and now situations. His own programing, his expectations, and the responses he evoked were all given more-or-less equal consideration.

There was an absolute minimum of interpretation and a far greater reliance on confrontation. Comments on the part of the analyst were either feedback responses or tentative statements designed to hear what they evoked in him as well as a judicious sharing of countertransferential response.

Dreams were woven into the context of overall communication rather than accorded a stellar position. Manifest content was discussed without overloading the significance of covert messages.

Transference and transferential distortions come in for their share of attention within and outside the analytic situation. The discussion of the intervention of anxiety and the manifestation of security operations played an active part in the therapeutic dialogue without being recorded here in any systematic way. A great deal of interest rested on affirming the ever-widening field of the patient's observational acumen pertaining to himself and others. Finally, emphasis was placed on the quality of interpersonal integrations which characterized the patient's present life situation.

He considers himself much improved, and people in his environment are even more impressed with positive changes on his part. The patient's capacity to look at himself and his immediate human environment in more objective terms can be demonstrated. His sensitivities have emerged with greater clarity, as evidence in significant environmental changes brought about by him. At the same time he is a more responsive partner in the analytic inquiry, and his prognosis is favorable in spite of a few more hurdles he needs and wants to work on.

Goals of Interpersonal Theory

It is difficult to state psychotherapeutic goals in general terms, because expectations of both patient and analyst usually emerge within the context of the therapeutic alliance. Each patient had needs and requirements that do not necessarily apply to other patients. Goals must also be geared to the particular life situation the patient finds himself in — his age, health, and social and economic position. To a certain degree goals are also culture bound and depend on a consensus between patient and analyst as to what legitimately can be expected under the prevailing conditions. Furthermore, it stands to reason that therapeutic goals are linked to sociopolitical currents rather than having genuine autonomy regardless of what goes on in the environmental setting.

One of the recurrent problems in the consideration of goals is the implicit or explicit understanding that patients are not supposed to run counter to the mainstream or established norm. There is always a potential risk involved whereby conformity is a hidden therapeutic goal, that is, conformity with the therapist's theoretical point of view and conformity with societal standards or both. Nevertheless, I wish to sketch a few more general expectations or goals that are associated with the interpersonal point of view.

1. A general therapeutic goal of the expectation that the patients's observational field expands, thus leading to a greater personal awareness of the interpersonal Self.

2. The goal of encouraging the patient to be in touch with his genuine needs and with his capacity to obtain satisfaction.

3. An increasing appreciation of the intervention of anxiety and of the host of concomitant security operations or defenses (parataxic phenomena).

4. The emphasis on improving communication in personally meaningful terms with a growing capacity to verbalize personal experiences to oneself and to others.

5. An in-touchness with transferential distortions and with countertransferential manifestations.

6. A sensitivity to relational patterns, to reciprocal role commitments, and to alliances as well as hostile integrations.

7. The awareness and recognition of anger in its multitude of manifestations.

8. A self-monitoring and consensual validation of cognitive patternings.

9. An effort to improve the quality of one's human environment (growth) and sensitivity to appropriate maintenance operations.

10. Experimentation with thoughts, dream work, and reveries in communicable verbal interchanges.

These ten points are a shorthand way of outlining areas of therapeutic expectations. They are by no means all-inclusive statements of appropriate goals in therapy, and each point requires definite elaboration, for it frequently covers a much larger territory.

Point 1. The conception of an interpersonal Self makes for increasing clarity about the way a person is embedded in his overall interpersonal field. It calls for a widening of the observational acumen as a means of monitoring the reciprocal transactions pertaining to the person's impact on his immediate environment as well as the environment's impact on the person. The therapeutic process provides the patient with confrontational experiences that make him increasingly more sensitive to environmental currents in terms of his own participation in them and in terms of their interpenetration with his overall attitude, behavior, and thought processes.

The underlying assumption is that the content of consciousness is determined by a person's clarity about the nature of his interpersonal transactions. This expansion of the Self as an expanding area of registering and noticing subtle interpersonal phenomena is related to the term consciousness raising processes, which is used widely today.

Point 2. One of the recurrent difficulties encountered with a large number of people in therapy is that they have lost touch with their own needs and requirements. They tend to be excessively programed by sociocultural and environmental expectation. A typical example of this conflict may be seen in the comment of a female patient who had been living with a new boy friend for a relatively short period of time. The boy friend had a never-ending desire or demand for sexual contact, which according to the patient bordered on compulsivity. He seemed to be unaware of the principle of Occam's Razor, which refers to an optimal quantity and involvement in a given task. For instance, an optimal dosage of aspirin happens to be 10 grains or ordinarily two pills. There is no advantage in taking an excessive amount, which from a certain point on may even be harmful. Conversely, nothing is accomplished by taking too little, since it clearly does not do the job.

The point is that people often get unduly involved in activities and performances that are not based on their actual needs but rather on false expectations by themselves or their environment. It is an essential task of therapy to explore this area in detail and have the patient become increasingly vigilant and sensitive to his actual needs. Hand in hand with the awareness of a need comes the thought and potential action of gaining appropriate satisfaction under the conditions which prevail.

Point 3. The significance of anxiety intervening as a restrictive force has been discussed in some detail in Chapter 3. It suffices here to stress the need to enhance a person's recognition of the presence of anxiety and of the resulting security operations or defenses that conceal the situation which has led to their appearance. In other words, the anxiety precedes the defenses, whereas conscious awareness tends to focus exclusively on the anxiety.

Point 4. In every form of therapy patients should be encouraged to improve personally meaningful communication. Many people find it difficult to verbalize recurrent experiences in a communicable fashion and tend to deprive themselves of being fully in touch with the experience, because they have inadequate tools for conceptualizing or expressing it.

Point 5. Related to the sphere of experience comes the growing recognition of transferential distortions, whereby situations may be seen either outside of their developmental, historical context or outside of their here and now significance. The task is to bring about a rapprochement between on-going and past events in such a fashion that their interrelatedness comes to the fore and assists the person in more objective tuning in to what goes on at the present time. Illustrations from transactional distortions within the psychoanalytic situations are useful in that respect.

Point 6. The therapeutic process is designed to focus on relational patternings between people. In this connection, reciprocal role commitments, alliances, as well as hostile integrations play a major part. This is a way of addressing oneself to an exploration of the quality of a person's human environment.

Point 7. In many situations it becomes necessary to direct focal awareness to the presence of anger, resentment, sulking, and its multitude of manifestations. Anger is frequently acted out without a direct awareness of the underlying feeling tone.

Accordingly, much attention must be placed on recognizing hostile attitudes before partial or total denial sets in.

Point 8. Another aspect of therapy centers on the element of consensual validation, which in turn is related to a variety of cognitive phenomena. I have often stated that consensual validation may be merely a *folie a deux*. There is a calculated risk in such an occurrence. However, a sensitive way of checking and verification can bring out the presence of faulty cognition or distorted cognition that affect the person's self-image as well as his understanding of the interpersonal situation at hand.

Point 9. Earlier in this chapter special emphasis was placed on the desirability of improving and maintaining the quality of a humanly rewarding environment. The necessity for seeking out contact and being able to be responsive to appropriate people, the capacity to integrate constructively even difficult relationships, and the awareness of stumbling blocks in that respect constitute an important aspect of the therapeutic endeavor.

Point 10. It is very useful to encourage people to experiment with thoughts, fantasies, reveries, and content of dream work in every conceivable form. The ability to place some of these experiences in a framework of communicable verbal interchanges is very helpful. It assists the patient more fully to appreciate the range of his thoughts, and permits freedom to have whatever thoughts he may have while being able to distinguish between thought and action.

I have worked with a number of patients who dutifully recorded and reported all their recalled dream material. In doing so they felt that they had discharged their obligation as psychoanalytic patients. It frequently did not occur to them to report their fantasy life in detail despite the fact that it took up a considerable amount of their waking life.

CHAPTER 6

Clinical Syndromes and Their Clinical Implications

The Need for Classifying Clinical Syndromes

Nosology or the systematic classification of diseases has been a helpful tool of the medical field. The process of determining by examination the nature and circumstances of a disease is medically called diagnosis. Once a diagnosis has been established, it tends to give information about the prognosis of the condition as well as about appropriate therapeutic interventions designed to treat, prevent, or cure the particular illness.

This medical model has been widely used in clinical psychiatry, in psychoanalysis, and in psychoanalytic psychotherpay. Every student and practitioner in the clinical, psychological field relies to some degree on clinical entities as diagnostic guidelines and therapeutic considerations. Technical procedures pertaining to the intervention in all forms of mental disorders depend largely on a systematic classification of clinical syndromes. Nevertheless, this procedure is still subject to considerable controversy. Objections are raised along two major lines. One argument centers around the pinning of labels on people who suffer from a variety of distressing psychological manifestations. Proponents of this argument reason that labeling tends to dehumanize people by placing them in categories that have been created for the benefit of society rather than the welfare of the patients.

The other side of the argument is that we hide our ignorance behind pseudomedical disease entities as if we could apply medical procedures to cure people in a state of personal or social human distress. At present we do not have particular information about the specific cause or nature of mental disorder. At the same time our overall knowledge of multiple dynamic factors in the genesis and manifestation of mental disorders is increasing. In addition, we still find much conflict in the realm of biological versus psychological and social causes of mental disturbances. There is a risk involved in creating an unnecessary dichotomy, for biological, hereditary, and other organic factors do not not in any way exclude the psychological side of maladaptations, malfunctioning, and a variety of thought disorders.

Emphasis on the myth of mental illness (as advocated by Thomas Szasz, Ronald D. Laing, and others) is a basically negativistic approach to an undeniable fact of life. Mental disorders exist as a particular manifestation of human existence regardless what names we apply to the range of observable behavior and thought disorders. We are not justified in denying the existence of a phenomenon merely because of our inability to explain the cause or nature of the phenomenon adequately.

Clinical terms are essential requirements for interprofessional communication as well mandatory tools for teaching and practicing psychotherapy at all levels. Nosological units constitute a valuable shorthand for a large body of observational data which enable us to approach mental disorders in a thoughtful and humanly sensitive fashion. Difficulty arises mainly when we concretize clinical syndromes, that is, when we objectify them excessively or treat the syndrome as if it were a thing, a clearly defined disease entity, or a rigidly demarcated configuration. Nosological categories must retain a relatively loose structure, a rough outline or Gestalt. Only when we view the syndrome as an open-ended system rather than as a predetermined pattern do we provide the opportunity for making the terms clinically useful.

A mental disorder cannot be confined within the context of a self-perpetuating, intrapsychic process. It is always embedded in the text of a person's life and mode of living. In psychiatry, psychoanalysis, and psychotherapy we are invariably dealing with fellows human beings in distress and not primarily with a circumscribed disease, a particular sickness, or a strictly internal defect. Alleviating a person's emotional suffering does not necessarily mean a removal of distressing symptoms. We are not dealing with humanly alien components in our patients. There are no emotional tumors to be extirpated; not all painful thoughts and experiences can be replaced by pleasurable sensations; successful and happy living cannot be guaranteed to any human being. In no way does this indicate that our essential therapeutic task consists in helping adjust to their limitation and make the most of things under the conditions that prevail. Up to a point the elements of adaptation and compromise formation have a place in the therapeutic intervention. However, this aspect is never central in the therapeutic task. We address ourselves clinically to a mutual appreciation by therapist and patient of how the patient's total life experiences have set the stage for his present interpersonal situation. Family dynamics, social and cultural factors, friendships, and helpful as well as harmful events in the individual's mode of living are brought to the fore. The continuum of transferential and countertransferential patterns is explored inside as well as outside of the analytic situation. Play acting, role committments, and acting out are studied carefully, together with the revelation of fantasies, daydreams, and night dreams. An appraisal of thought and action is made in conjunction with an increasing awareness of how decisions are made by the patient and to what degree they are implemented. Much interest is focused on the range of possible options by the patient. This is combined with an inquiry into the scope of emotional expressions ranging from anger and aggression, to tenderness, affection and ambivalence.

These points plus a number of other factors constitute a general foundation for dealing with mental disorders. The designation of clinical syndromes is a way of emphasizing one or another aspect of the general therapeutic repertory as a potentially helpful approach to a particular cluster of defenses. The nature of the defenses or security operations affects the analytic relationship, the mutual participants in the therapeutic endeavor and the quality of the transference-countertransference continuum. In other words, obsessional, hysterical, borderline, or schizophrenic security operations set in motion different interpersonal and different therapeutic relational patterns.

The Nature of Clinical Entities

The point of view outlined here differs from prevailing opinions on this subject. It is customary to look at clinical syndromes as entities with fixed boundaries that are causally related to specific events. Ordinarily, nosological units are described in terms of one to one correlations to circumscribed developmental and traumatizing occurrences. The result has been a powerful barrier to an unbiased exploration of ordinary as well as of warped psychological manifestations. The classical formulation of neurotic and psychotic disorders stresses the genesis of intrapsychic malfunctioning as a preponderance of immature strivings.

Neo-Freudian formulations have for the better part either rejected the nosological coding of mental disorders or added speculative explanations of their own. Previous reference has been made to Sullivan's ideas on the topic.

Descriptive psychiatry either harks back to the pioneering work of Kraepelin and others or treats mental illness as a strictly biochemical manifestation with predicatable behavioral patterns and predictable prognosis. Intervention in traditional psychiatry centers mainly on chemical, physiological, environmental, or behavior modifications.

One of the major pitfalls in present-day formulations of mental disorders is the excessive reliance on a theoretical platform with implicit causative and resulting remedial assumptions. The approach presented here stresses a different point of view. It centers on the fact that our assumptions about specific causes of mental disorders are largely unsupported by reliable empirical data. At best we can offer educated guesses and speculative assumptions about the origin of so-called psychopathology. Many patients will respond favorable to some explanatory deductions, even if they prove to be unfounded. A certain placebo effect is often radiated by the au fait tones of an "authority." In the long run, however, verbal positivism will bring diminishing returns. Telling a patient a theoretical assumption as if it were a fact has a reassuring but fleeting effect, and eventually it reveals itself to be in the category of the emperor's new clothing.

One cannot argue about the importance of etiological research. Clinically, however, it is recommended that patients be spared explanations that we as therapists are unable to support. We all have to live with a measure of uncertainty, whether we be therapists or patients. In my experience troubled people tend to respond well to factual information. We know what we know and we don't know what we don't know without having to feel defensive about it. In many instances we are unable to figure out why people suffer from certain problems. To be helpful to the patient we should not feel compelled to find answers on the basis of obscure past events. A thoughtful exploration of the past often suffices to bring events into clearer focus for the patient even if the investigation turns up little or nothing of major significance. In fact, even meaningful insight into distressing experiences in earlier life does not necessarily have a remedial effect. What seems to have a particular positive impact on the patient is the experience of being the focal point of interest in a setting where useful information is shared. The important consideration is to explore largely unchartered territory rather than wait for the patient to accept the therapist's interpretaion. In other words, successful clinical work does not depend on etiologic knowledge to a significant degree.

Our search for causative elements in the formation of clinical syndromes is vital and must be continued. However, our preoccupation with a direct connection between cause and symptom can lead us into a blind alley. Chances are that we are dealing with multiple and usually cumulative events in the genesis and maintenance of mental disorders. Our most reliabe guide in that respect is the observable impact and counterimpact of distorted relational patterns in people. A developmental tracing is helpful, particularly when it takes place hand in hand with an increasing awareness of how people erect communicative and emotional barriers which affect interpersonal integrations.

Technical Considerations

Accordingly, clinical syndromes have particular clinical implications pertaining to a variety of technical considerations. Each major clinical entity calls for an awareness of potential defenses and counterdefenses which characterize interpersonal patterns connected with the nosological unit at hand. The structure of the patient's security operations or defenses brings to the fore responses that call for sensitive self-monitoring on the therapist's part as well as a judicious sharing of responses for mutual consideration. What emerges are modifications in technique depending on the nature of the clinical syndrome that one encounters in the therapeutic situation. Care must be taken not to confuse technical procedures with a formula as to how to do it. The emphasis rests on an appreciation and alertness to complex emotional and relational aspects that are more prominent in one clinical syndrome compared to another. Invariably, a certain amount of overlapping clinical manifestations are involved. Nevertheless, each nosological cluster has a characteristic set of security operations that in one form or another permeate the therapeutic setting. Reference has already been made to the need for keeping clinical entities openended. In a similar vein technical procedures must not be dogmatized or turned into overly specific prescriptions. We should also keep in mind that technique and therapeutic structure, as important as they are, cannot go beyond the individual, human qualities of the analyst who applies them. In this connection we are still plagued by an unproductive controversy of depth psychology compared to more superficial psychological approaches. Up to a point there is merit in emphasizing significant developmental and dynamic occurrences, in exploring the emancipation of an interpersonal Self, and in studying the full range of the transference-countertransference continuum in daily life and in therapeutic situation. Practitioners in the field need to be thoroughly familiar with a wide range of psychotherapeutic modalities. It would be naive, however, to assume that depth psychology can be learned merely by following the rules of the particular theory of therapy. After all, depth is a quantitative term and cannot be measured by the adherence to psychological mystique. In the psychotherapeutic domain the genuine depth of the therapist's personality prevails over his allegiance to any psychoanalytic doctrine. It underlines a large body of empirical data indicative of a therapeutic truism, that is, technique and structure alone do not alleviate mental disorders. There has to be an additional element of caring for a person. Indeed, care stems from the latin word *carere,* and is the basis for the medical term cure. The kind of caring under discussion here considers the notion of neutrality in analytic work to be an unrealisitc concept. It also questions the vadility or desirability of a regressive transference neurosis as a therapeutic aid. There is no evidence that significant events of earlier years are relived mainly under the conditions that prevailed during the formative years. Indications are that childhood memories are not recalled through the eyes of the child alone, but are screened through the adult person's way of viewing the world (see Schachtel's studies on childhood memories).

My discussion of clinical syndromes deals largely with observable phenomena. It emphasizes relatively enduring patterns that are characteristic of a particular nosological unit. The material presented consists of rough sketches that are not intended to cover all aspects of a major syndrome. Clinical vignettes serve as illustrations of technical considerations.

A Descriptive Sample of Clinical Syndromes

Three clinical syndromes are presented as samples. The selection of obsessional, borderline, and hypochondriacal manifestations does not follow a reasoned exposition or principle. Initially I intended to include illustrations of schizophrenic, hysterical, depressive, and other nosological entities. However, it became clear that such an endeavor would cover material for an entire book rather than for part of a chapter. Accordingly, I chose three samples at random, primarily for the purpose of discussing certain technical principles.

The Obsessional Syndrome

Obsessional behavior constitutes a style of life that blends like a chameleon with a multitude of cultural phenomena. The camouflage is often quite effortless, and we can appreciate the psychoanalytic anecdote attributed to Karl Abraham, namely that the Swiss response to his description of the anal character was "Is that not just human nature?"

The fact is that no society can function without some degree of obsessionalism (paying bills on time, running trains, meeting deadlines, etc.). At the same time, it must be appreciated that certain obsessional practices constitute a tremendous waste of time, energy, and worthwhile human potential. Also, we need to recognize the fact that there is a major difference between a garden variety of obsessional attitudes and a full-blown obsessional neurosis.

There is no need in repeating the classical obsessional phenomena. Instead, I would like to group some of the familiar symptoms along two categories:

1. Along the lines of a noninterpretive, descriptive listing; and

2. Along experiential lines or on a cognitive level.

PHENOMENON I: OBSESSIVE DOUBTING

Included in this phenomenon are aspects of indecisiveness, procrastination, ambivalence, overattentiveness to detail, overcautiousness, and reluctance or inability to act spontaneously. Every issue has a measure of great complexity involved often with equal emphasis on opposing elements in the situation. The phenomenon of obsessive doubting may be compared to the well-known metaphor of "daisy picking" whereby each affirmation of he or she loves me is immediately followed by a negation of this assumption. The result is a type of chain reaction that covers a variety of behavioral, ideational, cognitive, and emotional manifestations.

Obsessive doubting takes place as regards (a) *action*, (b) *belief and faith*, and (c) *memory and observation*.

(a) *In regard to Action*. Hesitation, rumination, and excessive concern about consequences occur in many mundane or outright trivial situations. Deep concern may be experienced about doing or not doing something quite ordinary. To telephone or not to telephone a person, to see or not to see a friend, to date one girl or another, to buy or not to buy something, to wear or not to wear a particular garment, and so forth. There are endless variations on this basic theme.

(b) *In regard to Belief and Faith*. The doubting here centers around the question of whether to trust people (including oneself). Included here is also the recurrent concern of being understood and the constant fear of being misunderstood. Related doubts may include the area of intelligence or the lack of it, the soundness of judgement or its unsoundness, the feeling of competence or incompetence, of being well or ill thought of, and endless similar preoccupations.

(c) *In regard to Memory and Observation*. Thoughts in this category may center around did I or did I not lock the door the car, close the window, turn the gas off, mail a letter, remember the correct time for an appointment. Included here are also ruminative thoughts pertaining to the appropriateness of behavior, the correctness of attire, the adequacy of a tip, the sensation of having accepted or rejected as well as of having acted in a friendly or unfriendly fashion.

All these examples of obsessive doubting are descriptively endless efforts of checking and verification that never bring about the desired feelings of certainty in the prevailing situation.

PHENOMENON II: COMPULSIVE COUNTING

This compulsion may involve everything under the sun, such as counting lampposts, telephone poles, money; adding up the number of sexual conquests, telephone numbers, license plate numbers; up to hoarding things, and collecting articles of value or of no worth at all. In this category we find related compulsions of touching or not touching things, of stepping on or of avoiding the cracks in the pavement. We also find here compulsive attitudes toward being a spendthrift or a tightwad. One may wish to add the compulsion to take notes frequently with no desire to look at them.

PHENOMENON III: MORBID FASCINATION

This group covers the relentless preoccupation with a musical tune, a particularly unpleasant thought, the recurrent rumination about flinging oneself out of a window, throwing oneself in front of an oncoming car or train, using a sharp instrument to hurt a person, and so forth. Inherently we are confronted here with a phenomenon that is an intense temptation or fear to do something basically alien to oneself, to lose one's control and engage in destructive masochistic or sadistic compulsive activities.

Finally one may wish to mention the phenomenon of *morbid grieving,* which by no means concludes the list of obsessional defenses.

PHENOMENON IV: MORBID GRIEVING

Morbid grieving is a process of feeling chronically deprived, never fully satisfied, and experiencing the grass as invariably being greener elsewhere. Part of the phenomenon is a low-grade form of sulking, of feeling frustrated, not sufficiently appreciated, or outright ignored. The feeling of grief is a keen mental suffering over having lost or over being unable to obtain something personally meaningful. It covers the range of feeling anguish, heartache, woe, and sadness.

One of the characteristic manifestations of morbid grieving is to feel exceedingly needy without the capacity to feel genuinely satisfied. Interconnected sensations with the obsessional syndrome are feeling surrounded by insensitive and uncaring people. Included in the obsessional cluster are feeling imposed upon, feeling righteous, trying to elevate oneself by putting others down (Sullivan's poignant description of the obsessional person's motto "If I am a molehill, there shall be no mountains"), and being compulsively negativistic.

There are numerous theories concerning the etiology of the obsessional syndrome. Every major theoretician in the field has made some contribution to tracing the origin of this widespread defensive manifestation. This in not the place to discuss the large number of ingenious theories on the topic. Such a task clearly transcends the scope of this book. I only wish to make a brief reference to Sullivan's point of view on this topic because his formulations have been a primary focus in this text, and to do justice to his original ideas pertaining to the etiology of the obsessional dynamism — his term for the syndrome under discussion.

1. He placed the origin of the obsessional dynamism in the realm of interpersonal events occurring at the level when children learn how to talk. To Sullivan language behavior requires a form of consensual validation when autistic and baby talk give way to communicable language. According to Sullivan this is a time when the magic of words is discovered, that is, when people often use the words to conceal meaning rather than reveal the underlying thoughts and feelings. For instance, people may feel compelled to express regret and say that they are sorry when in reality they experience righteous indignation. Others may overtly speak in affectionate and loving terms as a thin veneer for hostile, resentful, and angry feelings. There may be verbal expressions of concern, of interest, of respect in a basically negative emotional atmosphere. The result is that children who witness outright verbal double binds in the environment or who are direct victims of it themselves tend to acquire obsessional security operations.

2. Sullivan traced the origin of the obsessional dynamism to family dynamics. He felt that obsessional people usually had parents who suffered from some kind of hostile integration, that is, a relational pattern in which the bond between the parents rests mainly on focusing on inadequacies of the partner, which evokes attitudes of fault finding and blaming. There is a prevailing inability to give each other support by affirming assets rather than by enlarging liabilities.

Sullivan told a fictitious story of a self-demeaning woman

married to a man who considered himself a bishop or at least a God-appointed superior person. According to Sullivan the "bishop" never forgave himself for having married his particular wife. He often insulted and mistreated her overtly or covertly, only to insist that she apologize for his misbehavior. The "bishop's" rationalization was always that he happened to be a worthy person. Invariably, he could prove that technically he was in the right by quoting some appropriate text in the holy scripture. Marital mismatches of the above described pattern have been described earlier in the text as hateful integrations. In this particular case the husband lords it over a self demeaning partner who is party to a most unfortunate warped interaction. Children who observe such blatant verbal manipulations become fascinated with the magic of words and thus are indoctrinated into the obsessional world.

3. Sullivan coined the term masking operation for the defensive hostility of obsessional people. He traced this phenomenon to the obsessional's never-ending doubt whether the most significant person in their life is basically their friend or foe. The inability to make up one's mind about benevolence or malevolence on the key person's part was considered by Sullivan to be the foundation of obsessive doubting.

4. Sullivan focused much clinical attention on the Self-system activity in obsessional people, that is, operations to play down or keep out of awareness the presence of anxiety based on feelings of worthlessness inculcated at the level of initial verbal learning. One of Sullivan's technical recommendations for working with obsessional patients was to be sure not to tell the patient what is wrong with him but rather to have the patient find out for himself what his difficulties are. He also tended to assume the role of the devil's advocate (the so-called paradigmatic approach) in communicating messages to negativistic patients.

A great deal more could be said about Sullivan's approach to obsessional disorders. His observation that under certain conditions obsessional security operations could fail and lead to overt psychotic episodes should be included, but the task at hand is a description of clinical syndromes and their clinical implications. My personal illustrations center around a few

examples of transference and countertransference phenomena, of symptoms and response to the symptom in terms of
therapeutic transactions.

At one time I saw a highly gifted and highly obsessional
professor of English literature as a patient. Our work pro-
gressed reasonably well, until the patient began to praise the
brilliance of my interpretations excessively. We had come to
deal with his sense of competition and what I belatedly recognized as his feeling of arrogance. Initially I took some pleasure in the praise of a person whom I respected. Then we
heard a dream that evoked different feelings in me. The
patient dreamt that he had mistakenly exchanged his hat with
mine in the closet located in my waiting room. To his surprise
he found that my hat barely covered the top part of his head.
He brushed the dream off as not having much meaning, but I
concluded that he saw himself endowed with a huge brain,
whereas my hat was only fit for a person with a bird's brain. In
other words, he considered himself to be brilliant, but that I
was limited in my intellectual equipment. When I confronted
him with my impression of his dream he blushed slightly but
did not overtly agree with me. The following week he came
back with another dream in which he had gone to an inferior
haberdashery where a salesman tried to sell him inferior
merchandise. This time he connected his dream to his
analysis, whereupon I inquired what realistic shortcomings he
had encountered in working with me. He made some valuable
criticism, which was acknowledged as valid. What emerged
was my awareness of counterdefenses to his ceaseless, concealed attacks on me. Once that situation was out in the open,
the quality of our therapeutic collaboration improved. It
should be mentioned that this man's father had committed
suicide by sticking his head inside a gas stove when the patient
was a young boy. His mother was an extremely domineering
person, as was the patient's wife. Anyhow, he felt that I would
desert him and eventually prove my inadequacy.

Another obsessional patient gave me a very hard time by
compulsively nodding her head in agreement before I had a
chance to utter a word. She had found a perfect way of
shutting me up or of making it clear that she had no intention
of listening to me. To add insult to injury, she would at the end

of my comments usually say "You happen to be 100% right." I explained that everybody likes to be right some of the time, but always being right is as unlikely an event as never being right or of being 100% wrong. The discussion did not get us very far until I unwittingly retaliated against the patient by giving her an appointment at the same time that I had scheduled another patient. When the patient saw what had happened I acknowledged that I had acted out strong feelings of futility and irritation and expressed regret about it. The patient knew that I scheduled appointments carefully and I explained that this had happened on only one previous occasion in my professional life (with an extremely suspicious patient). The incident helped in clarifying some important patterns in the patient's life. She became aware of the fact that she had been involved in a number of similar situations outside of the analysis. Nevertheless, we eventually reached some impasse, and I did not consider her analysis to have gone far enough when we terminated. Interestingly enough, the patient did not share my opinion.

Another brief clinical vignette may serve as an illustration of the response-counterresponse aspects in working with some obsessional patients. This young woman was in the habit of automatically cleaning the ashtrays in my office when entering the door. She usually came into the office poised with a handkerchief and quickly wiped the ashtrays before lying down on the couch. For one reason or another the matter did not come up for discussion until I found myself doing something unusual. In an automatic response I caught myself cleaning the ashtrays just before the patient entered. It was clearly a case of "one upmanship" designed to foil her intrusively compulsive behavior. I told the patient what I had done and the incident proved helpful in working on a number of important issues in the patient's life.

Finally, I wish to offer a description of some aspects relating to the reanalysis of a markedly obsessional patient. This successful, middle-aged bachelor had a classical analysis of long duration, including a second classical analysis of about 10 years prior to seeing me. This second analysis can be accurately described as an obsessional marathon, with both parties reaching a point of mutual exhaustion toward its unsuccessful end. It would be appropriate to refer to this previous analytic experience as a hateful integration (a term already described previously). In a sense the analyst's technique consisted of interpretations that basically pointed to the patient's alleged or real defects. It was then up to the patient to map out a defense that eventually wound up in a culpa mea confession with a yes-but comment. This sad analytic checkmate is an illustration of an unfortunate misuse of the analytic process. Such an occurrence results mainly from an obsessional analyst dealing with an obsessional patient in a therapeutic system overloaded with obsessionalism.

There were many obstacles in my work with this patient which are too extensive to be listed here in detail. Instead, I confine myself to the description of a few characteristic therapeutic transactions.

One of the first observations I made was the patient's amazing inability to concentrate on what was being said during the analytic hour. He was endowed with an excellent memory, and it was surprising to find a distinct lack of recall on his part not only to the analyst's comments but also to his own. He usually asked me what we had talked about the previous hour, which I usually declined to reveal. When he could not recall the most recent material, he proceeded many times to tell what he had talked about the last time. Often, he would tell me the same story again, each time giving a detailed description of the participants in the events after he already had described them to me an endless number of times. My repeated comments that I already knew the story as well as who was who in his life were politely ignored by him, or he would blush slightly, acknowledge my comment, and go on to repeat the details anyhow. At other times I would inquire "Do you recall having told me the story before?" which frequently led to an embarrassed smile with the comment "I am not sure but let me tell you again." Finally we taped his sessions regularly, and he was asked to take his tapes home and listen to them. The educational results of this procedure produced only a limited capacity to hear more than he had heard in the analytic session. Then we made it our business to listen jointly to some of the recordings. In listening to the tapes I observed a few salient points. It turned out that he heard a great deal of criticism, even when there was none. At the same time it became clear that he had much difficulty in hearing affirmative comments on my part or outright praise in a few instances.

Second, it became apparent that he was a most inattentive listener to his own verbalizations. He had the capacity to repeat his remarks verbatim many times without recalling the context in which they were said by him. It was like replaying a passage on a phonograph record without appreciating or recalling the theme of the song or even its title. There was one particular episode he took great delight in retelling. It had something to do with the exploration of his anal opening and having the extraordinary skill not to soil his fingers in the exploratory process. According to his tedious story he slipped up on one occasion and got a smudge of fecal material on his finger. When he ran to his mother (possibly for the purpose of shocking her, because he knew her sensitivities) she had a hysterical fit. Every time he repeated the story — which was almost weekly — and I inquired "Do you recall having told me the story before?" he would go on in his own inimitable fashion "I am not sure but let me just mention it once more." After a while I could not conceal my irritation and would say words to effect "You must have magical fingers to keep them unsoiled under circumstances when most mortals would be less skillful." Such comments on my part were duly ignored by him.

Another approach used by me was a reference to the fact that he must have pestered his previous analyst with the same nonsequitur tales. He muttered "maybe so," but reiterated how much time he and his analyst had spent discussing a request for a change of time in the analytic hour by a few minutes.

Anyhow, I experienced increasing difficulty in opening up communication with this patient when I found myself trapped by a request of his. I agreed to see him for a limited time four times a week instead of three. It turned out that this was more that I was able to handle, and I was ready to wish him on somebody else. Happily, I did not get unduly exasperated with him for he proved to be a very worthwhile, inherently likable person who in the end was a genuinely rewarding analytic patient.

The tide turned in our favor when I consistently confronted him with my reactions to his manipulative defensive operations. First I expressed my feelings of frustration and resentment by saying to his repetitive recitals: "You and I both know this is at least the bicentennial anniversary of you telling us this particular episode." His response was to claim poor memory or words to the effect that he just could not help it. I told him that he was driving me up the wall and that not many people were blessed with his highly developed memory. I made it plain that there was a limit to how much nagging I could do, and that there was also a limit to how many interpretations I could give him since he had become an expert in turning his hearing off. I told him that he evoked in me the compulsion to make speeches to him from time to time that I knew entered one ear and came out the other. Neither of us wanted to repeat his previous unbeneficial analytic experience.

What kind of collaborative effort could he suggest to us?

It was at this time that he requested the previously mentioned additional hour. The intensification of contact led to increasing clashes between us, which eventually brought his attitudes and my counterattitudes into clearer focus. The patient volunteered more information about his fear of stepping into his father's ineffectual shoes. He also became more aware of his distance-making operations with woman of his acquaintance. We encountered strong compensatory feelings of arrogance on his part and of my response to his lecturing to me. I informed him when I enjoyed his presentations which occurred not infrequently and also told him when I found it difficult to listen to him. As time went on he observed a widening of his sense of humor when he caught himself in one of his typical obsessional maneuvers. In particular he became aware of his gratuitous qualifying statements that followed the majority of his affirmative comments. Eventually we set a mutually agreeable time for termination of a reanalysis of relatively short duration compared to the excessive amount of time spent in two previous analytic contacts. It may be argued that this man still has problems to work on, which is undoubtedly true. The fact remains that he has benefited from his last analytic experience and that he needs to implement things on his own now. The major thrust in my work with him was to deal with his massive obsessional defenses by showing him the powerful impact of his security operations on the environment. He was more interested in unmasking his previous analysts' obsessionalism than constructively working on his own. I presented less of a target to him because I confronted him with when, where, and how he scored with me, thus revealing my counterdefenses to a much larger degree. It was also possible for me to communicate my areas of genuine acceptance of him and affirm a number of affectionate attitudes on his part toward me.

The obsessional syndrome has many more faces than can be discussed here. I have selected a few illustrations at random. The purpose of describing characteristic obsessional phenomena is to highlight some of the particular clinical manifestations involved in this syndrome. Case illustrations merely point to rather typical obsessional patterns and to some of the responses they bring to the fore in the analayst. The approach offered here centers around countertransference in the broadest possible sense as a most significant therapeutic medium. It confronts the patient with the type of reactions he brings into play and offers him an on-going feedback of how the analyst experiences the patient's obsessional behavior. The mutual observation of security-countersecurity operations is discussed against the patient's developmental background as well as against his present-day life situation. Eventually the here and now comes into sharper focus than the past, which gradually recedes from the center of awareness.

In discussing clinical syndromes we need to appreciate the fact that the configuration of mental disorders, like customs and fashions, may change their shape and form to a certain degree. For instance, the widely known phenomenon of *cerea flexibilitas* in catatonic patients has become a rarity in many parts of the world. Also, the highly dramatic manifestations of hysteria in Freud's era have become distinctly less common, and some of the classic hysterical cases probably would be classified as schizophrenic disorders today. It points to a certain dilemma of the increase or decrease of a particular syndrome at a given period of time in contrast to the diagnostic criteria used to make the diagnosis. In some instances it is difficult to tell whether we are confronted with an epidemiological manifestation, that is, the increase or decrease of a particular nosological unit, or with diagnostic criteria, ranging from greater sophistication to potential overkill in excessively diagnosing one clinical syndrome. Chances are that both factors can occasionally be at play in terms of epidemiological changes as well as in diagnostic considerations.

The Borderline Syndrome

The next syndrome to be discussed is a case in point. There has been growing popularity of the borderline syndrome. So far no genuine consensus on the validity of the term has been reached in spite of an ever-widening body of literature on the topic. My own persuasion is in favor of such a syndrome as long as the term does not become reified. There is merit in conceiving of a category which is neither a mini-schizophrenia nor a maxi-neurosis but a condition in its own right. We have a plethora of etiological constructs connected with borderline states. The most widely known theoretical foundation of borderline states is offered by Otto Kernberg whose work should be read by analysts even if one disagrees — as this author does — with a number of Kernberg's theoretical and technical formulations. (See "Recent Advances in the Concepts and Treatment of Borderline Patients" in *New Dimensions in Psychiatry,* Vol. I, Arieti and Chrzanowski, Eds., New York John Wiley & Sons, 1975). Again, I wish to confine myself here to a descriptive exposition of the syndrome and discuss some of the complex therapeutic transactions involved in this clinical entity without reference to its etiology. Furthermore, I consider the undue preoccupation with certain differential diagnostic categories to be a sterile procedure. There is considerable overlapping between some character disorders, narcissistic syndromes, certain schizoid manifestations, some depressive syndromes, severe obsessionalism, and borderline states. I doubt that any worthwhile clinical purpose is served by sorting out each of these categories and viewing them as basically separate units.

Descriptively we find a cluster of symptoms which make up the Gestalt of the borderline-syndrome.

Symptom 1 centers around the ability to cope with feelings of anger and of aggression. The emotional range may be restricted to the sensation of anger, or there may be a denial or concealment of spontaneous anger. We may encounter a form of pouting, that is, a chronic, low-grade sullenness which can have a depressive component in it. Most people within the borderline category shy away from overt aggressivity in themselves and in others. This fear of aggressivity usually extends to areas of legitimate self-assertion. The inhibition of standing up for their own rights can be a genuine problem to people manifesting borderline symptoms.

Symptom 2 deals with the tendency to engage in distance-making activities. The defenses are geared in such a fashion that personal and social intimacy is avoided to a large degree. There may be a compulsive rushing into contact without permitting a meaningful integration with another person. The result is often a play acting of relatedness without the actual freedom to build a foundation for more durable contact. Partners in such encounters are frequently self-invented, idealized images rather than the actual people who have been met. In other instances the person with borderline manifestations is overtly withdrawn and avoids people.

Symptom 3 is not easily reconciled with the two preceding symptoms because it points to the presence of powerful transference phenomena in people representing the nosological unit under discussion. The borderline patient's penchant toward intense transference-experiences presents a particular technical problem in the therapeutic situation. The use of the term transference in this connection deserves some explanation.

On the one hand, we observe that people exhibiting borderline manifestations confine most of their emotions to the narrow channel of anger. On the other hand, we notice their isolating tendencies, their withdrawal, or compensatory pseudorelational patterns. Yet we find indications of strong emotional currents in the realm of emotions referred to as transference. In my opinion it points to the necessity of redefining transference, as an experiential process that is modified by on-going events in life rather than primarily as a repetitive compulsion. It also requires a greater emphasis of transference as a universal emotional potential in people that is a basic ingredient of daily life. Countertransference, then, is of one piece with transference with no determination of which facet of the continuum comes first.

Symptom 4 has been referred to by some authors as an ahedonic manifestation. In my experience we are dealing more with a compulsion to seek inauthentic satisfactions or pseudogratifications. The pursuit of "as if" pleasures may cover a wide area of life, ranging from the quest for prestige; to the wish for conquest in the narcissistic, sexual, or social sphere; to the need for unending approval; to the involvement in sterile or outright hostile integrations. I have formed the opinion that people caught in this unrewarding, complicated syndrome are basically out of touch with their most elementary human needs or requirements and lack awareness of what gives them satisfaction. This concept may be illustrated by dreams of three individuals who manifested these borderline symptoms.

The first is a young married woman with children who was in a basically stable marital situation and who had a generous share of some of "the good things in life." She experienced a chronic feeling of apathy and ahedonia. At one point in her analysis she reported a repetitive dream in which she found her old childhood diary when clearing out a desk. Much to her surprise the diary was arranged in the form of a dictionary in alphabetical order. Each letter of the alphabet pointed to an entry of prescribed behavior. It told her how to conduct herself under any and all circumstances: when and where to smile, how to eat properly, what social attitudes and emotions to display under a variety of circumstances.

Another patient had a dream with a somewhat similar connotation. In her dream she wore one dress on top of another — from tennis attire to casual clothing to an evening dress. The idea was to be prepared for every eventuality while on top of it all she wore a sadly mismatched skirt and blouse.

Finally, a dream of similar content is that of a successful

young professional bachelor. In his dream he was invited to a party and was greeted by his hostess when he arrived. In the rest of the dream he was preoccupied with catching a glimpse of a list which the hostess held in her hand. Written on the list was the name of each invited guest. Behind the guest's name he noticed a number of comments which stated specifically each guest's preferred topic of conversation, favorite food, drink, and the general areas of the guest's spheres of interest. In his dream the patient spent the entire evening trying to figure out what he was supposed to talk about, what he was supposed to ask for in food and drink, and what areas of interest he was expected to display.

All three dreams center around the familiar concept of "I will be as you desired me" or as you expect me to be, with a distinct out-of-toucheness with personal wishes, desires, or needs.

Technical considerations in being confronted with borderline defenses are complex and cover a wide transactional territory. They require the creative use of countertransference, that is, a thoughtful way of monitoring one's own appropriate and exaggerated security operations in the face of the patient's relational patterns.

I have not found the use of parameters of classical technique to be clinically helpful. In particular, I have been at a loss to work successfully with the doctrine of Ego weakness, transference psychosis, and compromise-formation. In addition, I find the splitting of transference into negative and positive categories to be a hindrance rather than a help. Transference by its very nature is an ambivalent phenomenon, and we need to contend with its polarity in ourselves as well as in our patients. I have found the nondefensive revelation of the analyst's negative sensations and experiences opposite the patient to be a useful technical procedure. It often clears the way for the interchange of more tender emotions on both sides. In this respect I have been strongly influenced by Sullivan's early description of transference as published in "Schizophrenia as a Human Process. To quote him, "Abruptly, often without warning one finds oneself integrated by powerful motives of the type of hatred and primitive love and others for which our language is lacking a term" (reprinted form *American Journal of Psychiatry,* 1934/5, Vol. 91, pp.1117-1126, "Psychiatric Training as a Prerequisite to Psychoanalytic Practice"). At a later point in the same text Sullivan goes on to say: "I refer here to failures of the psychoanalyst to recognize the transference processes, the shifting emotional relationships which spring up in his work with each individual patient. Any blindness in this field produces great stress. It can lead to serious disorder and in fact to the appearance of more ominous symptoms than those preceding the attempt of psychoanalysis."

One of Sullivan's concluding observation is that "the phenomena of transference must be personally experienced before they can be grasped." At another point he comments that "the underlying reality of the 'transference' and 'repetition compulsion' of Freud is a ubiquitous complicating factor in interpersonal relations which cannot safely be ignored in any inquiry into human relations." (*The Fusion of Psychiatry and Social Science:* "A Note on the Implications of Psychiatry in the Social Sciences", reprinted from *American Journal of Sociology,* 1936/7, Vol. 42, pp. 848-861).

I would add one other point to Sullivan's conclusion that transference requires a genuine experiential platform on the part of the analyst before it can be dealt with clinically, that is, freedom and ability by the analyst to communicate to the patient verbally as well as nonverbally what he has grasped about the transference-countertransference continuum and how it applies to the ongoing therapeutic process. In other words, I have found that the judicious sharing of the analyst's emotional interplay with the patient is a reliable protection against the formation of a transference psychosis. Sharing does not in any way mean a free for all. This need is even more pronounced in working with some borderline patients. To set limits, to guard against becoming the excessive target of hostile operations, to be concerned with acting out, and to confront the patient with on-going difficulties in the analysis and elsewhere are essential technical considerations. Furthermore, the analyst needs to maintain his professional role committment in an unequivocal fashion. It does not mean that he has two inherently different faces as a person and as an analyst. He simply cannot lose sight of the fact that he is there to actively collaborate with the patient toward a goal that is of benefit to the patient.

Once more I wish to reiterate my firm belief that all technical considerations are variations on a basic theme. What emerges is a set of therapeutic transactions that tend to differ with each individual to some degree and related to the quality as well as the intensity of characteristic defenses and counterdefenses in the particular clinical syndrome that is in evidence.

At this point I wish to present two more clinical vignettes in connection with the borderline syndrome.

One patient in this category was a single woman in her mid 30s who had been successful in her career. She was in her early 30s when she had her first sexual experience, and most of her boyfriends were married men. The patient was appealing in both appearance and personality, and she never experienced difficulty in attracting men. Nevertheless, she had isolated herself to a major degree, had kept any manifestation of anger and aggressivity under rigid control, while curtailing her emotional involvement at the same time. Her ability to be in touch with her own needs and requirements was markedly kept outside of her awareness.

When she first came to see me she was involved with a married man who was totally settled in his lifestyle and had no intention of changing it. She met this man not more than once a week for a few hours in her apartment and spent every weekend in isolation, waiting for his phone call, which usually never came.

She was finally able to emancipate herself from this unrewarding situation after approximately one year of therapy. At that time she met a man on her vacation with whom she instantly fell in love. There were distinctly transferential components involved in her love affair that were subjected to detailed exploration in the analysis. We worked together reasonably well, until it became clear that she had fallen victim to a con artist who literally fed her pack of lies. It turned out that he had a wife and children. I pointed out the growing number of blatant contradictions, which she did not want to hear. The situation deteriorated further when she hired a private detective who confirmed the worst suspicions. This did not deter her deepening involvement in a distinctly destructive relationship. Finally, I felt compelled to confront her with the fact that I could not in good conscience lend my support to a person who was determined to put a noose around her neck. All efforts to stop her acting out and end her blind selfdestructiveness were to no avail. Accordingly, I suggested that she have a consultation, as a way of discussing the situation with another analyst, which she refused. At that point I informed her that I found myself unable to continue our work unless she found a way of extricating herself from an illusory and highly damaging love affair. All efforts to analyze her behavior were fruitless, and her analysis was terminated after I confronted her with my unwillingness to be a party to her unfortunate need to hurt herself. About one and a half years later the patient came back to me. It seems that she had to see her misery through to the last humiliating detail before she could let go of this man. Even then, she found it difficult to accept the obvious fact that the man had been a miserable psychopath. We worked our way through a number of cliff-hanging episodes in which she managed to come through with only minor scars. There was one danger-fraught situation when she expected to marry a man who proposed to her, but who knew her only in a most superficial and casual fashion. She had a relatively close call with disaster in this case but managed to extricate herself reasonably well. I recall a spontaneous and unexpected exclamation, "You can't be serious about this matter!" which surprised both of us. As time went on her dreams served as increasingly useful guidelines to her self-defeating behavior, which eventually included both her professional as well as her personal life. It was the patient's impression that I helped her the most when I "fired her from the analysis," as she put it. Her improvement was slow but steady, with a mutual appreciation of the nature of her defenses and my way of reacting to them. In retrospect I realize that I minimized a persecutory, paranoid trend on the patients's part. It is possible that I could have seen things through with her when I resigned as her analyst or "fired her," if I had faced with her more directly my feelings of intimidation associated with her paranoid fury. The thought occurred to me when I learned a significant aspect of the

patient's life experience. In connection with a dream association the patient informed me that there was considerable
evidence that her mother may have committed suicide. The
important consideration was not whether she actually did or
did not kill herself. What impressed me was the fact that the
patient always suspected it without permitting herself to
acknowledge her feelings about her mother's death. This
revelation was accompanied by a most unusual emotional
outburst on the patient's part as well as by an affirmation of
the feeling tone as it affected me at that time. Looking back, I
couldn't help receiving the impression, which I have since
shared with her, that her destructive acting out that led to the
temporary termination of her analysis was the equivalent of a
suicidal attempt on her part.

Here is another situation illustrative of a distinctly personalized transaction in the therapeutic process. It pertains to
a 19-year-old girl who had a history of frequently running
away from home in her early adolescence. She came from a
socioeconomic background where this type of behavior was
very rare. At one time she arranged to go to a foreign country
and lived with a family whom she expected to become her
substitute parents. It did not work out for her, and she requested her actual parents to bring her back home which they
did. The patient tended to ingratiate herself with people in
spite of basically being very much of a loner. Overt and covert
anger were areas of major difficulty for her, and she experienced distinct difficulties in being in touch with her own
genuine needs and requirements.

The patient encountered a host of problems in her
freshman year in college and dropped out after no more than
6 to 8 weeks. Upon returning home she made a serious suicidal attempt, which led to a 3-week psychiatric hospitalization.
I saw her directly following her release from the hospital. We
worked together reasonably well until the patient insisted that
she had lost her ability to mobilize emotional attitudes and
feelings. Furthermore, she wanted to have it clearly understood that there was no way in which her feelings could ever be
brought back to life again. Suddenly she informed me that she
had decided not to see me any longer. Interestingly enough,
her termination announcement coincided with the time of my

summer vacation, which she rejected as having any meaning to her. I arranged with her consent a "summit" meeting with her parents, and she left the possibility open of returning in the fall.

From then on there was a distinct improvement in the relational pattern between us, and she showed unmistakable progress in several areas. Suddenly we hit a stormy stretch when I had to leave town for a few days. Upon my return she telephoned me from the ward of a general hospital where she had been admitted as an emergency in the middle of the night because of an acute vaginitis complicated by an inability to urinate. I visited her at the hospital the day she called and found her reaction to me strange. It was not until a week later, when she resumed her sessions with me, that I learned what really happened. She had picked up a young Frenchman in New York and agreed to have him stay with her in her apartment. She had her first sexual relationship which took place before I had left and which she had concealed from me. However, she saw to it that her parents were informed about the sexual affair by the hospital's gynecologist. As it turned out later, she had told a different story to everybody, while at the same time withholding the information of her psychiatric contact with me. There were numerous transferential aspects involved which culminated in a lengthy letter to her gynecologist. This letter was clearly a displacement and was meant for me.

My initial reaction to her widely broadcast defloration was a distinctly protective attitude. Then I felt let down by her concealment of the earlier events, which coincided with a reduction of my contact with her. (It should be mentioned here that the parents had shown active resistance to her contact with me and had been responsible for cutting down the number of sessions. It should also be mentioned that her way of dressing had been rather bizarre and slovenly until very recently, when she suddenly paid attention to her appearance.) Next, she had a series of dreams with obvious sexual implications with the analyst lying nude on a bed while she was attentive to young men.

All these events were carefully explored and discussed in the therapeutic sessions. The understanding we reached was that she was gaining a measure of independence from her parents. We also learned that many events in her earlier life had been sexualized by the parents. The patient had what she called a lesbianlike contact with her prudish mother, whereas the father enjoyed embarrassing the patient by crude sexual references. In regared to the analyst, she spoke of a mixture of seeing him in the role of her painting teacher, her voice teacher, and her father. All this took place prior to the above-mentioned dramatic episode.

After the facts had become known to me, the patient reverted to an early pattern in her contact with me, that is, coming consistently late for her hour. My initial response to her acting out was a somewhat narcissistic feeling of failure. Her progress had been most encouraging, and I felt that I had missed something important since I had lulled myself in a false sense of believing things were going well. My mentioning this to the patient provoked two significant responses. First, she felt that she had play-acted by pretending more of a commitment than there actually was on her part. She said that she was basically too suspicious a person to get that much involved in any situation. Her second comment was that she has a way of getting overinvolved with one person that automatically pushed the other person out of the picture. She said "I really know better but that is the way I react" as if it were a quantitative measuring system. She also told me that she had talked to her voice teacher who, after having met the patient's mother, said that the patient had stepped into her mother's shoes and was behaving like her.

In regard to the countertransference, I became aware of several elements. One category of responses falls in the classic category of countertransference; that is, I unwittingly competed with her parents by overstressing my capacity to understand her while experiencing an excessive antagonism with their resistance to her progress. Furthermore, I did not sufficiently tune in to her "flight into health" as an indication of her deep-seated pessimism. I also assumed the narcissistic role of the successful "healer" with an overdose of satisfaction from it. By the same token, I did not uncover with sufficient consistency the patient's aggression, hostility, and emotional overinvolvement. For the better part, these attitudes were clearly within my therapeutic field of vision. My potential shortcoming here was the lack of courage or freedm to cut through an unwelcome protective layer on my part.

In this case the patient signaled the presence of a communicative barrier in the therapeutic relationship that I initially failed to notice. It led to conscious self-monitoring on the part of the therapist and a judicious sharing of the information with the patient. In discussing the above-described events, the therapist acknowledged an overprotective attitude on his part, as well as a need to desexualize the patient as if she were a little girl. This attitude played into the patient's need to conceal her sexual experimentation from the therapist. At the same time the patient began to speak about her feeling of a pseudocommitment to the therapy while giving evidence of a more genuine involvement than she had been aware of. We learned in this connection about her concern of overinvolvement with one single person as a one-way street that, to her way of thinking, automatically cut off all other contacts. She also confided deep-seated feelings of suspiciousness and anger that had not been clearly expressed before.

The Hypochondriasis Syndrome

In concluding this chapter I wish to discuss the syndrome of hypochondriasis. As a symptom it does not require any detailed description, because its manifestations and its widespread occurrence are common knowledge. The familiarity with this clinical syndrome tends to obscure its complexity and enables hypochondriacal phenomena to mask a host of mental disorders from mild to severe forms. Another technical problem is posed, because one frequently cannot outright dismiss the possibility of an obscure ailment. Neither is the field of medicine above the possibility of human error, nor have we reached clarity above all that can go wrong with our biological systems.

The way things are, hypochondriasis is a major challenge to most medical, psychiatric, and psychoanalytic practitioners.

It is also a dilemma with distinct social implications, for it reflects a society's attitude toward a form of misery that many times eludes tangible evidence of dealing with a known physical illness. Hypochondriasis should not be viewed as a form of malingering, because it does reflect a source of distinct personal distress.

There are many instances in which people with hypochondriacal manifestations experience great relief when a bona fide physical illness is diagnosed. They tend to feel vindicated when even serious organic conditions are discovered. A sensation of righteousness may appear in spite of sadness in receiving some grim medical news.

The field of psychiatry has known about the hypochondriacal syndrome for a very long time. With the advent of psychoanalysis the potentially morbid side of hypochondriasis was recognized. Freud thought that hypochondriasis had the same relation to paranoia as anxiety neurosis has to hysteria.

Sullivan had some interesting thoughts about the hypochondriacal syndrome. He viewed it as a particular kind of security operation. The self-esteem of the hypochondriac has been organized in such a fashion that bodily phenomena are given a great deal of highly pessimistic attention. For the hypochondriac, an intense, morbid preoccupation with his body serves as a distraction from a stressful interpersonal situation, and, concurrently, the recognition of anxiety is minimized or avoided. The hypochondriacal person has difficulty in achieving any genuine satisfaction, because he is constantly haunted by the shadow of impending doom. Hypochondriasis is further characterized by an implicit symbolism that is body centered and reflects a regression of cognition. It is this regression of the cognitive operations that links the hypochondriacal thought processes to certain schizophrenic thought processes. Sullivan formulated his ideas on the subject as follows: "It is as if the hypochondriacal patient had abondoned the field of interpersonal relations as a source of security, excepting in one particular. He has to communicate data as to his symptoms; the illness, so to speak, becomes the the presenting aspect of his personality.[1]

This compulsion to present the physical symptoms as the major part of the personality can present a difficult technical problem. I have encountered hypochondriacal patients who did not appear even to have abandoned the field of interpersonal relations as their source of security. They never came to experience the type of verbal communications that transcends somatization or body language as the only means of establishing contact. To be able to have a stomachache or some form of physical distress may serve as a safe channel of communication in families where spontaneous verbal rapport is not practiced or outright discouraged. Accordingly, some hypochondriacal people have an experiential void in uncomplicated, spontaneous verbal communication.

The difficulty in therapy is such cases centers frequently around the never-ending invitation on the part of the analyst to encourage the patient's awareness of a thought, feeling, or wish with the freedom to verbalize it. It is a tedious, time-consuming, and not always encouraging procedure. Chapter 5 contains an illustration of a patient with recurrent eye symptoms and discusses the course of therapeutic transaction with the patient's hypochondriacal phase.

More specifically, I have dealt with a number of patients who presented hypochondriacal manifestations. I worked for a Veterans Clinic immediately after World War II. At that time I was in the habit of making a short speech to the patients who complained of chronic back pain. All the patients had been carefully checked out for neurological, orthopedic, or internal problems. Each person knew that the medical findings had been negative. This gave me an opportunity to say that some people tend to experience physical tension symptoms when they are under personal stress and strain. We discussed their developmental and current life situations with an eye on discovering areas of conflict. At the end of such a session the patient would often express appreciation about my interesting comments only to inquire politely, "But how about my back? It hurts." As time went on I recognized the futility of my approach. Instead, I would make an effort to preempt the nature of the physical complaint by saying that I was not qualified to treat or cure their back condition. My expertise was in the field of psychiatry, which deals with human relations and a wide range of human feelings. Did they care to discuss any personal matters with me related to their emotions and their significant dealings with others? Some of them declined to do this or said there was really nothing they had to say in that respect. The majority, however, took up the invitation and began to verbalize various interpersonal experiences.

On a more analytic level, I saw a young married woman who had a number of children. Her tolerance for her mother's morbid preoccupation with physical illness was low, and she could not control her own florid imagination about her own as well as her children's state of ill health, or rather, the never-ending anxiety about it. The patient lived in a state of constant apprehension that an illness of fatal nature had befallen her, her children, or others about whom she cared deeply. Her fear of malignancies ranging from leukemia to every imaginable form of cancer tortured her mind morning, noon, and night.

Much of our early work centered on her symptoms, on the time and circumstances when they first occurred, and on the purpose they may have served, particularly on possible areas of displacement. Frequent reference was made to her relationship with her mother and some overlapping patterns that pertained to her husband. It required a considerable amount of time to transcend her compulsive hypochondriacal and phobic preoccupations. Gradually but slowly a minimum of personal information trickled through the maze of somatic metaphors. A few personal fantasies with a masochistic quality came to the fore while much of her communications were still fixated on a morbid level. It seemed as if my countertransference could not fully detach itself from her incessant need to deal predominantly with her thoughts of physical doom. Her presentations had a poignant quality to them, and I detected a mild note of morbid fascination with her symptoms on my part. The thought occurred to me when I realized that I neither got bored nor irritated with her endless, alarming dramatizations. Finally, I caught on to the fact that the patient's vivid imagination indicated a genuine gift on her part as a story teller. I realized that she was a highly talented individual who never had allowed herself to give vent to her creative side. It was a genuine pleasure to listen to her stories about people, about her personal observations and the scope of her emotional range in discussing other people's predicaments. I told the patient my impressions about her native gift, which she first tried to brush off, but she later came to understand what my opinion was based on.

A series of highly dramatic events took place in this woman's life, which are not relevant to my illustration of the hypochondriacal syndrome and certain technical considerations connected with it. What emerged with increasing clarity, however, was the remarkable widening of the patient's communicative channels. We fruitfully explored significant aspects of the transference-countertransference continuum. A wealth of intimate thoughts on the patient's past pertaining to her hopes, wishes, and fears emerged with considerable clarity. There were still minor flurries of hypochondriacal preoccupation without causing much commotion any longer. The analysis came to a satisfactory termination, and the presenting symptoms of hypochondriasis had receded to a nonmorbid level.

It is my conviction that the recognition of her finely tuned mind, her creative imagination, and her genuine gift as a story teller were significant therapeutic observations. She had not been in touch with the range of her imaginative capacities and had concentrated exclusively on the somatic channel to give vent to her variegated feelings. Many paranoid, frustrated, bitter and unhappy feelings had to be worked through before she could reveal the scope of her constructive sensitivities. The revelation that the patient had managed to hold the analyst's attention with basically unproductive material proved to be helpful. It was possible to demonstrate to the patient that her repetitive somatic and phobic complaints ordinarily would evoke somnolent detachment or selective. inattention.

Summary

In this chapter, three clinical syndromes have been sketched. No concerted effort has been made to delve into causative explanations of the entities under discussion. Instead, primary emphasis has been placed on descriptive, phenomenological manifestations of each nosological cluster.

Care has been taken to identify each syndrome by a set of characteristic phenomena that represent adaptational security operations based on unfortunate life experiences. The evolving clinical syndrome permits interprofessional communication and makes the consideration of technical procedures possible.

The hypothesis is advanced that the particular defenses or security operations that define a given syndrome evoke complex interrelational patterns within the observational field of contact between patient and analyst. In particular, it is the analyst's gamut of responses that need to be monitored by him and used as essential therapeutic material in the analysis. The therapeutic approach illustrated concerns itself with skillful self-observation and with an imaginative playback of countertransference experiences in the broadest sense of the term.

It may be argued that obsessionalism, borderline symptoms, and hypochondriasis are ubiquitous psychological phenomena that manifest themselves in one form or another in most mental disorders. This point is well taken and underlines the technical considerations discussed here with its focus on shared, basically familiar experiences rather than on dealing with terra incognita. In this connection it may also be taken into consideration that the overtly arbitrary selection of syndromes is not merely a matter of chance. It so happens that the entities chosen lend themselves particularly well to a discussion of certain technical procedures. The question arises, then, to what degree if any the therapeutic principles advocated here can be applied with more experience-distant manifestations as observed in schizophrenic, manic, psychopathic, and complex character disorders, to mention just a few psychopathological phenomena. There are significant variations of the basic therapeutic scheme proposed in this text. A detailed discussion of technical considerations to the above-mentioned syndromes, however, transcends the scope of this book by a wide margin and requires a separate text.

Now, I would like to sum up in greatly abbreviated form the essence of each nosological category included in the triad of syndromes outlined.

Obsessional defenses on the part of the patient tend to

mobilize obsessional aspects in the analyst's personality. His ability to confront the patient with mutually defensive operations when and where they occur in the analytic situation is a key factor in demonstrating reciprocal security operations. The uncovering of masking operations pertaining to both analyst and patient within the relational context constitutes a significant therapeutic modality. An interweaving between past and present events is not merely intended to bring back early memories. It usually serves the additional purpose of highlighting how people's life experiences contributed to making them into who they are today. By the same token, it illustrates how people tend to resist change, even if it be change for the better. Familiar defenses produce a false sense of security, and the risk of taking an untrodden psychological path often leads to resistance. A particular area of security operations centers around the freedom to permit appropriate tender and affectionate emotions to emerge without unduly hiding behind self-protective operations in the nature of setting up unnecessary distance-making attitudes.

Borderline manifestations call out a wide range of security operations in most analysts. The ability to evoke underlying anger and aggression in oneself as well as in the patient is a most difficult task. Dealing with social distancing and intense emotional involvements pertaining to both parties involved in the therapeutic situation is demanding, frequently threatening, and not free of pitfalls. Finally, the freedom to be in touch with one's basic needs, requirements, and satisfaction as an analyst is a prerequisite in confronting the patient with this common dilemma.

In hypochondriasis the analyst is often confronted with either feelings of overprotectiveness, irritation, or potential manipulation. The countertransference to a deluge of hypochondriacal complaints differs from analyst to analyst. It proves to be helpful, however, to recognize the symbolic, metaphoric quality of somatic language and be in touch with the experiential poverty this symptom frequently represents. A major therapeutic consideration rests in the analyst's ability to share with the patient the analyst's range of responses to the monosyllabic language of the hypochondriacal person.

Postcript

In bringing this book to a close I hope that the material presented has renewed some readers' interest in Sullivanian psychiatry and that others may have been encouraged to familiarize themselves with interpersonal theory and practice. The primary purpose of critically exploring Sullivan's contributions and expanding the range of their clinical application is to enlarge the extant body of knowledge in the psychiatric field, that is, psychiatry as defined as the study of interpersonal relations under ordinary as well as under morbid circumstances. The clarification and the coding of relevant data pertaining to the immensely complex process of people living with and among each other in workable patterns is a formidable task.

Personality cults have no place in any major discipline. The brilliant observations, speculations, and innovations by the pioneers in psychoanalysis represent historical landmarks and deserve lasting monuments to be built for them. Each and all of them to different degrees has played a part in remodeling the psychological profile of our era. It does not change the fact that the importance given to some of the psychoanalytic pioneers is often not what they deserve based on the merit of the contribution. For my part, I consider Sullivan next to Freud as the most significant figure in the field of psychological contributions. Regardless of the validity of my opinion about Sullivan's status or the lack of it, we are in no way entitled to reify his ideas and formulations. There is no longer viable living space for competing theories about mental health and mental illness. An urgent need exists for incorporating the growing body of empirical data in the overall structure of psychoanalytic theory and practice.

The next required step is to recognize the necessity for all psychoanalytic schools of thought to find a mutually productive *modus vivendi*. Excessive institutionalization and systematization of psychological tenets hinders progress in the overall field. We have lived too long with the illusion of building a science while relying on predominantly philosophical assumptions. Information must be shared by all psychoanalytic schools of thought in a spirit of genuine collaboration, lest we disintegrate into psychoanalytic splinter groups to the detriment of all. There is also an urgent need for a rapprochement and a dialogue with other disciplines. Social and cultural factors profoundly affect patients and practitioners alike.

It no longer suffices to have a psychoanalytic belief and to abide by it. Empirical data and clinical observations need to be brought on a common denominator toward an expanding general field of psychoanalysis. As in every major specialty, we are able to coexist with a number of divergent ideologies without setting up unproductive closed systems that weaken the field by unnecessary infighting.

Psychoanalysis is a derivative of philosophy ranging from the Age of Enlightenment to various other formative phases. It has emerged as a hybrid between philosophy, psychology, and medicine. As philosophy it rests on speculative assumptions that so far have eluded definite knowledge. As psychology it is caught between humanistic, behavioristic, and psychodynamic considerations. As part of medicine it has fallen heir to a mixture of biologic ideation, theoretical speculation, and a basically authoritarian doctor-patient model. In addition, psychoanalysis has been increasingly integrated into many socioeconomic and political currents of our time. Be that as it may, psychoanalysis is still torn between knowledge and dogma. By contrast, emerging open-ended, ecologically oriented systems point in a remedial, constructive direction for the overall advancement of psychoanalysis. A distinct shift from metapsychology to epistemology is under way and offers distinct hope for a specialty that has been unduly divided within its own ranks.

Going back in history we realize that the scientific thought of ancient philosophers had the virtue of wholeness. By intuition and philosophical assumption alone great minds felt competent to discuss any subject their intellectual powers would allow. They were as much religious thinkers as philosophers and physical scientists. There were no walls between metaphysical speculation and scientific observation.

What is called for in the words of the Nobel laureate Erwin Schroedinger is to expose errors of the past that have been perpetuated as unconscious presuppositions in ourselves.

Only by studying them carefully may we come to recognize our relationship with them and and liberate ourselves from an unrealized tyranny.

Harry Stack Sullivan
A Biographical Sketch

Harry Stack Sullivan was born in Norwich, a small upstate New York town, on February 21, 1892. The grandson of Irish immigrants who thought to better their lot in the New World, the son of a withdrawn, poor farmer and a complaining, semiinvalid mother — Sullivan was raised in the secluded atmosphere of a farm near his birthplace. In a region traditionally Protestant and Republican, theirs was the only Catholic family. Though his parents had three children, he alone survived infancy and had neither playmates or companions to mitigate the rigors of a sequestered existence.

Little else is known of his formative years except what has been recorded by a close friend and colleague, Clara Thompson. In an address[1] delivered at a memorial service for Sullivan on February 11, 1949, she mentions the isolation and loneliness of Sullivan's childhood, and she describes his mother as a chronically dissatisfied woman — who felt she had married beneath her — who offered little warmth or affection to her small son. Instead, she used him as a coathanger for her own fantasies. In contrast, the father is depicted as a shy, pensive man whose occasional words of approval meant a great deal to the boy.

As may be expected in one whose only companions were mind and imagination, young Sullivan had a mystical, sentimental side to his nature best illustrated by a special fondness for a tale told to him by the mother. In it, one of Sullivan's ancestors was the West Wind who, in the shape of a horse, ran towards the sunrise to meet the future. The impact of this tale was such that Sullivan made the horse a kind of symbol for himself. Possibly Sullivan's identification with his mother's feelings of a special ancestry indicates a stronger tie to her than Clara Thompson implies.

Upon reaching school age, he felt out of place with his peers and — as one would also expect — suffered greatly from his self-consciousness and isolation. Gradually, he began to develop a strong interest in a field that influenced some of his psychiatric formulations later in life — physics. However, he elected to enter medical school where, again, his poverty and social isolation distanced him from his contemporaries. After receiving his medical degree at the Chicago College of Medicine and Surgery in 1917, he served as a first lieutenant in World War I and remained in government service until 1923 as liaison officer at St. Elizabeth Hospital, Washington, D.C. It was here that he met Dr William Alanson White, a figure of major significance in his professional life.

Later that year, Sullivan went to the Sheppard Enoch Pratt Hospital in Baltimore where he first met Clara Thompson. Their friendship would persist "with unswerving loyalty over twenty-five years," and one of her favorite stories was a description of their initial meeting. Sullivan, it should first be said, was slow in making friends and subjected people to prolonged tests. Once a person had made it as "persona grata," that is, as a person who stood up under his careful scrutiny, Sullivan offered his unstinting support and loyalty. Self-interest never entered his mind where loyalty to a friend was involved. Also, he had a particular fondness for people who were schizophrenic or, at least, markedly schizoid. His compassion for severly troubled people went so far that he accorded them a special status. To Sullivan, being schizophrenic meant to be particularly sensitive and a potential member of a special class of human nobility.

As Clara Thompson's story goes, she was seriously ill with an attack of typhoid fever when she presented a paper on suicide in schizophrenic patients. Sullivan, listening to the presentation, was led by her afflicted appearance to the "happy conclusion" that Clara Thompson suffered from schizophrenia. "And so," she said, "an attack of typhoid fever is responsible for one of the richest friendships in my life."

Both had that mutual interest in people, which constituted a strong bond between them. Both shared a basic respect for people in distress as well as a strong sense of dedication to working with them. In her address, she adds that she "soon learned that this man, who in public could tear a bad paper to bits with his scathing sarcasm, had another side — a gentle, warm friendly one. This was the side he showed to his patients. Anyone who has seen him talk with a disturbed catatonic can know that he has seen the real Harry without pretence or defenses. There was nothing maudlin about his tenderness — it rather conveyed a feeling of deep understanding."

In 1925 Sullivan became Director of Clinical Research at the hospital where he devoted himself to the intensive study of schizophrenic disorders. At the same time, he was associate professor of psychiatry at the University of Maryland School of Medicine.

Here, the reader is referred to Helen Swick Perry's introduction to the posthumous publication of Sullivan's *Schizophrenia as a Human Process*. (Crowley ©126) In it she refers to a specially designed receiving ward for male schizophrenic patients which Sullivan set up for six patients within the hospital as a forerunner to a therapeutic community. Sullivan isolated the patients from the female nursing staff as well as from the convential hospital routine. He trained a number of hand-picked male attendants in the role of special therapeutic assistants, and he installed an intricate system of communication between the attendants, the patients, and himself. He changed the traditional role of the hospital attendants involved in the project by making them an integral part of the therapeutic endeavor. As an indication of the involvement of the attendants, it is stated that some of them underwent a personal analysis at that time. In other words, Sullivan was the mastermind of the therapeutic community, served as a supervisor, therapist, and communicative agent in an intensive, on-going communicative system, designed to study and improve the lot of people caught in a schizophrenic dilemma. Sullivan had a firm conviction that psychiatric study could render psychiatric data that was valid only if the study were conducted in an atmosphere specifically designed to improve the patient's Self-esteem. In the course of his research into schizophrenic ways of living, Sullivan came to recognize the impact of sociocultural factors in the dynamics of mental disorders. He focused his attention increasingly on the trans- action between native, human endowment and existential experience with people of emotional significance. To Sulli- van, the psychiatric field consists mainly of the constant in- terplay between the preordained stepladder of maturation and the process of socialization and acculturation. This con- cept formed the foundation for his interpersonal theory.

In 1931 Sullivan moved to New York City, where he en- tered private practice. His major psychiatric field of study during the New York years was the work with obsessional neurotic patients. He returned to Washington in 1939, where he became a consultant to the Selective Service System.

Sullivan had a major problem as a writer. He did not have the facile and productive pen of a Freud (Freud was awarded the Goethe Award for his brilliant prose). At one point, Sulli- van confided that he wrote for two kinds of an imaginary audience. He conceived of a group of readers who would be unable to understand him regardless how lucid his presenta- tion was. In his mind he called this group "wrong-headed idiots." By contrast, he imagined a group of geniuses who would make fun of the simplicity of the material. Be that as it may, Sullivan did not have a single book published during his life-time. Though he circulated a few copies of his con- templated book "Personal Psychopathology," its actual publi- cation had to wait for about 40 years. All the other books published in Sullivan's name were posthumously edited transcriptions of lectures that had been recorded during Sul- livan's lifetime (he carried a tape recorder along while lectur- ing). His other posthumous publications are collections of various papers previously published in professional journals.

Every major thinker has been stimulated, influenced, and affected by the thoughts of other original thinkers in his own or related fields. Sullivan is no exception in this respect, but it is a sterile preoccupation to trace every thought to its original source. This is not necessary, possible, or even helpful in many instances. For one thing, ideas do not always have a linear tracing to a particular root. An original mind frequently tends to make novel associations between known concepts, and creative thinking is not necessarily based on unchartered territory.

Sullivan was indebted to a number of predecessors and contemporaries. Only a few influential persons in connection with his interpersonal theory need be mentioned. No attempt is made to cover the entire field.

First of all it should be acknowledged that Freud's genius cast a strong shadow on Sullivan's psychological point of view. Among psychiatrists the influence of Adolf Meyer, William Alanson White, Edward Kempf, and David Levy can be cited.

Sullivan's rapprochment between psychiatry and the social sciences is the *leitmotif* of his interpersonal theory of therapy. Here, the impact of George Herbert Mead with his conceptualization of mind, society, and the self is very strong. One may want to add Cooley, Baldwin, and other early sociologists. Sullivan's friendship with cultural anthropologist Edward Sapir and with Ruth Benedict had a distinct impact on his formulations.

Sullivan had a strong interest in establishing an interdisciplinary basis for the study of psychiatry. He actively participated in the founding of the Washington School of Psychiatry, which was designed to foster a cross fertilization between a number of specialties connected with the study of man. The William Alanson White Institute in New York became an offshoot of the Washington School of Psychiatry until 1946, when it became an independent training center. Sullivan was also active as the co-editor and, later, editor in chief of *Psychiatry*, A Journal for the Operational Statement of Interpersonal Relations.

Finally, he was an active participant of the world Federation for Mental Health and was deeply concerned with world peace and promoting a constructive dialogue among nations.

Clara Thompson described this aspect of Sullivan as "a fire within him, which sustained his frail body in the last physically ill years of his life. Several times in the last few years he outwitted death in a way that seemed like a miracle. He wanted to live and he lived productively. He will go on living with us and through us, who have known him."

In January 1949 a UNESCO meeting was held in Paris which addressed itself to the alleviation of tensions leading to wars. Harry Stack Sullivan died while attending that meeting.

Harry Stack Sullivan
The Complete Bibliography[1]

BY RALPH CROWLEY, M.D.

1924
1. Schizophrenia: Its conservative and malignant features. *American Journal of Psychiatry,* **81:**77-91. Reprinted in #126, 7-22.
2. Varieties of repression (Paper read at American Psychoanalytic Association, December 28, 1921); abstract in (1925), *Psychoanalytic Review,* **12:**333-334.

1925
3. The oral complex. *Psychoanalytic Review,* **12:**30-38.
4. Peculiarity of thought in schizophrenia. *American Journal of Psychiatry,* **82:**21-86. Reprinted in #126, 26-99.

1926
5. Erogenous maturation. *Psychoanalytic Review,* **13:**1-15.
6. Regression: A consideration of reversive mental processes. *State Hospital Quarterly,* **11:**208-217, 387-394, 651-668; abstract in (1925), *Psychoanalytic Review,* **12:**463.
7. The importance of a study of symbols in psychiatry. *Psyche (London),* **7:**81-93.

1927
8. Affective experience in early schizophrenia. *American Journal of Psychiatry,* **83:**467-483. (See 1928.)

9. The onset of schizophrenia. *American Journal of Psychiatry,* **84:**105-134. Reprinted in #126, 104-136.
10. Discussion. The constitutional psychopathic inferior, by A. H. Bryant. *American Journal of Psychiatry,* **83:**684-685.
11. Mental hygiene and the modern world. *Modern World,* **1:**153-157.

[1] This attempt at a definitive bibliography of Harry Stack Sullivan was made possible by the contributions of Helen Swick Perry, editor of Sullivan's posthumous books, and Dr. N. Stockhamer.

12. The common field of research and clinical psychiatry. *Psychiatric Quarterly,* **1:**276-291. Reprinted in #126, 140-156.
13. Discussion—The narrowing of the gap between the functional and the organic by William Alanson White. *American Journal of Psychiatry,* **84:**228-229.
14. Discussion. Psychiatry and its relation to the social sciences, by William Alanson White. Proceedings, Social Science Research Council Conference, Dartmouth College, Hanover. N.H. Mimeographed. (See Addenda, 1931.)

1928
15. Affective experience in early schizophrenia. *Proceedings Association Research in Nervous and Mental Disease,* **5:**141-158 (see #8).
16. Tentative criteria of malignancy in schizophrenia. *American Journal of Psychiatry,* **84:**759-787. Reprtined in #126, 158-183.
17. Medical education—An editorial comment. *American Journal of Psychiatry,* **84:**837-839.
18. Politics in state hospital systems—An editorial comment. *American Journal of Psychiatry,* **84:**1077.
19. Psychiatric research—An editorial comment. *American Journal of Psychiatry,* **84:**1075-1077.
20. Query—An editorial comment. *American Journal of Psychiatry,* **85:**188-190.

1929
21. *Proceedings First Colloquium on Personality Investigation* (with the American Psychiatric Association Committee on Relations with the Social Sciences). Baltimore, Md.: The Lord Baltimore Press, 102 pages. (Sullivan present throughout conference. His own remarks are on pp. 59-63.) Reprints available from Xerox University Microfilms, Ann Arbor, Mich. 48106. Ask for #OP51673.
22. Research in schizophrenia. *American Journal of Psychiatry,* **86:**553-567. Reprinted in #126, 186-202.
23. Discussion. The relation of endocrinopathic states to conduct disorders of children, by Louis Lurie. *American Journal of Psychiatry,* **86:**305.
24. Discussion. The three levels of cortical elaboration in relation to certain psychiatric symptoms, by Samuel A. Orton. *American Journal of Psychiatry,* **85:**655-656.
25. *Proceedings Research Conference.* Chicago, Ill.: American Religious Education Association.

1930

26. Archaic sexual culture and schizophrenia. Ed. N. Haire. *Proceedings of the Third International Conference for Sexual Reform,* London, September 8-14, 1929. London: Kegan Paul, Trench, Trubner & Co., pp. 495-501. Reprinted in #126, 206-215.

27. Abstract. The socio-genesis of homosexual behavior in males. *American Sociology Society Papers,* **24:**281-282.

28. *Proceedings Second Colloquium on Personality Investigation* (with the American Psychiatric Association Committee on Relations of Psychiatry and the Social Science Research Council), Baltimore, Md.: The Johns Hopkins Press, 206 pages. (Sullivan present throughout the conference; his own comments are interspersed with others pp. 43-154.) See also Selected bibliographies, *American Journal of Psychiatry,* **87:**146. Reprinted in #126, 218-232. Complete reprints available from Xerox University Microfilms, Ann Arbor, Mich. 48106. Ask for #OP51674.

29. *Farewell Lectures.* Sheppard & Enoch Pratt Hospital. Privately circulated. Reprinted in *Personal Psychopathology,* #35 and #128. (See Addenda, 1965.)

1931

30. The relation of onset to outcome in schizophrenia. In *Schizophrenia* (Dementia Praecox), Proceedings, Association for Research in Nervous and Mental Disease, Dec. 27-28, 1929. New York: Williams and Wilkins. **10:**111-118. Reprinted in #126, 236-244.

31. Environmental factors in etiology and course under treatment of schizophrenia. *Medical Journal and Record.* **133:**19-22. Reprinted in #126, 246-255.

32. Socio-psychiatric research: Its implications for the schizophrenia problem and for mental hygiene. *American Journal of Psychiatry.* **87:**977-991. Reprinted in #126, 256-270.

33. The training of the psychiatrist. IV: Training of the general medical student in psychiatry. *American Journal of Orthopsychiatry,* **1:**371-379.

34. The modified psychoanalytic treatment of schizophrenia. *American Journal of Psychiatry,* **88:**519-540. Reprinted in #126, 272-294.

1932

35. *Personal Psychopathology.* Privately circulated. Available later in mimeographed form by William Alanson White Psychiatric

Foundation. See #28 and #128; pp. 205-235 of Chapter 7 reprinted in #126, 321-351. (See also #128 and Addenda, 1965.)

1933

36. Mental disorders. *Encyclopaedia of the Social Sciences,* **10:**313-319. Reprinted in #126, 297-307.
37. Psychoanalysis and psychiatric education. *Proceedings National Committee for Mental Hygiene; Conference on Psychiatric Education.*

1934

38. Psychiatry. *Encyclopaedia of the Social Sciences,* **12:**578-580. Reprinted in #127, 7-12.

1935

39. Psychiatric training as a prerequisite to psychoanalytic practice. *American Journal of Psychiatry,* **91:**1117-1126. Reprinted in #126, 309-318.
40. Abstract of discussion. *Proceedings National Research Council Conference on Personality and Culture.*
41. *Proceedings First Conference National Research Council Sub-Committee on Training Fellowships.* Dec. 21, 1935. Unpublished; privately circulated; in files of the William Alanson White Psychiatric Foundation, Washington, D.C.

1937

42. A note on the implications of psychiatry, the study of interpersonal relations, for investigations in the social sciences, *American Journal of Sociology,* **42:**848-861. Reprinted in #127, 15-29. Also in part in Eds. S. J. Beck and H. B. Molish. *Reflexes to Intelligence: A Reader in Clinical Psychology* (1959). Glencoe, Ill.: Free Press, pp. 101-107.
43. William Alanson White—1870-1937. *American Journal of Psychiatry,* **93:**1480-1482.

1938

44. Psychiatry: *Introduction to the study of interpersonal relations. Psychiatry,* **1:**121-134. Reprinted in (1949): Ed. P. Mullahy *A Study of Interpersonal Relations.* New York: Hermitage, pp. 98-121, and in #127, 32-55.
45. The William Alanson White Psychiatric Foundation—An editorial, *Psychiatry,* **1:**135-140.

46. The Washington School of Psychiatry—An editorial. *Psychiatry,*
     1:140-141.
47. This journal—An editorial. *Psychiatry,* **1:**141-143.
48. Discussion. Section meeting on culture and personality. *American Journal of Orthopsychiatry,* **8:**608-609.
49. Security of the American commonwealths—An editorial.
     Psychiatry, **1:**419-420.
50. Antisemitism—An editorial. *Psychiatry,* **1:**593-598. Reprinted
     in #127, 76-84.

1939
51. Intuition, reason and faith—An editorial. *Psychiatry.* **2:**129-
     132. Reprinted in #127, 60-65.
52. Psychiatry and the national defense—An editorial, *Psychiatry,*
     2:133-135.
53. Psychiatry and the national defense. *Naval Medical Bulletin,*
     37:273-276.
54. A note on formulating the relationship of the individual and
     the group. *American Journal of Sociology,* **44:**932-937. Reprinted in #127, 67-73.
55. Edward Sapir, Ph.D., Sc.D., 1884-1939. *Psychiatry,* **2:**159.
56. The support of psychiatric research and teaching—An editorial. *Psychiatry,* **2:**273-279.
57. Summary and critique—A formal discussion of physical and
     cultural environment in relation to the conservation of mental health." In: Eds. F. R. Moulton and P. O. Komora *Mental
     Health.* Lancaster, Penna.: The Science Press, No. 9, Chapter 5, pp. 276-278.
58. Responsibility—An editorial (with Ernest E. Hadley and
     Thomas Harvey Gill). *Psychiatry,* **2:**599-602.

1940
59. Conceptions of modern psychiatry. The First William Alanson
     White Memorial Lectures. *Psychiatry,* **3:**1-117; Washington,
     D.C.: William Alanson White Psychiatric Foundation,
     vii + 147 pages. (See #97 and Addenda, 1953.)
60. Memorandum on a psychiatric reconnaissance, and a psychiatric gloss on a sociological study. Studies for the American
     Council on Education. Washington, D.C. (See #61 and
     #76.)
61. Discussion of the case of Warren Wall. A psychiatric gloss on a
     sociological study. In: Ed. E. F. Frazier *Studies of Negro Youth:
     Negro Youth at the Crossways.* Washington, D.C.: American

Council on Education, pp. 228-234. Reprinted in #127, 100-107.

62. National solidarity: Bulletin from the William Alanson White Psychiatric Foundation to psychiatrists and other physicians. *Psychiatry,* **3:**326-327.

63. The eagle, the lion, and the giant squid—An editorial. *Psychiatry,* **3:**437-441.

64. Memorandum on the utilization of psychiatry in the promotion of national security (from the William Alanson White Psychiatric Foundation). *Psychiatry,* **3:**483-492.

65. Endocrinoneuropsychiatry. *Psychiatry,* **3:**561-563.

66. Psychiatry and the national defense (with a Committee of the Southern Psychiatric Association). *Psychiatry,* **3:**619-624.

67. A minimum psychiatric inspection of registrants: William Alanson White Psychiatric Foundation Bulletin (largely incorporated in *U.S. Selective Service System Medical Bulletin, No. 1*). *Psychiatry,* **3:**625-627.

68. Propaganda and censorship: William Alanson White Psychiatric Foundation Memorandum. *Psychiatry,* **3:**628-632. Reprinted in #127, 111-119.

1941

69. Selective Service Psychiatry—An editorial. *Psychiatry,* **4:**118-120.

70. Psychiatry and the national defense. *Psychiatry,* **4:**201-217. Pages 201-212 reprinted in #127, 124-145.

71. A seminar on practical psychiatric diagnosis (for Selective Service System Psychiatrists). *Psychiatry,* **4:**265-283.

72. Sective Service Psychiatry (an extract from the President's annual report to the Board of Trustees of the William Alanson White Psychiatric Foundation). *Psychiatry,* **4:**440-464.

73. Psychiatry in the emergency. *Mental Hygiene,* **25:**5-10.

74. Psychiatric aspects of morale. *American Journal of Sociology,* **47:**277-301. Reprinted (1951) in Eds. A. Stanton and S. Perry *Personality and Political Crisis,* Glencoe, Ill.: The Free Press (cf. #88).

75. Mental hygiene and national defense. *Mental Health Bulletin of Illinois Society for Mental Hygiene.* **19**(March 1, 1941).

76. Memorandum on a psychiatric reconnaissance. In: Ed. C. S. Johnson *Growing Up in a Black Belt.* Washington, D.C.: American Council on Education, pp. 328-333. Reprinted in #127, 89-95.

110. Two international conferences of psychiatrists and social sciences. *Psychiatry,* **11:**223-229.
111. Psychiatry, education, and the UNESCO "Tensions Project." *Psychiatry,* **11:**371-375.
112. The school and international prospects—Address given at 1948 Convocation of Washington School of Psychiatry. *Psychiatry,* **11:**xvii-xx.
113. Ruth Fulton Benedict, Ph.D., D.Sc., 1887-1948. *Psychiatry,* **11:**402-403.

1949

114. The study of psychiatry; 1948 orienting lectures. *Psychiatry,* **12:**325-337. Pages 325-331 reprinted in #127, 256-266; abstract in (1953) *Psychoanalytic Review,* **40:**86.
115. The theory of anxiety and the nature of psychotherapy. *Psychiatry,* **12:**3-12; abstract by L. Rangell in *Psychoanalytic Quarterly,* **18:**553; in *Psychoanalytic Review,* **40:**73-74.
116. Discussion of *The Management of a type of institutional participation in mental illness* by Stanton and Schwartz. *Psychiatry,* **12:**23-25. Reprinted in (1954), Ed. H. Brand *The Study of Personality: A Book of Readings.* New York: Wiley: London: Chapman and Hall.

1950

117. Multidisciplined coordination of interpersonal data. In: Eds. S. Stansfield Sargent and Marian W. Smith *Culture and personality.* New York: Viking Fund (Now: Wenner-Gren Foundation for Anthropological Research), pp. 175-194.
118. The illusion of personal individuality. *Psychiatry,* **12:**317-332. Reprinted in part in #127, 98-126; abstract in (1954) *Psychoanalytic Review,* **41:**81-83.
119. Tensions interpersonal and international: A psychiatrist's view. In: Ed. Hadley Cantril *Tensions That Cause Wars.* Urbana, Ill.: University of Illinois Press, pp. 79-138. Reprinted in part in #128, 293-331, and in part in #123, 367-374 and 375-382.

1951

120. The psychiatric interview. *Psychiatry,* **14:**361-373. Reprinted with changes in #124, changes on 3-27; abstract by L. Rosengarten in (1953) *Psychoanalytic Quarterly,* **22:**456-457.
121. Psychiatric aspects of morale, In: Eds. Alfred Stanton and

Stewart E. Perry *Personality and Political Crisis.* Glencoe, Ill.: The Free Press, pp. 44-60. (Reprinted from (1941) *American Journal of Sociology,* but contains additional material.)

1952

122. The psychiatric interview. II. *Psychiatry,* **15:**127-141. Reprinted with changes in #124, see especially 28-34.

1953

123. *The Interpersonal Theory of Psychiatry.* (Eds. Helen Swick Perry and Mary L. Gawel introduction by Mabel Blake Cohen). New York: W. W. Norton, 393 pages. Chapter 16, Preadolescence, pp. 245-255 and 257-262; Chapter 17. Early Adolescence, pp. 263-276. Reprinted in (1955), Eds. C. Thompson, M. Mazer, and E. Witenberg *The Outline of Psychoanalysis,* revised ed. New York: Random House, pp. 248-274. Chapter 22, Towards a Psychiatry of Peoples, reprinted in (part): (1964) Eds. L. Bramson and G. W. Goethals *War Studies from Psychology, Sociology and Anthropology.* New York: Basic Books, pp. 105-118.

1954

124. *The Psychiatric Interview* (Eds. Helen Swick Perry and Mary Ladd Gawel; introduction by Otto Allen Will). New York: W. W. Norton, 246 pages. Reprinted in part in (1954), Basic concepts in the psychiatric interview, *Pastoral Psychology,* **5:**39-46.

1956

125. *Clinical Studies in Psychiatry* (Ed. Helen Swick Perry, Mary Ladd Gawel, and Martha Gibbon; foreword by Dexter M. Bullard) New York: W. W. Norton, 386 pages. Pages 371-376 reprinted in: (1959) The inefficient wife, Ed. Harold Greenwald *Great Cases in Psychoanalysis.* New York: Ballantine, pp. 201-207.

1962

126. *Schizophrenia as a Human Process* (Introduction and Commentaries by Helen Swick Perry). New York: W. W. Norton, 363 pages. (Reprints of papers from 1924-1935.)[2]

2. The first six of the Sullivan books are now available in paperback editions. (See also Addenda, 1953.)

1964

127. *The Fusion of Psychiatry and Social Science* (Introduction and Commentaries by Helen Swick Perry). New York: W. W. Norton, 346 pages. (Reprints of papers from 1934-1949.)[2]

1972

128. *Personal Psychopathology* (Introduction by Helen Swick Perry). New York: W. W. Norton. (See also #35 and Addenda, 1965.)

REVIEWS

(Published in *Psychiatry*)

Man Against Himself, by Karl Menninger, 1938, **1:**149.

After Freedom, by Hortense Powdermaker, 1939, **2:**142.

The Startle Pattern, by Carney Landis *et al.,* 1939, **2:**298.

The Exploration of the Inner World, by Anton T. Boisen, 1939, **2:**424-427.

Medical Diseases of War, by Sir Arthur Hurst *et al.,* 1940, **3:**442-443.

Psychiatry for the Curious, by George H. Preston, 1940, **3:**565.

The Psychology of Fear and Courage, by Edward Glover, 1940, **3:**565-567.

Psychological Effects of War on Citizen and Soldier, by R. D. Gillespie, 1942, **5:**443-447.

The Chrysanthemum and the Sword, by Ruth Benedict, 1947. **10:**214-216.

ADDENDA[3]

1925

REVIEWS

Practical Clinical Psychiatry for Students and Practitioners, by Edward A. Strecker and Franklin G. Ebaugh. *American Journal of Psychiatry,* **82:**331-335.

The Theory and Practice of Individual Psychology, by Alfred Adler. *Mental Hygiene,* **9:**827-835.

---

3. Most of the items herein, as well as corrections for inaccuracies in the main list are from a bibliography prepared by the William Alanson White Psychiatric Foundation, Inc., 1610 New Hampshire Avenue, N.W., Washington, D.C. 20009. I am indebted to Gloria Parloff, Managing Editor of *Psychiatry,* for making available to me this bibliography.

1926

Certain prepotent notions in schizophrenia. Unpublished; in files of William Alanson White Psychiatric Foundation. Presented at a meeting of the Washington Society for Nervous and Mental Diseases, November 18, 1926.

REVIEWS

Old and New Viewpoints in Psychology, by Knight Dunlap. *American Journal of Psychiatry,* **82:**442-447.

An Introduction to Objective Psychopathology, by G. V. Hamilton. *American Journal of Psychiatry,* **82:**447-459.

Elementary Psychology, by Arthur I. Gates. *American Journal of Psychiatry,* **82:**667-670.

The Organization of Life, by Seba Eldridge, *American Journal of Psychiatry,* **82:**670-671.

Outline of Abnormal Psychology, by William McDougall. *American Journal of Psychiatry,* **83:**191.

Experimental Psychology, by Mary Collins and James Drever. *American Journal of Psychiatry* **83:**191-193.

Animals Looking into the Future, by William Allison Kepner. *American Journal of Psychiatry* **83:**194-195.

An Introduction to the Mind in Health and Disease for Students and General Practitioners Interested in Mental Work, by T. Waddelow Smith. *American Journal of Psychiatry,* **83:**195-198.

1927

Dr. Kline's address at Cincinnati. *American Journal of Psychiatry,* **84:**159-161.

REVIEWS

Problems of Personality: Studies Presented to Dr. Morton Prince, Pioneer in American Psychopathology, Eds. C. Macfie Campbell and others. *American Journal of Psychiatry,* **83:**605-607.

Psychologies of 1925: Powell Lectures on Psychological Theory, American Journal of Psychiatry, **83:**607-608.

The Physiology of Mind, 2nd ed., by Francis X. Dercum. *American Journal of Psychiatry,* **83:**609-611.

Child Guidance, by Smiley Blanton and Margaret G. Blanton. *American Journal of Psychiatry,* **84:**166-168.

Shell Shock and Its Aftermath, by Norman Fenton. *American Journal of Psychiatry,* **84:**367-368.

The Gang Age, A Study of the Preadolescent Boy and His Recreational

Needs, by Paul Hanly Furfey. *American Journal of Psychiatry*, **84:**368-370.

The Psychology of Mental Disorders, by Abraham Myerson. *American Journal of Psychiatry*, **84:**530-532.

The Invert and His Social Adjustment, by "Anomaly." *American Journal of Psychiatry*, **84:**532-537.

1928

REVIEWS

The Laws of Social Psychology, by Florian Znaniecki. *American Journal of Psychiatry*, **84:**674-685.

The Phenomenology of Acts of Choice: An Analysis of Volitional Consciousness, by Honoria M. Wells. *American Journal of Psychiatry*, **84:**686-687.

1929

The sociogenesis of homosexual behavior. Unpublished; in files of William Alanson White Psychiatric Foundation. Presented to Section on Sociology and Psychiatry, American Sociological Society, Washington, D.C., December 27, 1929. (See 1930.)

Discussion—The study of personality, by Lawson G. Lowrey. *American Journal of Psychiatry*, **85:**700-702.

Discussion—Schizophrenia and psychotherapy, by A. A. Brill. *American Journal of Psychiatry*, **86:**538-541.

REVIEWS

Lectures in Psychiatry, by William Alanson White. *American Journal of Psychiatry*, **85:**1182-1183.

Ideal Marriage, by Th. H. Van De Velde. *American Journal of Psychiatry*, **86:**218-223.

Manual of Psychiatry, by Aaron J. Rosanoff. *American Journal of Psychiatry*, **86:**223-227.

1930

REVIEWS

Psychopathology and Politics, by Harold D. Lasswell. *American Journal of Psychiatry*, **87:**363-364.

Psychiatric Word Book, by Richard M. Hutchins. *American Journal of Psychiatry*, **87:**364.

Epilepsy, by William G. Lennox and Stanley Cobb, and *Treatment of*

Epilepsy by Fritz B. Talbott. *American Journal of Psychiatry*, **87**:735-736.

1931

Personality differentials as antecedents and consequences of acculturation. Proceedings Hanover Conference, Social Science Research Council. (See #14.) (Not confirmed.)

REVIEW

The Morbid Personality, by Sandor Lorand. *International Journal of Psychoanalysis*, **12**:497-499.

1932

REVIEW

The Morbid Personality, BY Sandor Lorand (translation of above minus final sentence). *Internationale Zeitschrift fur Psychoanalyse*, **18**:550-551.

1934

Discussion—Experimental analysis of the psychopathological effects of intoxicating drugs, by Erich Lindeman and William Malamud. *American Journal of Psychiatry*, **90**:879-881.

REVIEW

Towards Mental Health, by Charles Macfie Campbell. *International Journal of Psychoanalysis*, **15**:346-347.

1937

Discussion—A study of cases of Folie à Deux, by M. H. Grover. *American Journal of Psychiatry*, **93**:1061-1062.
The William Alanson White Psychiatric Foundation. A note. *American Journal of Psychiatry*, **93**:1456-1459.

1938

Discussion—The effect of adrenalin and mecholyl in states of anxiety in psychoneurotic patients, by Erich Lindeman and Jacob E. Finesinger. *American Journal of Psychiatry*. **95**:366-367.
Discussion—Early schizophrenia, by D. Ewen Cameron. *American Journal of Psychiatry*, **95**:578-580.
The application of the principles of mental hygiene to the practice of

medicine. Scheduled but apparently not published; in files of the William Alanson White Psychiatric Foundation. Presented to the Michigan Society for Mental Hygiene, April 7, 1938.

What is this psychiatry? Scheduled but apparently not published; in files of the William Alanson White Psychiatric Foundation. Annual address, Kentucky State Medical Society, October 3, 1938.

1939

The language of schizophrenia. Presented at Round Table, American Psychiatric Association, May 12, 1939, Chicago. (See #92.)

Psychiatry and civil rights—An editorial. *Psychiatry*, **2**:415-416.

Adequate personnel for mental hospitals and other treatment agencies. Scheduled but apparently not published. In files of the William Alanson White Foundation. Presented to Michigan Society for Mental Hygiene. April 21, 1939.

1940

Psychiatric mobilization in the U.S.A. *American Journal of Psychiatry*, **97**(supplement):2-4.

Therapeutic aspects of the psychiatric consultation with special reference to obsessional and schizophrenic states. Scheduled but apparently not published. In files of the William Alanson White Psychiatric Foundation. Presented to Neuropsychiatric Section, Baltimore City Medical Society, November 8, 1940.

Some facts about psychiatric therapy and schizophrenia. Scheduled but apparently not published. In files of the William Alanson White Psychiatric Foundation. Presented to Washington-Baltimore Psychoanalytic Society, February 10, 1940.

Wars—Nerves and the public. Unpublished. In files of the William Alanson White Psychiatric Foundation. Presented to Annual Scientific Assembly, Medical Society of the District of Columbia, October 16, 1940.

Reference list: Harry Stack Sullivan. *Psychiatry*, **3**:172-174.

1941

Mental health in defense. *Community Service*, Washington, D.C., Council of Social Agencies, **6**:20 (November).

1943

Selective Service psychiatry—An editorial. *Psychiatry,* **6:**442-444.

1947

The World Health Organization—An editorial. *Psychiatry,* **10:**99-103.

1948

Social responsibility and psychiatrists—An editorial. *Psychiatry,* **11:**87-89.

World Federation for Mental Health—An editorial. *Psychiatry,* **11:**401-402.

1953

Conceptions of Modern Psychiatry: The First William Alanson White Memorial Lectures (Foreword by the author, critical appraisal of the theory by Patrick Mullahy.) New York: W. W. Norton. (See #59 and #97.)

1965

Personal Psychopathology. Mimeographed. Washington, D.C.: William Alanson White Psychiatric Foundation, 332 pages. (See #35 and #128.) (No longer available.)

1969

Bibliography. In *Psychologie der Zwischenmenschlichen Beziehungen: Eine Einführung in die Neo-psychoanalytische Sozial Psychologie von H. S. Sullivan,* by Joseph Rattner. Olten: Walter-Verlag, pp. 207-215.

7 West 96th Street
New York City, New York 10025

References

1. Arieti, Silvano. *The Intrapsychic Self.* Basic Books, New York, 1967.
2. Arieti, Silvano and Chrzanowski, Gerard, (Eds.), *New Dimensions in Psychiatry: A World View Volume I.* John Wiley & Sons, New York, 1975.
3. —— *New Dimensions in Psychiatry: A World View Volume II.* John Wiley & Sons, New York, in press.
4. Breger, Louis. "Motivation, Energy and Cognitive Structure in Psychoanalytic Theory," in Judd Marmor (Editor), *Modern Psychoanalysis: New Directions and Perspectives.* Basic Books, New York, 1968.
5. Brenner, Charles. *An Elementary Textbook of Psychoanalysis.* New York, International Universities Press, 1955.
6. Bridgeman, P. W. *The Way Things Are.* Harvard University Press, Cambridge, 1959.
7. Bruch, Hilde. *Learning Psychotherapy.* Harvard University Press, Cambridge, 1974.
8. Burton, Arthur (Editor). *Operational Theories of Personality.* Brunner/Mazel, New York, 1974.
9. Chapman, A. H. *Harry Stack Sullivan: The Man and His Work.* G. P. Putnam & Sons, New York, 1976.
10. Chrzanowski, Gerard. "Success and Failure in the Treatment of Obsessional Disorders," in *Progress in Psychoanalysis* Vol. II, C. G. Hogrefe, Goettlingen, Germany, 1964.
11. —— "The Family Environment of Schizophrenic Patients," Congress Report of 2nd Int. Congress of Psychiatry, 1957, pp. 42-47.
12. —— "Psychotherapy — Cure, Self-Deception or Social Submission," Congress Report, Montreal.
13. —— "Sexuality in Schizophrenia," Congress Report of the IInd Int. Congress for Psychiatry, Zurich, Switzerland, Sept. 1957, Vol. III.

14. ———— "Treatment of Asocial Attitudes in Ambulatory Schizophrenic Patients," *Schizophrenia in Psychoanalytic Office Practice,* Alfred H. Rifkin (Ed.) Grune & Stratton, New York 1957.

15. ———— "What is Psychotherapy? The Viewpoint of the Sullivanian School," *Annals of Psychotherapy* (Journal of American Academy of Psychotherapists), Vol. I, No. 1, July 1959.

16. ———— "Neurasthenia and Hypochondriasis," in *American Handbook of Psychiatry,* S. Arieti (Ed.). Basic Books, New York, 1959.

17. ———— "A Presentation of the Basic Practical Features in the Application of the Psychoanalytic Method," in *Current Approaches to Psychoanalysis,* Jules Masserman (Ed.). Grune & Stratton, New York, 1960.

18. ———— "Termination in Psychoanalysis: Goals and Technical Principles Evolving from Sullivanian Conceptions," *American Journal of Psychotherapy,* Vol. XIV, No. 1, pp. 48-62, Jan. 1960.

19. ———— "The Impact of Interpersonal Conceptions of Psychoanalytic Technique," *Progress in Psychoanalysis* Vol. I, C. G. Hogrefe, Goettingen, Germany, 1964.

20. ———— "Training Analysis: Past, Present and Future," *American Journal of Psychoanalysis,* Vol. XXIII, No. 2, 1965.

21. ———— "Panel Discussion on Depression," *Contemporary Psychoanalysis, Vol. 2, No. 1, 1965.*

22. ——— *"The Management of Depressive States,"* Panel Discussions in Contemporary Psychoanalysis, Vol. 2, No. 1, 1965.

23. ———— "The Psychotherapeutic Management of Sociopathy," *American Journal of Psychotherapy,* Vol. XIX, No. 3, July 1965.

24. ———— "Symptom Choice in Schizophrenic Manifestations," *Contemporary Psychoanalysis,* Vol. 4, No. 1, Fall 1967.

25. ———— "The Independent Roots of Ego Psychology and Their Therapeutic Implications," *Science and Psychoanalysis,* Vol. XI, Jules Masserman (Ed.). Grune & Stratton, New York 1967.

26. ———— "An Interpersonal View of Phobias," *Journal of the American Academy of Psychotherapists,* Vol. 3, No. 3, Fall 1967.

27. ———— "Einige Grundpositionen der Interpersonellen Theorie," *Zeitschrift fur Psychosomatische Medizin und Psychoanalyse,* 14. Jahrgang -4. Vierteljahrsheft, Oct.-Dec. 1968.

28. ———— "On the Nature of Therapeutic Dialogue in Psychoanalysis," *Contemporary Psychoanalysis,* Vol. 6, No. 1, Fall 1969.

29. —— "Die Berucksichtigung der Familie-dynamik in der Individuellen Psychoanalytischen," *Progress in Psychoanalysis* Vol. IV, C. G. Hogrefe, Goettingen, Germany, 1970.

30. —— "An Absolute Diagnosis of Neurasthenia: A Critical Evaluation," *International Journal of Psychiatry*, Vol. 9, 1970-71.

31. —— "Devi and Transcultural Psychiatry," *Contemporary Psychoanalysis*, Vol. 8, No. 2, Spring 1972.

32. —— "The Changing Language of Self," *Contemporary Psychoanalysis*, Vol. 7, No. 2, Spring 1971.

33. —— "Psychotherapy with Patients with Phobias," *Theory and Practice of Psychotherapy with Specific Disorders*, Max Hammer (Ed.). Charles C. Thomas, Springfield, Ill., 1972.

34. —— "Editorial: Psycho-Politics and International Psychoanalysis," *Journal of the American Academy of Psychoanalysis*, Vol. 1, No. 2, 1973.

35. —— "Implications of Interpersonal Theory," *Interpersonal Explorations in Psychoanalysis*, E. Witenberg (Ed.). Basic Books, New York 1973.

36. —— "The Rational Id and the Irrational Ego," *Journal of the American Academy of Psychoanalysis*, Vol. 1, No. 3, 1973.

37. —— "Neurasthenia and Hypochondriasis," *American Handbook of Psychiatry*, 2nd edition, S. Arieti (Ed.). Basic Books, New York 1974.

38. —— "The Merits of Short Term Psychotherapy," Published by Bleuler Psychotherapy Center Inc., New York, Nov. 1974.

39. —— "Recent Advances in the Concepts and Treatment of Borderline Patients," *New Dimensions in Psychiatry: A World View*, Vol. I, S. Arieti and G. Chrzanowski, (Eds.). John Wiley & Sons, New York, 1975.

40. —— "On the International Forum," *Contemporary Psychoanalysis*, Vol. II, No. 1, Jan. 1975.

41. —— "On the Complexities of Teaching and Learning Psychotherapy: In-Group Dangers," *Contemporary Psychoanalysis*, Vol. II, No. 2, April 1975.

42. —— "The Way Things Are in Psychoanalytic Training and Practice," *Contemporary Psychoanalysis*, Vol. II, No. 3, 1975.

43. —— "Interpersonal Treatment Method with the Difficult Patient," in *International Encyclopedia of Neurology, Psychiatry, Psychoanalysis and Psychology*, Benjamin B. Wolman, (Ed.) in press.

44. —— "The Psychoanalytic Work of Erich Fromm, Karen

Horney and Harry Stack Sullivan," in *Encyclopedia: Psychology of the XXth Century*, Vol. II and Vol. III, Kindler Verlag, Munich, 1976.

45. Cohen, Mabel Blake (Ed.). *Advances in Psychiatry.* W. W. Norton & Company, New York, 1959.

46. Crowley, Ralph M. "Harry Stack Sullivan: The Complete Bibliography," Contemporary Psychoanalysis, Vol. II, No. 1, Jan. 1975.

47. Fairbairn, D. and Ronald, W. *An Object-Relations Theory of the Personality.* Basic Books, New York, 1954.

48. Freud, Sigmund. *Collected Papers.* The International Psycho-Analytic Press, London, 1946.

49. Fromm-Reichmann, Frieda. *Principles of Intensive Psychotherapy.* University of Chicago Press, Chicago, 1950.

50. Green, Maurice E., (Ed.). *Interpersonal Psychoanalysis.* Basic Books, New York, 1964.

51. Green, Maruice R. "The Interpersonal Approach to Child Therapy." In *Handbook of Child Psychoanalysis,* edited by B. Wolstein (Ed.). Van Nostrand-Reinhold, New York, 1972.

52. —— "Prelogical Processes and Participant Communication," *The Psychiatric Quarterly,* Oct., 1961, State Hospitals Press, Utica, New York.

53. —— "Suicide: The Sullivanian Point of View," *American Journal of Psychoanalysis.*

54. Guntrip, Harry. *Schizoid Phenomena, Object Relations and the Self.* International Universities Press, New York, 1969.

55. Hartman, Heinz. *Ego Psychology and the Problem of Adaptation.* International Universities Press, New York 1958.

56. Havens, Leston L. *Approaches to the Mind.* Little, Brown & Co., Boston, 1973.

57. Hook, Sidney. *American Philosophers at Work.* Criteriorn Books, New York, 1956.

58. Jacobsen, Edith. *The Self and the Object World.* International Universities Press, New York, 1964.

59. Jaensch, Erich R. *Eidetic Imagery,* trans. Oscar Oeser, Kegan, Paul, Trench, Truebner, London, 1930.

60. Jung, C. G. *The Undiscovered Self.* Atlantic — Little Brown, Boston, 1957.

61. Kernberg, Otto. *Borderline Conditions ana Pathological Narcissim,* Jason Aronson, New York, 1975.

62. Khan, R., Masud, M. *The Privacy of the Self.* International Universities Press, New York, 1974.

63. Kohut, Heinz. *The Analysis of the Self.* International Universities Press, New York, 1971.
64. Kvarnes, Robert (Ed.). *A Harry Stack Sullivan Case Seminar.* W. W. Norton, New York, 1976.
65. Laing, Ronald D. *Self and Others.* Penguin Books, London, 1961.
66. —— *The Divided Self.* Penguin Books, London, 1962.
67. MacKinnon and Michels. *The Psychiatric Interview in Clinical Practice.* W. B. Saunders Co., Baltimore, 1971.
68. McDougall, William. *Outline of Psychology.* Charles Scribner's Sons, New York, 1924.
69. Marmor, Judd (Ed.). *Modern Psychoanalysis: New Directions and Perspectives.* Basic Books, New York, 1968.
70. Mead, George H. *Mind, Self and Society.* University of Chicago Press, Chicago, 1934.
71. Moustakas, Clark E. (Ed.). *The Self.* Harper & Bros., New York, 1965.
72. Mullahy, Patrick (Ed.). *A Study of Interpersonal Relations.* Science House, New York, 1967.
73. ——*Psychoanalysis and Interpersonal Psychiatry.* Science House, New York, 1970.
74. Pfuelze, Paul E. *The Social Self.* Bookman Assoc., 1954.
75. Racker, Heinrich. Transference and Countertransference. International Universities Press, New York, 1968.
76. Rapaport, David. *Organization and Pathology of Thought.* Columbia University Press, New York, 1959.
77. Rothgeb, Carrie Lee (Ed.). *Abstracts of the Standard Edition of the Complete Psychological Works of Sigmund Freud.* Jason Aronson, Inc., New York, 1973.
78. Schachtel, Ernest. *Metamorphosis.* Basic Books, New York, 1959.
79. Thompson, Clara and Mullahy, Patrick. *Psychoanalysis: Evolution and Development.* Hermitage Press, New York, 1950.
80. White, Mary Julian. "Sullivan and Treatment," in *The Contributions of Harry Stack Sullivan,* Patrick Mullahy (Ed.). Hermitage Press, New York, 1967.
81. Will, Otto A., Jr. "Paranoid Development and the Concept of Self: Psychotherapeutic Intervention,"*Psychiatry,* Vol. 24 pp. 74-86, 1961.
82. Witenberg, E., Rioch, J. and Mazer, A. M. "The Interpersonal and Cultural Approaches," in*American Handbook of Psychiatry,* Vol. II, S. Arieti (Ed.). Basic Books, New York, 1959.
83. Wyss, Dieter. *Psychoanalytic Schools.* Jason Aronson, Inc., New York, 1973.

Notes

Preface

1. From "A Note on the Implications of Psychiatry," reprinted in *The Fusion of Psychiatry and Social Science*. See Crowley #127.

Chapter 1

1. Jaensch, E. *Eidetic Imagery,* London, Paul, Trench, Traebner; New York, Narcourt Brace, 1930. See also Rappaport, David: *Organization and Pathology of Thought:* Columbia University Press, New York 1959.
2. Freud's early theory of unconscious, preconscious, and conscious as the required road toward insight.
3. The postulate of Id, Ego, and Superego as mental structures.

Chapter 2

1. Zetzel, E. and Meissner, W.W.: *Basic Concepts of Psychoanalytic Psychiatry,* Basic Books, New York 1973.
2. Imprinting is a concept from the field of ethology and refers to animal behavior as described by Tindbergen and Lorenz.

Chapter 3

1. Double-bind is Gregory Bateson's term for messages with inherent contradictions.

Biographic Sketch

1. The complete text can be found in *Psychiatry,* Vol. 12, pp. 435-437, 1949.

Chapter 6

1. See "Neurasthenia and Hypochondriasis," G. Chrzanowski, in *American Handbook of Psychiatry,* edited by S. Arieti, Ed. New York, Basic Books, 1959. Chapter 7.

Index

Abraham, K., 182
Adolescence, 11
Anger, 13, 70
Anti-anxiety, 2, 12, 74
Anxiety, 2, 5, 9, 12, 13, 22ff., 45,
  47ff., 58, 60-65, 81, 102-105, 108,
  170, 172
Apathy, 9
Association, free, 36, 41
Arieti, S., Preface

Bad Mother, 8, 66, 98
Bad Me, 8, 12, 13, 66
Baldwin, 217
Beckett, T., 112
Bowlby, J., 67
Borderline syndrome, 193-203, 209
Brazil, H.V., 134
Brentano, F., 92
Bridgeman, P.W., 7, 14, 39

Cannon, Walter., 62
Childhood, 9
Cognition, 7, 45, 46
Confrontation, 156, 157
Consensual validation, 9
Cooley, 217
Countertransference, 76-89, 133,
  141, 150, 151, 155, 158, 178, 187,
  192
Culture, 5

Dannevig, E.T., 134
Determinism, 6
Developmental epochs, 5, 6, 8ff.
Dewey, John, 25
Dostoevsky, F., 110, 111
Dubos, René, 134
Dynamism, 22

Ecology, Preface, 16ff.-18, 115, 144,
  154
Ego psychology, Preface, 1, 15, 34,
  68, 92, 93, 101, 102, 104, 106,
  128, 129ff., 130
Eldridge, Seba, 18
Empathic, 8
Energy transformation, 21
Epigenetic, 5
Eurphoria, 12
Experience, 5-8, 12, 13, 21, 66, 101,
  102, 138, 172

Fear, 62
Field-oriented, 3, 14
Freud, S., Preface, 1, 5, 26, 27,
  32-34, 38, 40-42, 49, 51, 60, 76,
  78, 82, 85, 93, 97, 107, 110, 111,
  116, 128, 160
Fromm, E., 51

Good Me, 8, 12, 13, 66
Good Mother, 8, 66
Greenson, R., 36, 38, 132
Guntrip, H., 93

Hartman, H., 34, 94
Hateful integration, 7
Holt, Robert R., 128
Horney, K., 51
Hume, 91
Hypochondriacal syndrome, 203-
  207, 208, 209

Infancy, 3
Intentionality, 19
Interpersonal, 1-7, 10, 13-16, 18,
  22-24, 26, 29-31, 34, 37-37, 45,
  47, 52-53, 55-56, 58, 61, 63,
  65-66, 68, 74, 81-82, 84, 94, 101-
  102, 120, 138, 153
Interpersonal field, 4, 14ff.
Intimacy, 10ff.
Intrapsychic, 14, 29, 31-34, 43, 55,
  84, 130, 176, 178
Introject, 66, 93